Digital Preservation for Libraries, Archives, and Museums

D1522349

Digital Preservation for Libraries, Archives, and Museums

Edward M. Corrado and
Heather Lea Moulaison

ROWMAN & LITTLEFIELD
Lanham • Boulder • New York • Toronto • Plymouth, UK

Published by Rowman & Littlefield
4501 Forbes Boulevard, Suite 200, Lanham, Maryland 20706
www.rowman.com

10 Thornbury Road, Plymouth PL6 7PP, United Kingdom

British Library Cataloguing in Publication Information Available

Library of Congress Cataloging-in-Publication Data

Corrado, Edward M., 1971-
  Digital preservation for libraries, archives, and museums / Edward M. Corrado and
Heather Lea Moulaison.
    pages cm
  Includes bibliographical references and index.
  ISBN 978-0-8108-8712-1 (pbk. : alk. paper) — ISBN 978-0-8108-8713-8 (ebook) 1.
Digital preservation. 2. Preservation metadata. 3. Electronic information resources—
Management. I. Moulaison, Heather Lea. II. Title.
  Z701.3.C65C67 2014
  025.8'4—dc23
                                                                        2013034021

∞™ The paper used in this publication meets the minimum requirements of
American National Standard for Information Sciences—Permanence of Paper
for Printed Library Materials, ANSI/NISO Z39.48-1992. Printed in the
United States of America

Contents

Figures

Tables

Foreword

Michael Lesk

Digital preservation is not a problem; it is an opportunity. Until recently we accepted that many creative activities, from poetry reading to broadcast interviews, would be transitory. Even the average written piece of paper would be lost, not because the paper would necessarily turn yellow (we have learned how to make acid-free paper) but because nobody could afford the costs of retaining the paper, describing what was on it, and remembering where it was. Today digital technology is cheap and accessible to everyone. Architects today neither have to worry about the space required to store models of buildings nor about the permanence of cardboard, balsa wood, and foamboard; instead, computer-aided design (CAD) models are universally used and stored. Digital cameras today are so small and cheap that the BBC put cameras on the collars of fifty cats in a rural town and recorded what the cats did all day, producing a program called *The Secret Life of the Cat* (BBC Horizon).

The explosion in quantity produces an explosion in our need to preserve and organize. The cats may be able to take pictures but not yet to tag these pictures with descriptions (and, my wife observed, these cats need to learn about composition). I'm not worried about the BBC, which has an admirable record of retaining its history. We can still hear what William Butler Yeats sounds like because he read his poems on BBC radio in the 1930s. But how does one make this kind of preservation happen?

Unfortunately a large fraction of what has been said about digital preservation has focused on technology: tapes wear out, disks have head crashes, and so on. I am one of the authors who wrote too much about this twenty years ago, not realizing that the media problems would become insignificant compared to the organizational issues. Digital copies are perfect: they are exactly the same as the original, and so multiple copies are nearly always the best answer to the fear of information loss. And so long as the price of disk drives declines by half every eighteen months we can afford to keep the copies of anything we could afford to copy in the first place. But, to repeat, the problem is not about the weaknesses of media; it is about the weaknesses of organizations and knowledge.

The late Jim Gray used to say, "May all your problems be technical," expressing his frustration with the complexities of economic, legal, social, and organizational issues. Digital preservation is a fine example: it is not about knowing the mean time to failure of a flash drive but about creating an organizational system that will make our information available in the future. Carving hieroglyphic inscriptions into stone blocks on pyramids did not guarantee intelligibility centuries later; only the accidental survival of the Rosetta Stone, with the same text in both hieroglyphs and Greek, enabled that. Worse yet, we still have difficulty with ancient Mayan texts as a result of deliberate destruction of most of the codices after the conquest of Mexico. Preservation today similarly requires organizational survival, knowledge of formats, understanding of content, and competence in technology.

As a contrast, there are two versions of the U.S. census that have posed preservation issues. The 1890 census records were destroyed by a fire in 1921. More frequently we read about the loss of some digital information from the 1960 census, the first to use digital magnetic tape. The tapes were from an early Univac system, and the drives to read them became obsolete quickly. However, we lost less than 1 percent of the census data, and that mostly because two of the tapes were physically lost. The response to the 1921 fire was in part a new organization, the National Archives. And the response to the tape problems was a managed program of backup copies, now that it was recognized that the very detailed data was in fact worth keeping. Until this episode, the census had routinely discarded the "microdata" as not worthy of preservation. So, in both cases, the answer is organizations and procedures, not a discussion of sprinklers as opposed to night watchmen or tape durability compared to disk.

The greatest danger to digital materials is that we forget the meaning of them. Preservation depends on our knowledge: we may have bits but be unable to interpret them. Keeping knowledge, rather than objects, is an organizational problem. This book is an excellent description of the issues involved in developing a digital preservation program. It will be useful to people who work in cultural heritage institutions—libraries, archives, and museums—or in institutions that perhaps have not been focused on preservation, such as theater companies or orchestras, but wish to exploit their legacy.

Both the knowledge and organizational issues described in this book are complex and well-explained. A variety of kinds of knowledge must come together in a digital preservation program: knowledge of the content, knowledge of the technology, and knowledge of the procedures used. This poses issues for human resources and educators, and one of the most valuable aspects of this book is its ample references to courses, conferences, and other resources for learning about digital preservation. Even if an organization follows a teamwork model in which different people are handling each aspect of the digital preservation process, it is still important to understand what the other team members are doing.

The importance of copies and of searching in digital preservation makes the organizational problems more serious. To enable other organizations to share copies of material, and to have search engines operate across all of our stored resources, we need interoperable representations and common protocols. This book describes the interworking of the various standards bodies, professional associations, and government or university groups that have created procedures and policies to encourage and facilitate sharing. These policies also reduce the workload of individual organizations and increase the chance of long-term survival.

The book also touches on many of the most delicate organizational issues: legal permissions, sustainable funding, and institutional survival. The habit of doing digitization as "soft money" has led to fears for long-term survival. Examples are the end of funding for the Arts and Humanities Data Service in the United Kingdom (taken over by Kings College London) and the Arabadopsis Information Resource (becoming a consortium). Various strategies are mentioned, but we don't have a general answer yet.

Sometimes there is an organizational tension between access and preservation. Libraries have always seen this tension when they acquire personal papers that must be kept confidential for a long period; some of Mark Twain's papers were under a 100-year embargo, requiring preservation activities helping no current users. A 1993 British Library strategic review noted that the library did both access and preservation, access for today's users and preservation for tomorrow's users. Only today's users, however, helped pay the bills. A preservation plan must balance priorities over time.

Finally, the book ends with some of the most important opportunities in the area of data preservation. As of mid-2013, the "big data" craze has demonstrated the importance of keeping large raw-data files from many areas around, and that subject has merged with national policies for preservation of research data that apply in the United States and other countries. Institutional staff not historically concerned with the details of scientific research projects may find themselves with enormous files of data. For example, the Sloan Digital Sky Survey primary site has moved from Fermilab to the University of Chicago Library. That's 100 terabytes of data, which is far more than the number of bytes you would get if you typed out every book that library owns. Its management involves a knowledge of astronomy and instrumentation and has to be coordinated with astrophysicists around the world.

The authors have tackled the complexity of digital preservation in an intelligible and useful way. Their recommendations apply to both large and small organizations, since they deal with the strategic and policy problems impacting long-term access and storage. The prospects for digital preservation of "big data" may be daunting, but they are exciting. If you wish to learn the area, there is no better introduction than this book.

Dr. Michael Lesk, professor at Rutgers University, has been at the forefront of research in digital libraries since completing his Ph.D. at Harvard in the 1960s. Prior to joining Rutgers University, he headed the Division of Information and Intelligent

Systems at the National Science Foundation. Dr. Lesk received the Flame award for lifetime achievement from USENIX in 1994, is a fellow of the Association for Computing Machinery, and in 2005 was elected to the National Academy of Engineering. He has written extensively on digital libraries and on issues relating to digital preservation, including his 1997 book, *Practical Digital Libraries: Books, Bytes, and Bucks*, and his 2004 book, *Understanding Digital Libraries*, now in its second edition.

Preface

Digital Preservation for Libraries, Archives, and Museums offers librarians and other library and cultural heritage professionals, including administrators, a new approach to thinking about and getting started with digital preservation.

It presents digital preservation as a triad of interrelated activities: management-related activities, technological activities, and content-centered activities. While other books about digital preservation address technology to a certain extent, technology cannot—and should not—be the sole concern of digital preservation. There is much more to digital preservation than that. Digital preservation means gathering, organizing, authenticating, and allowing long-term access, all of which needs to be carefully thought-out in advance. It is concerned with the life cycle of the digital object in a robust and all-inclusive way. Many Europeans and some North Americans may refer to digital curation to mean the same thing, taking digital preservation to be the very limited steps and processes needed to ensure access over the long term. *Digital Preservation for Libraries, Archives, and Museums* views digital preservation in the broadest sense of the term: looking at all aspects of preserving curating and preserving digital content for long-term access.

This is not a how-to book giving step-by-step processes for certain materials in a given kind of system. Guides can be useful when implementing a given system in a specific environment; this book, instead, takes a broader perspective on requirements, giving readers the tools necessary to make big-picture decisions about digital preservation on their own.

In this way, this book addresses managing, caring for, and building a collection of resources that could be housed in any number of digital preservation systems. The intention is to provide readers with things (not technology, not how-to, not theory) that seasoned digital preservationists would have wished they had known before they got started.

Digital Preservation for Libraries, Archives, and Museums is written for people working in libraries and archives and museums, since, when it comes to digital preservation, they share many of the same concerns:

- How can I preserve the digital content available in my institution for the future?
- What do I need to know to carry out this work?
- How can I plan for the future in terms of the technology, human resources, and collections?
- How do I know if I'm on the right track with my digital preservation efforts?

The answers for an archivist working with digitized versions of her files, a museum curator wishing to use 3-D imaging to support virtual visits to his museum, and a librarian providing digital access to locally created audio files share certain qualities in common.

The information in this book is presented in a way that is readable straight through as a comprehensive primer. Although the chapters follow a logical sequence, each chapter can also be consulted on its own as an independent resource on the topic being covered.

Anecdotally, museum professionals have been slower than those in the pure information professions to dedicate their energy to the intricacies of digital preservation. We feel that this book, while being of use to all information professionals, will be especially useful to museum curators and to any cultural heritage professionals wishing to increase their understanding of digital preservation as it pertains to their digital assets.

SCOPE AND STRUCTURE OF THIS BOOK

Following the triad model of digital preservation, this book is divided into four parts:

  I. Introduction to Digital Preservation
 II. Management Aspects,
III. Technology Aspects, and
IV. Content-Related Aspects

Part I introduces the basics of digital preservation. Chapter 1 identifies what digital preservation is and what it is not before giving concrete reasons for investing in digital preservation. Chapter 2 outlines a strategy for getting started with digital preservation, including an overview of the process based on the notion that digital preservation is a tripartite approach involving management, technology, and content.

Part II continues the discussion of the importance of management in any digital preservation initiative. Chapter 3 focuses on the OAIS model, the foundational model at the center of most digital preservation initiatives. Chapter 4 focuses on human resources in the digital preservation context, listing resources of interest to digital preservationists at various stages in their careers. Finally, chapter 5 focuses on sustainability of a digital preservation project, the ultimate goal of any digital preservation initiative.

Part III delves into some of the most important technical aspects of digital preservation: the repository, its metadata, and the files that are stored in it. Building on the content in part II, chapter 6 looks at aspects of the trusted digital repository, including considerations for documentation. The concern with documentation and technology continues through chapter 7, which focuses on the importance of documenting information about digital objects through the use of metadata as a way of supporting long-term access. Finally, chapter 8 discusses in some detail the files that comprise the digital objects in systems, providing strategies for supporting them in the digital preservation system.

The last section, part IV, focuses on the actual content: that which is preserved digitally. As with the other parts, part IV begins with chapter 9, an overview that is management-oriented in tone describing considerations for collection development of digital content. Chapter 10 describes content of interest to researchers in the sciences; chapter 11 looks at the humanities and approaches being taken with the digital humanities movement.

An appendix provides additional information and resources for digital preservationists wishing to continue their study in the field. The appendix includes websites for organizations devoted to digital preservation that maintain relevant content, listings of reports and white papers, listings of webliographies identifying online resources supporting digital preservation, a section on additional books on digital preservation, and a summary of some education-based resources including research centers.

To support a robust understanding of the terminology used in the book, especially for readers new to digital preservation, a glossary is provided. Terms in the glossary relate to this book, and many are also taken from standard digital preservation glossaries, reports, and other foundational documents. To provide readers with a quick glimpse at the resources cited in the creation of this book, a bibliography has been compiled that will surely serve as an additional resource if further reading is desired.

As mentioned earlier, this book is meant to convey crucial information and guidance that should be known before getting started with digital preservation. We hope that readers will find many answers to questions about digital preservation they may not have even known they had, leading to more successful digital preservation initiatives.

Acknowledgments

We would like to thank our reviewers, along with Alex May, Metadata Librarian at Tufts University, for their instructive comments and invaluable insights. We would also like to acknowledge C. Sean Burns, assistant professor at the University of Kentucky School of Library and Information Science, for his input, feedback, and suggestions. Additionally, we owe a debt of gratitude to University of Missouri Ellis Library reference librarians and to contacts in local museums for assistance with research. Finally, we would like to thank our administrators and coworkers at our respective places of employment for their help and support, and Coda.

I

INTRODUCTION TO
DIGITAL PRESERVATION

1

What Is Digital Preservation?

The Library of Congress defines *digital preservation* as "the active management of digital content over time to ensure ongoing access."[1] This is a good start, but what does this really mean for the libraries, archives, and museums (LAM) community? Digital preservationists struggle with this and related questions in their day-to-day work: How does one actively manage digital content to ensure ongoing access? Who is managing the digital content? What are the best tools for managing digital content? And, perhaps more importantly, in light of the many obligations libraries and cultural heritage institutions have in fulfilling their missions, is digital preservation truly worth the investment? In many respects, what digital preservation is and the reasons why it is essential are abstract concepts that do not fit neatly into a short definition, but working through them is a reality in institutions wishing to preserve content in electronic formats. In beginning to formally approach the topic of digital preservation, it might be better to ask first, What is digital preservation *not*?

DIGITAL PRESERVATION IS *NOT . . .*

Digital preservation is not only the technical aspects of storing data, it is not purely about access, and it is not a one-shot effort to be added to a staff-member's workload as a temporary assignment. The following gives some details about why it is important to keep in mind what digital preservation is not.

Digital Preservation Is Not Only about Backups and Recovery

A common misconception is that having backup copies of files is digital preservation. While having a well thought-out backup and disaster recovery strategy is a key component of any digital preservation program, having backups by itself is not enough to "ensure ongoing access" and cannot be considered a digital preservation strategy. Backup copies are a response to short-term risks associated with failure of digital media—be they actual physical items like magnetic tapes of audio recordings or electronic items like born-digital files. When executed correctly, backup copies are able to provide bit stream preservation (preserving the ones and zeros that make up a digital file), but they do not address things like the availability of software to access the file, obsolete file formats, questions of rights, and issues of authenticity and provenance. Backups can protect data from accidental deletion, accidental changes, the effects of viruses and hackers, and catastrophic disasters such as floods and fires.[2] They can recover data from this morning, yesterday, last week, or perhaps even last year depending on the backup strategy in place. Having a disaster recovery plan that details the process of recovering data and information technology systems (both hardware and software) after a natural or man-made disaster will certainly be valuable in the event of a fire or flood. However, like less complicated backup strategies, disaster recovery plans are not by themselves digital preservation plans. As library technology expert Marshall Breeding reminds us, however, backup and disaster recovery are more about the "ability to maintain the continuity of the organization, focusing on the restoring of data in its current state," than they are about long-term access.[3] A backup copy of data does not protect against changes in technology. Older digital copies can be rendered unreadable or incomprehensible because newer versions of software or hardware may not be able to access the information correctly, if at all, and because the context of the original is completely lost. Of course, without backup and disaster-recovery policies that are followed faithfully, any digital preservation strategy is likely to be doomed.

Digital Preservation Is Not Only about Access

Simply by creating an infrastructure to house digital content an institution is not engaging in digital preservation. Digital libraries including institutional repositories excel at providing access to electronic content, yet they do not inherently provide for the kind of active management that is necessary to ensure long-term, ongoing access. Providing ongoing access requires crafting policies and devising the procedures necessary to support them. In spring 2010, 78 percent of respondents to Yuan Li and Meghan Banachs's survey of academic libraries that had an Institutional Repository (IR) and that belonged to the Association of Research Libraries (ARL) said that that they are committed to providing long-term preservation for their IR content. It is unclear, however, how all of these institutions are going to ensure that this will happen. About half, or "51.5 percent of respondents indicated that their IRs have preservation policies,"[4] and "only 16.7 percent reported that they were already providing long-term digital preservation."[5] Without the policy and practices in place to ensure long-term access, these institutions are not engaging in digital preservation. Additionally, less than half of the respondents of Li and Banach's survey said they had adequate staffing, and over one-third did not have or did not know if they had sustainable long-term funding. Creating a repository to house content is one aspect of a digital preservation strategy; it is not, however, the only aspect.

The goal of digital preservation is also not about *open access* to electronic content. Open access is a concept being considered by the scholarly communications community as a possible model for the circulation of ideas via the Web; fundamentally, in this regard, it is a copyright issue. SPARC, the Scholarly Publishing and Academic Resources Coalition, defines *open access* as "immediate, free availability on the public Internet, permitting any users to read, download, copy, distribute, print, search, or link to the full text of these articles, crawl them for indexing, pass them as data to software, or use them for any other lawful purpose."[6] At meetings and conferences about digital repositories, one will typically hear multiple speakers advocating for open access.[7] A digital preservation system is digital library software that includes a preservation component. Digital preservation systems and institutional repositories can support open access materials, and open access may be a worthy goal. Digital preservation, however, should be considered independently of an open access repository. In fact, open access could actually work against the digital preservation of some, particularly smaller, journals since it may be harder to preserve them in a digital preservation initiative like the Global LOCKSS (Lots of Copies Keep Stuff Safe) Network or CLOCKSS (Controlled LOCKSS) because there are voting and monetary restrictions to what gets included in these repositories.[8] As the Blue Ribbon Task Force on Sustainable Digital Preservation and Access (BRTF-SDPA) points out in their final report, "Open access is like any other form of access: without preservation, there will be no access, open or otherwise."[9]

Digital Preservation Is Not an Afterthought

Digital preservation is not accomplished in isolation by staff in remote parts of the institution unfamiliar with the mission, goals, users, content, and culture of the organization. For users to be able to use content effectively in the future, appropriate content needs to be collected and stored in ways that are supported and accessible into the future. As the National Library of New Zealand's Steve Knight has commented, "Digital preservation requires interaction with all the organisation's processes and procedures."[10] A digital preservation department or even a whole academic library or archive would find it difficult, if not impossible, to implement any wide-scale digital preservation program in a vacuum. Without support from an institution's parent body, there may not be available resources, human or capital, to implement and maintain a sustainable digital preservation program.

In summary, digital preservation is not merely a technical problem that can be solved via backups or through the acquisition of a turnkey repository. Certainly there are many aspects of digital preservation that require a complex technical infrastructure and the skilled people necessary to operate it; but above and beyond all of that, ensuring ongoing access to digital content over time requires careful reflection and planning. In terms of the technology, digital preservation is possible today. It might be difficult and require extensive, institution-wide planning, but digital preservation is an achievable goal given the proper resources. In short, digital preservation is in many ways primarily a management issue.

ELEMENTS OF DIGITAL PRESERVATION

According to the Digital Preservation Coalition (DPC), digital preservation is a "series of managed activities necessary to ensure continued access to digital materials for as long as necessary."[11] These activities are the actions required to keep digital information accessible and useable at some later date despite the "obsolescence of everything."[12] Everything includes software, hardware, file format, people, and more. The *Jisc* (formerly the Joint Information Systems Committee [JISC]) *Beginner's Guide to Digital Preservation* elaborates on the DPC definition of digital preservation given above by highlighting and explaining five key words, or aspects. The key words they choose to distill the definition are *managed, activities, necessary, continued access,* and *digital materials.*[13] These key aspects should be kept in mind when planning any digital preservation initiative. In table 1.1 we explain these aspects and present some possible policy implications.

The *JISC Beginner's Guide* goes on to quantify three different lengths of digital preservation. They are *long-term, medium-term,* and *short-term,* and each has different requirements of the preservation repository. Long-term preservation is when continued access to digital objects is desired indefinitely. It is the most challenging of the three. Medium-term preservation is when continued access to digital objects is desired beyond changes in technology; it typically has a defined time length that continued access is required, and the duration is not indefinite. Short-term preservation is when continued access to digital objects is desired but does not extend into the future beyond changes in technology.[14]

WHY DIGITAL PRESERVATION?

The Library of Congress's Digital Preservation website includes a short video that attempts to answer *Why Digital Preservation is Important to Everyone* (the video's title). They point out that "traditional information sources such as books, photos, and sculptures can easily survive for years, decades, or even centuries, but digital items are fragile and require special care to keep them useable."[15] Paper documents, artwork, and other information containers can remain readable for centuries or even millennia. Because of the rapid rate of technological change, however, electronic documents may be inaccessible just a few years after they were created. As information continues to go digital and new technologies are developed, formats that are older or outdated become obsolete and content may not be accessible using new software.[16] Because of our dependence on technology, digital information is at great risk of loss if digital preservation is not a consideration.

Table 1.1. JISC's Key Aspects of the DPC Digital Preservation Definition

Key Aspect	Explanation	Policy Implications
Managed	Jisc is emphasizing that digital preservation really is a management problem. Digital preservation projects need to be properly managed, and they require support from upper administrators in order to be successful.	All planning, resource allocation, and use of technology needs to be thought through. It is important to have high-level strategy and polices.
Activities	Certain activities need to take place in order to ensure digital preservation. These activities should be broken down to individual tasks that can be performed in well-defined ways at specified times. These activities and their corresponding tasks should be well documented so that someone else can perform them if necessary.	An activity is any action taken for digital preservation or for maintaining a digital preservation system. These actions can include emulation, format migration, or normalization.
Necessary	What needs to be done? It is necessary to have discussions about what activities are necessary to achieve a desired level of digital preservation.	The outcome of these discussions should be included in an institution's digital preservation policies.
Continued Access	It is vital to ensure continued access to digital objects over time. This is especially true when considering publicly funded scholarship and other objects in the public sphere or made available as a public good. Related to continued access are the concepts of search and retrieval. By not only storing the file but also making sure it is retrievable and accessible, digital preservation supports the long-term use of the content.	How long access to digital content is required needs to be included in an institution's policy, which should also look at how to respond to format obsolescence, and include obtaining permissions to modify files over the long term.
Digital Materials	Digital materials are the objects being preserved. Some examples of digital materials include images, datasets, audio recordings, videos, three-dimensional files, and text-based content such as newspaper articles.	Different types of digital materials may require different processes to preserve or to provide access to them.

As presented in Jisc, *JISC Beginner's Guide to Digital Preservation*, accessed September 1, 2012, http://blogs.ukoln.ac.uk/jisc-beg-dig-pres/.

Even big and well-funded projects can go awry if digital preservation is not a primary concern at the outset. An oft-cited example about the failure to ensure digital preservation is the tale of the Domesday Book and the BBC Domesday Project. The original Domesday Book, the result of a survey of a large part of England and parts of Wales, was completed in 1086 A.D. under the order of William the Conqueror. To commemorate the 900th anniversary of the Domesday Book, the British Broadcasting Company (BBC), along with partners Acorn Computers, Philips, and Logica, launched the BBC Domesday Project. The goal of the project was to create a modern, multimedia version of the book. The BBC Domesday Project contained a new survey of the United Kingdom "that would harness some of the potential of multimedia and provide a detailed snapshot or time capsule of British life in the mid-1980s, as seen by the people themselves."[17] Over one million people, mostly school children, submitted nearly 150,000 pages of article text and over 23,000 photographs that described "what it was like to live, work, and play in their community."[18] The BBC Domesday Project was stored on two interactive video discs and cost approximately £2.5 million to create.[19] The interactive video discs themselves were virtually indestructible, but by the beginning of the new millennium the BBC Domesday Project was on the brink of complete technological obsolescence because the disc players were not so indestructible and the discs could not be read by the computers of the time.[20] The original Domesday book had lasted nearly a millennium, but the modern one was only accessible for a decade and a half.

Luckily for future generations, in 2002 a team of researchers from Leeds University and the University of Michigan worked to make the digital contents of the BBC Domesday Project accessible. Ultimately, however, the researchers were unable to make the results of their work publicly available "due to the complex copyright situation surrounding Domesday."[21] But all is not lost. The spirit of the BBC Domesday Project continues today as a new Domesday Reloaded project undertaken by the BBC and the National Archives to republish the BBC Domesday Project on the BBC's dedicated website. This time, the National Archives are "working closely with BBC Learning to. ensure this valuable resource will be available to the public for generations to come."[22]

Digital obsolescence can affect anyone working in digital media. For example, consider a professor who wrote her dissertation in the early 1980s using WordStar, which was one of the most popular word processing applications of the period. She had her dissertation stored on a floppy disk, which she saved. Recently she wanted to consult her dissertation saved on the floppy disk, but she no longer had a disk drive that could read it. At this point she asked around to see if someone had any equipment to read the disk, assuming it was still in readable condition. Even if she were able to find someone with the appropriate legacy hardware and if the floppy disk were still readable, that would not guarantee that she could have retrieved and read the file containing her dissertation. She would also need access to a software program that could interpret the zeros and ones in the file as a WordStar file and then display them on a computer monitor. Luckily for this professor, the university where she earned her doctorate had the foresight to preserve her dissertation both in print and on microfilm in the library, saving her from the need for drastic digital recovery operations. The library was able to scan the document, save it as a Portable Document Format (PDF) file, and e-mail it to the professor. Now she has a digital copy of her dissertation in a modern file format that she can read. The question remains, though, as to how long that PDF will be readable. If the document is a PDF/Archive (PDF/A) file, we assume that it will be more accessible than the WordStar format, since PDF/A is an International Organization for Standardization (ISO) standard (ISO 19005-1) designed for long-term archiving.[23] If it is a nonarchival PDF document used in digitization, in thirty years she may well find herself in a similar situation all over again.

Digital preservation can be pertinent in institutional settings as well. Consider the case of an information organization that supports the work of a performing arts institution. Performers at most performing arts institutions are members of unions. Their performances are works for hire, and their contracts in many cases stipulate that the institution where they are performing must make a copy of their performance and retain it as part of their professional record. After surveying a number of performing arts archives, Tom Evens and Laurence Hauttekeete concluded that "many organizations lack any systematic preservation policy for safeguarding their collections."[24] If not properly preserved, recordings can literally pile up, undocumented over time, impossible to search. Digitized versions of poorly preserved audio-visual content might provide access but may not be able to ensure authenticity, accurately describe provenance, or record information about actors and rights. The jury is still out in the above scenario, but unless there is a huge influx of resources that will permit the proper digital preservation of this recorded content, it is unlikely that the content will remain accessible and usable in the long term.

All of the above cases are instances of digital preservation problems. The people involved did not take the appropriate steps beforehand to prevent technological obsolescence; instead they made decisions (or neglected to take actions) that ultimately harmed long-term accessibility. The BBC Domesday Project may have been doomed to become obsolete from the beginning, thereby requiring extensive "digital archeology" to make the content accessible again. The project relied on a specially developed software interface, and data was saved in proprietary formats and relied on proprietary hardware (a special Philips LVROM player—a forerunner to CD-ROM) that was not widely used. There were also cost overruns that made the end product more expensive, decreasing the number of BBC Domesday Project video discs that were bought and sold. Many of these things were not necessarily the project team's fault, however. Digital versions of dissertations were perhaps not the norm in the 1980s, and with the reliance on paper as the copy of record it is not unreasonable that a disk would fall into obsolescence without a researcher's knowledge. Recordings on multiple file formats (both analog and digital) may ensure access to performances into the future, but, when not organized and made available in a system, essential information documenting rights, actors, and uses are difficult to ascertain without necessary information about the context. As content is increasingly digital in nature or being preserved in a digital environment, libraries and cultural heritage organizations can use these and similar tales of woe to help make the case for digital preservation initiatives and funding. As warns Adam Farquhar, head of Digital Library Technology at the British Library and cofounder of the library's Digital Preservation program, "if we're not careful, we will know more about the beginning of the twentieth century than the beginning of the twenty-first century."[25]

DIGITAL PRESERVATION: A MANAGEMENT ISSUE

As mentioned earlier in this chapter, digital preservation is in many ways a management issue. Often people involved with planning or running a digital preservation system focus on the technology. This is understandable because without the appropriate technological infrastructure it would be impossible to preserve digital materials. Additionally, since digital preservation is a relatively new field, much of the technology is still evolving. However, one needs to look no further than the international guidelines for trusted digital repositories to see that most of what is required to becoming certified or receiving a seal of approval is establishing appropriate, documented management procedures.

Trusted digital repositories will be discussed in detail in chapter 6, but it is insightful to briefly explore the major themes covered at this point by the *Trustworthy Repositories Audit and Certification: Criteria and Checklist.*[26] There are three major sections to the criteria and checklist—(1) Organizational Infrastructure, (2) Digital Object Management, and (3) Technologies, Technical Infrastructure, and Security. The first set of responsibilities, Organizational Infrastructure, has very little to do with technology. Instead, as its name suggests, it focuses on organizational issues like governance, financial sustainability, and legal issues, such as contracts and licensing. Digital Object Management has both organizational and technical components, but, even so, many of those technical components are more managerial or administrative decisions than they are technical. For example, one of the checklist items relates to the minimal amount of descriptive metadata necessary. While technology can create or help create descriptive metadata, it is not a technical decision as to what level or amount of descriptive metadata is deemed necessary. It is ultimately a management decision. Even the last theme, Technologies, Technical Infrastructure, and Security, is not all about technology. For example, many of the specific checklist items start with phrases like "Repository has a documented . . ." and "Repository has defined processes."[27]

Digital preservation is not something that can be done once and then be forgotten. Projects need to be managed throughout their *life cycles* (sometimes written *lifecycles*, as one word). The Life Cycle Information for E-Literature (LIFE) Project defines *life cycle collection management* as "a way of taking a long term approach to the stewardship of collections. It defines the different stages in a collection item's existence over time."[28] In order for a digital preservation initiative to be successful over time, there needs to be institutional commitment. This includes ensuring that enough financial resources are available to sustain the initiative. Sustaining an initiative includes funding for both staff and equipment, and such a commitment over the long term can be daunting.

Earlier in this chapter we demonstrated that digitization for access alone is not digital preservation. The BRTF-SDPA warns us, however, that "economists tell us that without the demand for access, there will be no preservation."[29] Another way of looking at this is that, without a marked return on investment (ROI) for the digital content deposited in a preservation system, there will be no incentive to maintain the preservation system. In institutions that do not explicitly have the goal of preserving content in perpetuity, making a case for long-term digital preservation has the potential to be challenging. Without demand, it is less likely that upper management will commit the long-term resources necessary to sustaining a digital preservation program. Because of this, it is important to have buy-in from content providers, potential content providers, and users; in many cases, it is possible to demonstrate that the preservation of stakeholder content does in fact support the institution's mission. Having buy-in from content providers will help populate the digital preservation system with items that will be in demand by the users the institution serves.

For a digital preservation initiative to be successful in serving an institution's clients no matter what the institution's overall mission and goals, a collection development policy that outlines what types of objects will be preserved and under what conditions they will be accepted is important. Collection development is the selection and deselection of objects for a collection, and designating a policy for the selection of digital resources to be preserved as part of a digital preservation initiative is important to the overall success of the project. Collection development policies for digital preservation are no different than policies for acquiring print materials in a library or art works in a museum. An archive or museum cannot accept everything that someone may wish to donate to it. While a Salvador Dalí painting would be a great addition to any modern art museum, a museum that specializes in Renaissance art would probably not add it to their permanent collection. The same principles apply to digital content retained for preservation. Collection development is discussed in further detail in chapter 9.

Steve Knight believes that digital preservation requires interaction with the process and procedures of all parts of an organization. He has identified seven specific areas where interaction is necessary based on his experience at the National Library of New Zealand: (1) business processes, (2) capacity and capability, (3) performance measures, (4) internal training, (5) producer management, (6) business and technical support, and (7) communication.[30] The first area he identifies is *business processes*, which includes workflows and policies. For example, information professionals who make collection development decisions in a library or a museum will have to adjust their policies and procedures for digital content. The second area, *capacity and capability*, refers to resources, which can either be human resources (and the skills they possess) or physical resources, such as money to purchase additional hardware.

Performance measures are likewise affected. How is the organization going to report and measure its effectiveness as it relates to digital preservation? When implementing a digital preservation system, *internal training* is affected. How are new staff going to be trained and existing staff retrained? What resources are available to train systems staff? In the case of the National Library of New Zealand, much of their content comes from producers outside of the library. This is likely to be true of many libraries and other cultural heritage organizations as well. *Producer management* fills a number of necessary roles, like marketing the preservation system and providing training to people who wish to deposit materials. *Business and technical support*, as Knight identified in his talk, is especially important between departments. Last, as always, the need for *communication* is a constant.

WHY LIBRARIES, ARCHIVES, MUSEUMS?

As the term implies, *digital preservation* is deeply entrenched in the modern technologies allowing for long-term digital access and consumption of content and also the preservation work traditionally carried out in archives and other cultural heritage institutions. In archives where one-of-a-kind unpublished works represent the bulk of the collections, the principle of the sanctity of evidence and the principle of provenance are two of the basic tenets. The principle of provenance is the primary principle of archival science; it states that the authenticity of items should be maintained through the retention of original order and their placement in their original collections.[31] The related principle of the sanctity of evidence requires that chain of custody must be ensured and that the document's intrinsic properties be intact. Maintaining these tenets of archival science in the digital realm through the process of preservation is what all LAM institutions must now attempt to do if they wish to preserve their digital content. Modern libraries house published works but increasingly are being tasked with the organization of unique content. Already as of 2008 a report to the Library of Congress called for libraries to organize and make their unique content accessible.[32] It is reasonable to think that in the future libraries will focus increasingly on organizing, providing access to, and preserving their own unique content.

The importance of preservation is not a new concept to information professionals in libraries—it is almost unthinkable that a large academic or research library would not have a preservation program for physical objects. Although there are some earlier works, according to Maja Krtalic and Damir Hasenay preservation in libraries has only been studied since the 1950s.[33] Preservation is a core value of librarianship,[34] and libraries have extensive experience in preservation management in the analog world.[35] In 1990 the American Library Association (ALA) adopted a preservation policy, discussing both physical and digital preservation, which states that "the preservation of information resources is central to libraries and librarianship."[36]

As information and libraries move into the digital realm, why would this core value not apply anymore? John Meador Jr., Dean of libraries at Binghamton University, often points out that it does still apply but that in the past many libraries rushed into digitization with a mind to access without taking into account the core value of preservation.[37] This is confirmed by a 2002 joint report by Online Computer Library Center (OCLC) and Research Libraries Group (RLG) on digital preservation that says that "often, those creating digital materials or designing digital content management systems do not take great interest in their long-term preservation."[38] While this report was published all the way back in 2002, it is clear that many systems still do not take long-term preservation into account. For example it is considered that digital asset management "consists of management tasks and decisions surrounding the ingestion, annotation, cataloguing, storage, retrieval and distribution of digital assets."[39] The word *preservation* is nowhere to be found in the main body of the article, referenced only in the *see also* section at the bottom of the page. So, despite the recognition by information professionals of the importance of digital preservation, many libraries and other cultural organizations have not been able to make it a high priority.

Some information professionals (and developers who program institutional repository software) are undertaking projects to retrofit digital preservation into their systems and workflows, and others are implementing digital preservation–ready systems. While these are indeed positive developments, the results of Li and Banach's survey of ARL libraries with digital libraries, mentioned earlier, show that many institutions have a long way to go before digital preservation is fully integrated. Digital preservation furthers the role of information professionals to the digital realm. It is not a new idea; it is merely a new set of rules.

CONCLUSION

In this chapter we have demonstrated what digital preservation is not: it is not about backups and recovery, it is not just about having access to content, and it is not an afterthought. Digital preservation, instead, is mostly a management issue, one that combines knowledge of users, technology, content, and the host organization. Planning to preserve content indefinitely as the goal of long-term preservation is the focus of the rest of this book. In the coming chapters we will look at all of the aspects necessary for long-term digital preservation as we explore the emerging, challenging, and rewarding field of digital preservation.

NOTES

1. Library of Congress, "About Digital Preservation," para 1, accessed September 29, 2013, http://www.digitalpreservation.gov/about/.

2. AHDS History/UK Data Archive, "Planning Historical Digitisation Projects," last modified June 21, 2005, http://chnm.gmu.edu/digitalhistory/links/pdf/preserving/8_32.pdf.

3. Marshall Breeding, "From Disaster Recovery to Digital Preservation," *Computers in Libraries* 32, no. 4 (May 2012): 22.

4. Yuan Li and Meghan Banach, "Institutional Repositories and Digital Preservation: Assessing Current Practices at Research Libraries," *D-Lib Magazine* 17, no. 5–6 (2011), "Preservation Policies," para 2, http://www.dlib.org/dlib/may11/yuanli/05yuanli.html.

5. Li and Banach, "Institutional Repositories," "Sustainability," para 4.

6. Scholarly Publishing and Academic Resources Coalition (SPARC), "Open Access," para 1, accessed September 1, 2012, http://www.sparc.arl.org/issues/open-access.

7. For example, the SPARC Digital Repositories 2010 meeting consisted of fourteen presentations. In the abstracts on the conference website, five of the fourteen mention open access, and another three belong to an open data track. None of the abstracts mentions the word *preservation*. Scholarly Publishing and Academic Resources Coalition (SPARC), "Abstracts," *Digital Repositories Meeting 2010*, accessed September 1, 2012, http://jlsc-pub.org/cgi/viewcontent.cgi?article=1042&context=jlsc.

8. Martin Paul Eve, "The Problems for Small Open Access Journals in Terms of Digital Preservation," *Martin Paul Eve*, March 30, 2012, accessed August 21, 2012, https://www.martineve.com/2012/03/30/the-problems-for-small-open-access-journals-in-terms-of-digital preservation/.

9. Blue Ribbon Task Force on Sustainable Digital Preservation and Access (BRTF-SDPA), *Sustainable Economics for a Digital Planet: Ensuring Long Term Access to Digital Information* (San Diego: San Diego Supercomputer Center, 2010), 23, http://brtf.sdsc.edu/biblio/BRTF_Final_Report.pdf.

10. Steve Knight, "Securing the Future: Digital Preservation at the National Library of New Zealand" (paper presented at the annual conference of the International Group of Ex Libris users [IGeLU], Madrid, September 8–10, 2008), slide 30, accessed September 1, 2012, http://igelu.org/wp-content/uploads/2010/10/12a_knight.pdf.

11. Digital Preservation Coalition (DPC), "Introduction: Definitions and Concepts," in *Digital Preservation Handbook* (York, Eng.: DPC, 2008), accessed September 1, 2012, http://www.dpconline.org/advice/preservationhandbook.

12. Michael Factor, "Long Term Digital Preservation" (paper presented at IBM Haifa Research Lab, Haifa, Israel, November 2008), slide 3, accessed August 30, 2012, http://www.ndpp.in/presentation/National_Workshop2008/Mr._Vijay_K_Garg.pdf.

13. Jisc, "Definition of Digital Preservation," in *JISC Beginner's Guide to Digital Preservation*, accessed September 1, 2012, http://blogs.ukoln.ac.uk/jisc-beg-dig-pres/.

14. Ibid.

15. Library of Congress, "Why Digital Preservation Is Important for Everyone," video, 2 minutes and 50 seconds, accessed September 1, 2012, http://www.digitalpreservation.gov/multimedia/videos/digipres.html.

16. For example, Microsoft Word 2010 dropped support for the following file formats: Microsoft Word for Windows 1.*x* and 2.*x*, Microsoft Word for Macintosh 4.*x* and 5.*x*, and Microsoft Word 6.0 and Word 95 Binary Documents and Templates.

17. Douglas Brown, "Lost in Cyberspace: The BBC Domesday Project and the Challenge of Digital Preservation," *CSA Discovery Guides*, para 2, June 2003, http://www.csa.com/discoveryguides/cyber/overview.php.

18. British Broadcasting Corporation (BBC), "Story of Domesday," para 4, accessed August 1, 2013, http://www.bbc.co.uk/history/domesday/story.

19. Robin McKie and Vanessa Thorpe, "Digital Domesday Book Lasts 15 Years Not 1000," *Observer*, March 3, 2003, accessed August 20, 2012, http://observer.guardian.co.uk/uk_news/story/0,6903,661093,00.html.

20. Brown, "Lost in Cyberspace."

21. Paul Wheatley, "Digital Preservation and BBC Domesday" (paper presented at the annual meeting of the Electronic Media Group's American Institute for Conservation of Historic and Artistic Works, Portland, June 14, 2004), p. 8, accessed September 1, 2012, http://cool.conservation-us.org/coolaic/sg/emg/library/pdf/wheatley/Wheatley-EMG2004.pdf.

22. National Archives, "Domesday Preserved in New BBC Project," "Past to Present," para. 2, May 12, 2011, accessed September 29, 2013, http://www.nationalarchives.gov.uk/news/573.htm.

23. PDF Standards, "PDF/A," accessed July 15, 2013, http://pdf.editme.com/pdfa.

24. Tom Evens and Laurence Hauttekeete, "Challenges of Digital Preservation for Cultural Heritage Institutions," *Journal of Librarianship and Information Science* 43, no. 3 (2011): 161.

25. "Digital Archiving: History Flushed," *Economist*, April 28, 2012, para 2, http://www.economist.com/node/21553410.

26. Online Computer Library Center, Inc., (OCLC) and the Center for Research Libraries, *Trustworthy Repositories Audit and Certification: Criteria and Checklist* (Chicago and Dublin, Ohio: OCLC and the Center for Research Libraries, 2007), http://www.crl.edu/PDF/trac.pdf.

27. Ibid.

28. Life Cycle Information for E-literature (LIFE), "LIFE: Glossary and Reference," s.v. "Life Cycle Collection Management," accessed July 15, 2013, http://www.life.ac.uk/glossary/.

29. Blue Ribbon Task Force, *Sustainable Economics*, 17.

30. Knight, "Securing the Future," slide 30.

31. See Anne J. Gilliland-Swetland, *Enduring Paradigm, New Opportunities: The Value of the Archival Perspective in the Digital Environment* (Washington, D.C.: Council on Library and Information Resources, 2000), http://www.clir.org/pubs/abstract/pub89abst.html; see also Patsy Baudoin, "The Principle of Digital Preservation," *The Serials Librarian* 55, no. 4 (2008): 556–59, doi:10.1080/03615260802291212.

32. Library of Congress, *On the Record: Report of the Library of Congress Working Group on the Future of Bibliographic Control* (Washington, D.C.: Library of Congress, 2008), http://www.loc.gov/bibliographic-future/news/lcwg-ontherecord-jan08-final.pdf.

33. Maja Krtalic and Damir Hasenay, "Exploring a Framework for Comprehensive and Successful Preservation Management in Libraries," *Journal of Documentation* 68, no. 3 (2012): 353–77.

34. American Library Association (ALA), "Core Values of Librarianship: Preservation," accessed June 8, 2013, http://www.ala.org/advocacy/intfreedom/statementspols/corevalues#preservation.

35. Barbara Sierman, "Organizing Digital Preservation," in *Business Planning for Digital Libraries: International Approaches*, edited by Mel Collier (Leuven, Belg.: Leuven University Press, 2010), 113.

36. American Library Association (ALA), "ALA Preservation Policy," 2001, preamble, para 2, http://www.ala.org/alcts/resources/preserv/01alaprespolicy.

37. John Meador Jr. has repeated this concept while describing the future academic digital library at various meetings and conferences as well as in person. Some conference presentations of note include the July 17, 2012, meeting of the Rosetta Advisory Group, held in Hannover, Germany ("Building Our Digital Library Using Rosetta and Primo: The First Year," copresented with Edward M. Corrado and Sandy Card); and the annual conference of the International Group of ex Libris Users (IGeLU), held September 11–13, 2012, in Zurich ("Rosetta and the 21st Century Academic Digital Library," copresented with Edward M. Corrado).

38. Research Libraries Group (RLG), *Trusted Digital Repositories: Attributes and Responsibilities; An RLG-OCLC Report* (Mountain View, Calf.: Research Libraries Group, 2002), 18, http://www.oclc.org/resources/research/activities/trustedrep/repositories.pdf.

39. Wikipedia, s.v. "Digital Asset Management," accessed 13 August 2012, http://en.wikipedia.org/w/index.php?title=Digital_asset_management&oldid=507130560.

2

Getting Started with the Digital Preservation Triad

The prospect of starting a digital preservation program can seem daunting. The technology may be mystifying, the ongoing financial commitment may be difficult to obtain, use scenarios might be difficult to imagine, and it can be hard to determine where to begin with the process. Getting started with digital preservation, however, is not an insurmountable challenge, and there is no time better than the present to begin. Although physical collections of books, manuscripts, or artifacts can be neglected for years without significant loss or additional expense, the same cannot be said of digital collections. Digital collections need attention in the near term. They cannot sit around on an archive's virtual shelf without being cared for due to digital-specific issues like bit rot, media decay, software and hardware obsolesce, and other issues that will not plague paper. Additionally, if the digital objects are not well organized or documented, "input from creators will be key" to knowing what the digital files are about, how they came to exist, and how they can be used.[1] Much of the challenge lies in thinking about digital preservation, in planning the process, in managing the content, the resources, and the staff, and in securing content.

Though having access to appropriate technology is one of the challenges of digital preservation, there are others that are equally important. Various digital preservationists have offered different models for breaking down digital preservation into smaller, more comprehensible chunks. The Digital Preservation Management Workshops and Tutorial, for instance, describes digital preservation as a three-legged stool—supported by technology, organization, and resources—two legs of which are management-related.[2] The three-legged stool is a good metaphor for digital preservation, especially if the focus is not on content preservation. We prefer, however, to approach digital preservation as a triad of interrelated activities: management-related activities, technological activities, and content-centered activities. As shown in figure 2.1, a Celtic knot, all three parts of the Digital Preservation Triad are interconnected.

Management

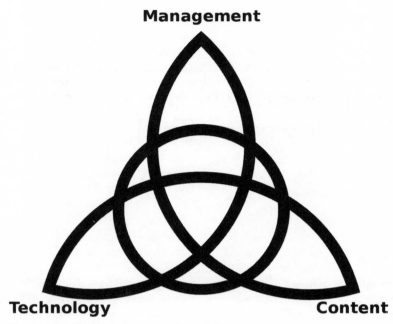

Technology   Content

Figure 2.1. The Digital Preservation Triad

Management is at the top of the triad, for without management in the form of re-sources and policies there is no impetus to preserve digital objects. The cornerstone to the left of the triad is technology, without which there is no digital preservation in the most practical sense of the term. Finally, to the right on the triad is content, which gives the repository value, as value comes in the access and use of the digital objects over time. The Digital Preservation Triad is the metaphor we have adopted throughout this book.

Digital preservation is a complicated, multifaceted endeavor, and many digital preservation activities will not fit neatly into only one area. For instance, in order to operate a complicated digital preservation software program, (a Technology issue), sufficient human and financial resources must be made available (a Management issue) to secure and organize digital objects that have been curated (Content). Still, breaking down digital preservation to these three major aspects makes it possible to examine smaller chunks in a systematic way.

This chapter begins with a brief overview of the digital preservation process; then it describes in additional detail some of the elements of that process using the Digital Preservation Triad described above as a framework. In short, this chapter serves as a practical introduction to digital preservation that will be fleshed out further in the rest of the book.

STEPS IN THE DIGITAL PRESERVATION PROCESS

Sometimes it is helpful to begin with a simplified but overarching view of where a project is going. This section will lay out the steps to digital preservation as a kind of a road map for understanding the more intricate discussion that follows. This section, therefore, should be taken as it is intended: as a preliminary overview that is perhaps overly simplistic yet provides the kinds of signposts that will be beneficial for a high-level understanding of the practical goals of digital preservation; many of these topics will be revisited later in the book. This chapter also presents and addresses some topics that are not meaty enough to be revisited in later sections.

Chronologically, the first step in performing digital preservation is to identify a collection or set of objects for digital preservation. Digital preservation does not have to cover every single item in an institution's care; it can first address a single collection, for example, and be expanded to include other items after the institution gains some experience with digital preservation. The items selected for digital preservation may be slides or photographs from a museum, born digital organizational records in an archive, or special collection materials from a library. Most libraries, archives, and museums (LAMs) have a collection development or similar policy for their organization that describes what types of objects are appropriate for their physical collection, and this ideally will be the case in the digital world as well. Some organizations may decide that their physical collection development policy is sufficient to guide them in their digital collection development with little or no modification, while others may wish to create a distinct digital preservation collection development policy. Policies and the plans that go with them are discussed later in this chapter.

Once a collection is identified for digital preservation, it should be evaluated to determine what actions are necessary before a digital version of the collection can be ingested into the digital preservation system that has been chosen. *Ingest* is defined as the "process by which a digital object or metadata package is absorbed by a different system than the one that produced it."[3] Besides looking at technical and systems-related issues, a review of the digital collection from someone familiar with copyright and licensing issues should be performed, particularly if the digital collection was not created locally. Some of the technical issues include determining whether the digital objects need to be migrated into a more preservation-friendly format before ingestion or determining, if objects are physical objects, how and by whom they will be digitized. If the collection is large, someone familiar with the technical details of the digital preservation system should review it to determine whether or not additional storage, hardware, or software will be necessary process and preservation. This is also a good time to evaluate the descriptive metadata needs of the collection. If the collection comes with metadata, can it be deposited into the digital preservation system with little or no modification? If extensive modification of existing descriptive metadata or original descriptive metadata needs to be carried out before the digital objects are deposited into the preservation system, who will be responsible for making sure that happens, and will additional funding be required? These aspects of organizational, technical, and resource issues are also discussed later in this chapter.

If the collection is coming from an external department or organization, an agreement or *Memorandum of Understanding* (MOU) that describes the collection and the responsibilities of both the department in charge of the digital preservation system and the originator of the content should be created. Additional information about MOUs will be provided in chapter 5 on sustainability. After a MOU or similar agreement is created, the actual work of depositing the collection into the digital preservation system can begin. At this stage, the objects will be digitized or converted to different formats if necessary. This is also when descriptive metadata should be created if it does not already exist. If descriptive metadata does exist, it may need to be augmented or migrated to a different metadata schema. In some cases it will be necessary to provide metadata and digitization training to people working on the project before digitization and descriptive metadata creation can begin. These elements of technology and resources are likewise addressed in a preliminary way later in this chapter; the topic of metadata for digital preservation is treated in greater detail in chapter 7.

If the collection's digital contents are going to be batch loaded into the digital preservation system, it may be advisable to load the digital objects into a test system first if possible. This way, stakeholders can review the batch load in the test system and agree if the load was successful. If the load was not successful, the problems can be corrected and another test load performed. One reason to do a load into a test system is that some digital preservation systems, by design, make it rather difficult to remove objects and, even when objects are straightforward to remove, they create an audit trail that can unnecessarily clutter or complicate future audits and system maintenance. Even if this is not a concern, having everyone look at the digital objects and metadata in a test system, or at least early in the process if no test system is available, is advisable if for no other reason than that it may prove more difficult, time consuming, and expensive to correct an erroneous or faulty load at a later date. At this time any discovery- and access-related issues should be examined as well.

Once all of the identified stakeholders (content creators, information professionals, subject specialists, etc.) agree that the test load is satisfactory, the digital objects should be loaded into the production digital preservation system. Stakeholder should likewise review and approve the load into the production system at this point whenever possible. It is important to do this soon after the load is complete because fixing problems down the road may be more difficult and time consuming, especially if the original people that worked on the collection are no longer available. Below, however, we will see that this somewhat simplistic and technology-heavy chronological approach to digital preservation contains a great deal of interrelated strategies that requiring planning, foresight, and documentation. It is those big-picture aspects of digital preservation initiatives that are the focus of the rest of this chapter.

THE DIGITAL PRESERVATION TRIAD

As demonstrated, the Digital Preservation Triad is comprised of three primary areas: Management, Technology, and Content. Each of these areas is essential to the functioning of the digital preservation initiative, yet each is complex and reliant on the other two. Because all three areas of the Digital Preservation Triad are interrelated and, in some ways, inseparable, any discussion of one will likely bring in considerations from the other areas as well. Below we investigate all three areas broadly, presenting them in the order in which they will be discussed in the book. Special attention is paid here to addressing foundational issues particular to each area of the triad that are not addressed later in the book. Necessarily, though, some content presented here will be elaborated in subsequent chapters.

MANAGEMENT

The first area of digital preservation identified through the Digital Preservation Triad is Management. Management aspects include planning for the Technology and the Content, making sure they are able to work successfully. Practically speaking, Management requires the creation of polices and documentation as well as the oversight of resource issues. Resource issues can be further broken down into human resources and financial resources. This section gives a valuable overview and strategies for dealing with digital preservation policies and planning, describing some issues relating to rights for digital objects. It then talks about both human and financial resources and describes the benefits of outreach in the Management context. Because of the importance of Management to the digital preservation process, this section will necessarily be longer than the other two.

Policies and Planning for Digital Preservation

Policies are high-level documents reflecting the mission of the institution. Accordingly, they are fundamental to making good decisions. More specifically, policies guide in the creation of action plans or guidelines and best practices. To go back to the example from chapter 1, an institution with a mission focusing on certain styles of painting will likely have selection and preservation policies that reinforce that mission. If the mission (or goals, when the mission is not specific) concentrates on a certain group of stakeholders, policies will probably include working with that community of stakeholders to carry out needs assessments to guide the plans that are put in place. Policies should take into account the mission and the goals of the institution and should be revisited less frequently than the more practical documents they inspire. Many institutions post their policies online, making the policies easily accessible for use as templates; for museums wishing to write a policy from scratch, the Canadian Heritage website's "Checklist for Creating a [Digital] Preservation Policy" will provide useful information for getting started.[4]

Plans, unlike policies, are directly actionable and can be case- (or collection-) specific. Although policies are vague, plans or guidelines contain particulars; although policies are guiding documents, plans are road maps that take into account the constraints of the institution. Plans are not voted on or approved at a high level and are often very specific in nature. Institutional policies that address long-term access will be the ones guiding the bulk of the digital preservation planning since plans for digital preservation will often stem from the official policies in place. Alternatively, plans can also be directly based on missions, goals, or objectives of an institution, bypassing a formal written policy.

Christoph Becker and his colleagues have done an outstanding job of exploring the idea of digital preservation plans, within the framework of the Planets (Preservation and Long-term Access through NETworked Services) project (http://www .planets-project.eu/) from the European Union.[5] After four years of incredibly active existence, the Planets project officially came to a close in 2010.[6] Becker and colleagues identify nine elements of a digital preservation plan:

1. identification—of the plan in relation to the collection it defines, facilitating access to the plan at any moment by employees
2. status and triggers—including documentation of the plan's status and the reason for its creation/revision
3. description of the institutional setting—outlining the context in specific terms relevant to the collection at hand
4. description of the collection—information about the objects themselves
5. requirements for preservation—such as information to evaluate potential impacts, costs, and, potentially, rights issues
6. evidence of decision for a preservation strategy—including documentation of alternative actions, objective evaluation, the decision, and the effect of the decision on the collection
7. costs—arising from the preservation plan
8. roles and responsibilities—including the reevaluation of the plan
9. preservation action plan[7]

Though not all digital preservation plans may be this intricate, this level of detail provides the sort of documentation needed to explain decisions and the rationale for those decisions. It also ensures the usability of the collections well into the future by documenting essential information in human-readable form. Ironically, digital preservation plans if recorded electronically need to be preserved as much as the digital objects they describe. Documentation to assist with digital preservation is, however, quite different from the digital objects housed in a digital preservation repository. These plans are revised and revisited regularly, bringing forth questions of versioning. *Versioning* can be defined as "a system for tracking and managing such changes explicitly so as to avoid accidentally replacing a current file with an obsolete previous version and so as to permit comparison of different versions, reversion to an earlier state of the file, and similar actions."[8] Yet these digital preservation plans do not necessarily require the kinds of metadata to ensure authenticity and provenance that other resources do. Detailed plans work within the idiosyncrasies of a collection, allowing for both training of staff and upper-level decisions. They also provide the evidence necessary for distinguishing between collections, highlighting differences and similarities in the various holdings of an institution.

One of the most unnerving things about digital preservation is the requirement on the part of the information professional to see into the future, not only in terms of the technologies needed to maintain and provide access to a resource but also in terms of the actual institution holding the digital objects, its mission, and primary stakeholders, such as users. Policies and plans are created with certain parameters in mind, but over time many things may change. At the most basic level, plans need to be adapted regularly to be certain they respond to the real, actual need for digital preservation.

Becker and his colleagues identify five events that will likely trigger a planning activity: (1) a new collection, (2) a changed collection profile, (3) a changed environment, (4) a changed objective, and (5) periodic review.[9] While it might seem more or less obvious that new and changed circumstances call for the creation of an explicit plan, the fifth trigger may be less apparent. In fact, it may not be obvious at all that periodic review is essential for the health of a collection's digital preservation plan. But without periodic reviews, it is impossible to make sure practices and the rationale for those practices reflects the current state of affairs. We can imagine a scenario where a collection is created for a specific stakeholder—say, a collection development policy is put into place to support the long-term study of Italian politics. If, after a certain number of years, the stakeholders change and no one is interested in Italian politics anymore, it would be opportune to reexamine the collection development policy, the collection itself, future additions to the collection, and current strategies for deciding what to do with the items held.

Technology Decisions

Many, if not most, digital preservation systems rely on the Open Archival Information System (OAIS) Reference Model (see chapter 3 for more information about the model). Someone beginning a digital preservation project should be aware of this model and ideally understand the basics of the OAIS Reference Model; however, it can become very complex very quickly. In reality, as Dr. William Kilbride of the Digital Preservation Coalition says to aspiring digital preservationists, "you don't need to understand or do *all* of this, and, even if you do, it doesn't all have to exist at the same time."[10] There are different technologies available to assist with digital preservation, including, among other technologies, preservation software, servers, storage, and backup devices. The decision to use any should be governed by policies, should be planned, and ultimately should be documented and revisited according to the established schedule. Chapter 3 addresses the Management aspects of the OAIS Reference Model and its relationship to planning a successful digital preservation initiative.

The Question of Rights

When concentrating on the preservation task at hand, it may be possible to lose sight of the fact that digital preservation copies of items are a form of intellectual property. Often text or images are copyrighted or copyrightable content. Digital objects could also represent the text of patents or images associated with trademarks, held by the parent institution. Digitized versions of intellectual property in digital repositories differ from other kinds of property because they can be shared without any aspect of the original being lost. With physical property, we can have an apple and give it to you, but if we do that, we will no longer have an apple. If, on the other hand, we have an idea about how to slice apples, we can share that idea with you while continuing to use the idea ourselves. Our creativity has benefited you as it has us. As shown in figure 2.2, slicing an apple length-wise means that there is no core and that more of the apple can be consumed.

When intellectual property is embodied in a digital format, it can be copied and shared infinitely, much the same way that the idea about apple slicing can be shared. Digital preservationists have the obligation to protect the rights of the creators and other rights holders while carrying out the missions of their institutions and promoting access. The balancing act can be difficult, but with thoughtful reflection and adherence to policies, the digital preservationist will be able to do the right thing.

Figure 2.2.   Cutting an Apple Crosswise with a Paring Knife

In the digital preservation of content in archives, the obligation to maintain records detailing information about ownership, chain of custody, and rights is essential for current and future use of the content. It is simply the responsible choice to document information about rights for each item when possible, to carry out due diligence with seeking information about rights for collections, and to be law-abiding cybercitizens and to comply if asked to removed content or to limit access where appropriate. Part of the process of documenting rights involves exploring copyright issues, which will be discussed as part of the content-centered aspects of digital preservation later in this chapter.

Resource Issues

Of concern primarily to management, resources cover such topics as human resources and the skills necessary for operating the preservation system, financial resources, and outreach. These three topics are addressed below:

Human Resources

As with any project, digital preservation requires human resources. Many institutions may already have the skills necessary to perform digital preservation, but these skills might not reside in any one place or department. The main skills required for digital preservation are technical (systems), concern metadata creation (cataloging), and involve selection and appraisal (collections). It may also be necessary to have staff that can digitize physical items or can perform format migration services for born-digital objects or to have someone who can work on intellectual property issues such as copyright. In some cases, staff may be involved in multiple areas.

The information technology (IT) skills involved will vary depending on the digital preservation system being used. If a museum is developing its own system or implementing an open source system with little or no support agreements, it may need to hire an applications developer familiar with the programming language(s) used by the system. Even if a proprietary system is used, an applications developer may be employed to help create custom submission and display tools. Most digital preservation systems run on a GNU/Linux or UNIX-based system, so someone with GNU/Linux or UNIX systems administrator skills needs to be available. Of course, if a system runs on an alternative operating system, such as Microsoft Windows Server, someone with the skillset to administer that system must be available. One of the most important system administrator responsibilities with digital preservation is backups and disaster recovery. At smaller organizations, the administrator of the digital preservation system may perform this task, but some organizations may have a centralized backup infrastructure that can be utilized.

No matter how well a digital file is protected, if it cannot be found and retrieved it is not digitally preserved. For this reason it is important to have descriptive metadata. It provides attributes of the content being described, including information such as author, title, and subject. The level and type of digital preservation will vary depending on organization and the intended audience. Within a single repository the level of description of digital objects may vary. For example, if an object is being preserved but for intellectual property or other reasons is not available to the general public, it may not be necessary to make sure there is complete subject metadata, whereas a different object in that same repository may be accessible, making full metadata desirable. Chapter 7 of this book investigates metadata in more detail, but it is important to remember that someone needs to be responsible for metadata. In some cases, the person responsible may be a subject expert or even the creator of the content while in other cases it may be a cataloger, digitization staff member, or the person responsible for *ingest*—or uploading the file to the digital preservation system. When the person creating the metadata is not a professional metadata or cataloging specialist, training is normally required. While this training can be provided in many ways, in some cases a cataloger who also acts as a project manager for individual collections is well positioned to provide the training.

Just as it is impossible for most libraries to collect every book ever written, it is usually not possible or even desirable to collect and preserve all digital objects produced by an organization. For this reason it is advisable to have a collection development policy and people responsible for determining what objects or collections to add into the repository.

The number of employees—or FTEs (Full Time Equivalents)—required to maintain the digital preservation system will vary by organization and preservation system used. The National Digital Stewardship Alliance (NDSA) Standards and Practices Working Group conducted a survey of organizations responsible for digital preservation, looking at, among other things, staffing levels. The average institutional respondents to the survey said their organizations had 11.4 FTEs working on digital preservation. They also said, however, that they were understaffed and felt that on average they really need just over 21.1 FTEs for this work. The highest number of FTE staff (both current staffing and needed) involved were in software development, content analysis, electronic record analysis, and cataloging/metadata–analysis functions. According to the survey, the highest-rated qualification when hiring a digital preservation manager was passion/motivation for digital preservation (58 percent said this is extremely important; 34.57 percent said it is very important). The second-highest qualification was knowledge of digital preservation standards, tools, and best practices (57.32 percent said this is extremely important; 37.8 percent said it is very important).[11]

Although some libraries, archives, and museums have rather large digital preservation staffs and want more, not all institutions have teams of almost a dozen or more FTEs working on digital preservation. In 2012 Binghamton University Libraries reported that they had four people playing significant roles related to digital preservation. These people included the Director of Library Technology, who performed most of the system configuration and maintenance, and three librarians from the Cataloging Department who worked with the descriptive metadata for the digital

preservation system. None of these librarians worked full time on digital preservation issues, and Binghamton estimated that a total of only 1.5 FTEs have worked
on implementing and managing Rosetta, its digital preservation system. Additional
library staff have also been involved with Binghamton's digital preservation system
to lesser extents. Special Collections, and University Archives, for example, works to
identify, digitize, and describe library materials to be preserved, while the librarian
responsible for the library's website has worked on issues related to end-user interface
design issues.[12]

Financial Resources

Long-term digital preservation is a complex endeavor, and developing cost pre-
dictions can be a difficult task even for large repositories. This does not mean that
one should not attempt to figure out the costs of long-term preservation, however,
as correctly estimating the long-term digital preservation costs can be crucial to the
endeavor's success. Several projects have attempted to look at long-term preservation
costs. While one might tend to look at prices for hardware and software, studies
have shown the most significant factor in the costs of digital preservation is staffing.
The Costs of Keeping Research Data Safe was a study concluding that in some cases
70 percent of the actual costs went to staffing.[13] The staff costs for one study participant, the Archaeology Data Service, were broken up between access (c. 31 percent),
outreach/acquisition/ingest (c. 55 percent), and archiving (c. 15 percent). As can be
seen by this example, the follow-up study found that costs of archiving activities is
"consistently a very small proportion of the overall costs and significantly lower than
the costs of acquisition/ingest or access activities for all our case studies."[14] Likewise,
Richard Wright, Matthew Addis, and Ant Miller observed that "storage costs are typically a small part of a preservation project or strategy (labour is always the dominant
cost), and storage cost is dropping by 50 percent every eighteen months."[15] We assume that digital preservation will continue to include human intervention and that
no automated procedure will replace readers of this book in the foreseeable future.

One of the most important investigations into creating a cost model for long-
term digital preservation is the LIFE (Life Cycle Information for E-literature)
Project, which is funded by Jisc and is a collaborative effort between the University
College London (UCL) Library Services and the British Library. The project was
designed to look "at the life cycle of the collection and preservation of digital material"[16] and was completed in three separate phases. The LIFE's first phase "created
a digital lifecycle model [and] applied the model to real-life collections, modeling
their life cycles and studying their constituent processes," while the second phase,
LIFE², "reviewed and refined the costing model and associated tools, making it
easier for organizations to study cost and compare their digital lifecycles in a useful
way."[17] LIFE³ continued this work by developing a model and predictive-costing
tool that can be used to estimate the preservation costs of a digital object across the
object's life cycle. Based on a series of real-world case studies, LIFE³ produced "a

series of costing models for each stage and element of the digital lifecycle."[18] There are six stages in the LIFE model, each broken down further in up to six elements. The stages are (1) Creation or Purchase, (2) Acquisition, (3) Ingest, (4) Bit-stream Preservation, (5) Content Preservation, and (6) Access. Figure 2.3 shows the LIFE model and both the stages and the elements of each stage. For digital preservation-ists interested in investigating costing models further, the LIFE³ models predictive costing tool is available as an Excel spreadsheet that can be refined and customized. That LIFE³ costing model is nonetheless based on the stages and elements of the LIFE model shown in figure 2.3. There is also a Web-based prototype version of the costing tool, aimed at "[making] the LIFE model both easily accessible and easy to operate for all levels and backgrounds of users."[19]

Another organization that has undertaken extensive investigations into cost mod-els of long-term digital preservation is the California Digital Library. In the second version of their report on the total cost of preservation (TCP), the UC Curation Center at the California Digital Library developed a formula for the total cost of digital preservation and applied it to two specific pricing models.[20] The first pric-ing model is pay as you go (i.e., a subscription service), and the second is a paid-up model where long-term digital preservation costs are funded upfront. The TCP model divides preservation environments and activities into ten high-level cost com-ponents. In the model, the costs of operating an archival (digital preservation) system are considered fixed costs while other costs are considered marginal costs, since they will vary depending on the size or number of units. Some of the marginal costs in the model include costs associated with necessary services, servers, staff, storage, monitoring, and preservation interventions.

Creation or Purchase	Acquisition	Ingest	Bit-stream Preservation	Content Preservation	Access
....	Selection	Quality Assurance	Repository Administration	Preservation Watch	Access Provision
....	Submission Agreement	Metadata	Storage Provision	Preservation Planning	Access Control
....	IPR & Licensing	Deposit	Refreshment	Preservation Action	User Support
....	Ordering & Invoicing	Holdings Update	Backup	Re-ingest	
....	Obtaining	Reference Linking	Inspection	Disposal	
....	Check-In				

Figure 2.3.   The LIFE Model v2.1
Image used by permission of the LIFE Project, www.life.ac.uk.

Outreach and Sustainability

One important, but sometimes overlooked, factor in securing the necessary human and financial resources for digital preservation is outreach. The Society of American Archivists (SAA) defines an outreach program as "organized activities of archives or manuscript repositories intended to acquaint potential users with their holdings and their research and reference value."[21] *Outreach for digital preservation* could be defined as a set of organized activities of a digital preservation program intended to acquaint stakeholders and potential stakeholders with digital preservation and its value. Digital preservationists need to make sure that stakeholders understand the importance of digital preservation and are aware of the services that staff involved with operating the digital preservation system are able to provide. A stakeholder can be described as a "person, group, or organization that has interest or concern in an organization."[22] This definition of stakeholders is somewhat generic but adequately emphasizes that there are other people and organizations that will and can affect or be affected by an organization. Each organization needs to define its own set of stakeholders. For a publicly funded museum, the stakeholders may include "tax payers, museum visitors, legislators, arts administrators, museum professionals, [and] museum scholars."[23]

Various groups of stakeholders will have different needs and may need to be approached differently and at different times. Outreach to some of these groups can sometimes be difficult and time consuming but, when successful, can go a long way toward making digital preservation a sustainable activity for the organization. The specific way a LAM initiates and maintains an ongoing dialogue with its stakeholders will depend on its relationship with the stakeholders, the nature of the stakeholders, and the local culture. If the organization already has other outreach and public-relations initiatives, it may make sense to combine any digital preservation outreach messages with these existing outreach efforts. Another effective method of raising awareness of digital preservation efforts is to have stakeholders explain to other stakeholders what digital preservation is and how the digital preservation program is important to them. For example, if the digital preservationist is working with a professor to preserve her datasets, and if the professor is happy with the work, it is likely she will let other faculty members know about this service and she may become an advocate for the digital preservation program with administrators and other funders. In other words, have the stakeholders become the organization's champions.

Digital preservation implies a serious financial commitment, and adequate funding is necessary to ensuring digital preservation's sustainability; therefore "it is necessary to have sufficient management buy-in. A communication plan is also needed to gain this buy-in."[24] Part of this communication, or outreach, plan is to be able to communicate with administrators and not just at them. Many, if not most, administrators will be concerned about costs and returns on investment. The digital preservationist should be able to communicate the multiple ways in which digital preservation brings value to the organization. Value is not only demonstrated by preserving digital objects for the future but also in protecting past investments in digital content. As noted by the Alliance Permanent Access to the Records of Science in Europe Network (APARSEN), "quite a lot of organisations understand the need to protect their investment of time, money, and effort put into creating digitized and born digital content, while others organisations have valuable intellectual assets and important collections now in digital format and need to ensure that they are available in the future."[25]

TECHNOLOGY

Digital preservation is not all about technology. It is not possible, however, to undertake digital preservation without the use of complex technology. Although the concepts and underlying technologies are in many ways complicated, the technology involved does not have to be overwhelming.

Trustworthy Digital Preservation Systems

In order to make use of resources and implement the policies described in the management section, a trustworthy digital preservation repository has to be in place. Although the process to become a certified trusted digital repository is long (see chapter 6), the basis for any trustworthy digital preservation initiative is choosing carefully, staffing thoughtfully, and fully supporting the system.

The size and type of server and storage will depend on many factors, including anticipated collection size and the digital preservation software utilized. Many organizations have decided to create their own digital preservation systems, while others have chosen to implement open source or proprietary solutions. Digital preservation software systems are improving every day, but it is important to keep in mind that digital preservation is still a new discipline and a rapidly evolving field. A few of the prominent software systems in this area include (1) Rosetta, a commercial offering from Ex Libris, (2) Tessella's various digital preservation solutions, (3) DAITSS (Dark Archive in the Sunshine State), an open source application developed by the Florida Center for Library Automation (FCLA) with funding from the Institute of Museum and Library Services (IMLS), and (4) Archivematica, an open source system designed for standards-based, long-term access to digital materials, each of which we examine in the following.

Rosetta is a proprietary digital preservation system designed by Ex Libris in collaboration with the National Library of New Zealand. Enabling organizations to preserve and provide access to digital collections in the near and long-term, Rosetta is a highly scalable and expandable solution. Its design was based on the OAIS Reference Model and is meant to conform to the Trusted Digital Repositories (TDR) requirements. Unlike some other systems, Rosetta does not include a discovery interface for end users, instead relying on a digital publishing system that, by default, uses the Open Archives Initiative Protocol for Metadata Harvesting (OAI-PMH) to allow a discovery interface to harvest the metadata. The Binghamton University Libraries use this method to transfer metadata to its discovery layer (Primo, also from Ex Libris), where end-users can search metadata from Rosetta along with records from the libraries' automation system.[26] Rosetta is extremely scalable, equally capable of handling small and large collections with ease. According to a white paper available on Ex Libris's website, tests conducted by the Information and Communications Systems department of the Church of Jesus Christ of Latter-day Saints showed that Rosetta can ingest 200,000 files of 100 KB each in under six hours and that one installation of Rosetta "could easily accommodate fifty million records."[27]

Tessela is a company whose various digital preservation services, including digital preservation technology, consulting, and research, allows them to offer multiple digital preservation solutions. One of their offerings, which they describe as a first step, is the Basic Repository, which collects "information in a central, managed location that is indexed and backed up."[28] The Basic Repository, however, does not offer full-blown preservation, only ensuring bit-level preservation. Two more complete offerings from Tessela are the Safety Deposit Box and Preservica. The Safety Deposit Box solution features includes ingest, data management, storage, a Web-based access module that enables end users access to content, full implementation of active preservation activities including preservation planning and action, and administration functions. For those who prefer a cloud computing–based solution, Preservica is a full-featured, pay-as-you-go digital preservation solution that runs on Amazon Web Services.[29]

DAITSS is an open source digital preservation system built, with some support from the IMLS, by the Florida Center for Library Automation (FCLA). The Florida Digital Archive (FDA) has used DAITSS since late 2006, and as of June 2011 it held 87 TB of storage for a single copy of the repository.[30] According to the FCLA, DAITSS "was the first preservation repository in the United States to implement active preservation strategies based on format transformation."[31] This is still largely true in the United States "where the lion's share of public funding has gone into Private LOCKSS [(Lots of Copies Keeps stuff safe)] Networks and other storage-based approaches."[32] In April 2010, DAITSS 2 was released, a completely rewritten version of DAITSS, utilizing "a series of RESTful Web services coded in Ruby."[33] Although the software was rewritten, the functionality does not differ from the original version of DAITSS.

Archivematica is an open source digital preservation system managed by Artefactual Systems, Incorporated, in collaboration with a number of governmental and nongovernmental organizations. Archivematica takes a microservices design approach, where the output of one task can be directed to the input of the next. The idea behind this methodology is to help prevent technological obsolesce of the software since it is easier to replace a microservice with a new or updated microservice than it is to rewrite or retrofit the whole application. The Archivematica Archival Information Package (AIP) makes use of standards-based systems and metadata standards including Metadata Encoding and Transmission Standard (METS), Preservation Metadata: Implementation Strategies (PREMIS), and Dublin Core, because they believe doing so will lower the cost of migrating to a new system in the future. Archivematica stores AIPs in the BagIt hierarchical file packaging format, an Internet Engineering Task Force Internet draft specification developed by the Library of Congress and the California Digital Library "to simplify large-scale data transfers between cultural institutions."[34] Another feature of Archivematica is that it is designed to use existing storage systems including LOCKSS and cloud-based storage. Archivematica 1.0 was released in January 2014.

Other open source digital library software applications that include some level of digital preservation functionality are CDS-Invenio, DSpace, EPrints, Fedora, Greenstone, and MyCore. A 2012 study appearing in *The Journal of Academic Librarianship* showed that, although these programs have varying levels of digital preservation support, open source digital library software still generally falls short when it comes to support for digital preservation.[35] Many of these open source systems are being actively developed, however, and, in some cases, are being retrofitted or even rewritten with digital preservation in mind. They may offer most of the functionality needed for digital preservation and, for this, are worth evaluating as part of a digital preservation initiative. Additionally, there are a number of digital asset management systems that may not have all of the components of a complete digital preservation system but are being used by organizations for at least part of their digital preservation needs. Digital preservationists should evaluate these and other digital preservation systems with open eyes to determine whether the systems meet their needs, what resources (human and financial) will be necessary to implement them, and what their limitations might be.

Because this is a rapidly changing environment, this book does not go into depth about any particular digital preservation system. The systems described above are only examples that highlight some of the key components of digital preservation systems someone may want to consider and should not be the only systems considered. Besides software functionality, it is also important to consider sustainability. Some sustainability factors involving technology, such as the strength of the user community, the rate of ongoing development, and issues affecting open source and proprietary systems, will be discussed in further detail in chapter 5.

Servers, Storage, and Other Computer Equipment

The type, size, and number of servers, storage, and other hardware will vary depending on the digital preservation software used and the size of the collections. Many of the digital preservation systems run on a GNU/Linux– or UNIX–based operating system and the hardware will need to be compatible with the operating system.

New digital preservationists ought to keep in mind that multiple copies of data should be stored in multiple places in order to keep it safe. There is not an agreement about how many copies are necessary, and the number of copies recommended could be anywhere from two to six depending on who is making the recommendation. In practice, the level of resources available often determines the number of copies of digital objects kept and where they are stored.[36] An additional factor to consider when attempting to determine the amount of data storage necessary is that in many cases multiple versions of a digital object are kept. This occurs because when digital objects are migrated or normalized into new formats the original files are usually not deleted. Instead an additional file is created, and both versions are preserved in the digital preservation system. For example, if a document is provided to a digital preservation repository in WordPerfect (.wpd) format, the digital preservationist may choose to normalize the file in the PDF/A format. As mentioned in chapter 1, PDF/A is an International Organization for Standardization (ISO) standard, making it a good choice, since a document in the PDF/A format can preserve its "visual appearance over time, independent of the tools and systems used for creating, storing, or rendering the files."[37] In the case where PDF/A would be chosen for use in a digital preservation repository, it is possible that some data could be lost in this format migration process. In order to ensure provenance, the institution's policies may call for both the PDF/A and original WordPerfect document to be stored. This means that the amount of storage needed can be significantly higher than if only the migrated copy was kept.

Many technologists believe it is also necessary to make sure that data is kept in geographically diverse places. It is probably obvious to most people that it is not prudent to have backup copies of data in the same room or building as the actively stored and managed data, but it may not be as clear that it is wise to have copies of the data stored in different geographic regions. For example, if your organization has copies of data in two different locations but both locations are in Los Angeles, it is possible an earthquake could destroy both locations simultaneously. Therefore, your organization may want to move one of those copies to a data center located in the Midwest or along the Eastern seaboard of the United States.

Metadata

Anyone who has ever tried to search for image files on the Web knows that metadata is an essential aspect of information storage and retrieval. Photos that have not been tagged or given a title are difficult to search. Though some systems may make up for a lack of text-based keywords by allowing for queries based on the visual content of the image (predominate color, shape of main item, etc.), users will still not know the specifics of an image's subject, who the author is, and if it is possible to use it when metadata is lacking. *Metadata*, digital information about digital files that ultimately permits their retrieval and use, is also key in the suite of tools necessary for using technology to preserve digital objects. Metadata will depend on a variety of aspects, including the digital preservation system chosen, the needs of the users, the content being preserved, and the capacities of the institution for devoting resources, financial and human, to its creation. Chapter 7 will delve into great detail about metadata and the specific metadata needs of digital preservation systems.

File Formats

In order to address problems that arise with format obsolescence, one must know what format a file is in. New digital preservationists just beginning to work with digital preservation projects may not realize how many different file formats there are. Take, for example, the Word Document Format (.doc) that was the de facto standard for Microsoft Office users before the XML-based .docx format was introduced in Word 2003. There are actually four different versions of the .doc format: (1) Word for DOS, (2) Word for Windows 1 and 2 and Word 4 and 5 for Mac, (3) Word 6 and Word 95 for Windows, with Word 6 for Mac, and (4) Word 97, 2000, 2002, 2003, 2007, and 2010 for Windows, and Word 98, 2001, X, and 2004 for Mac.[38] Therefore, one cannot just look at a file extension and know the file format. This is where file format registries like PRONOM come into play.

First released in March 2002, PRONOM was developed in the digital preservation department of the United Kingdom's National Archives. As of this writing, the current version of PRONOM is 6.2 and a linked data version is in development. According its website, "PRONOM is a resource for anyone requiring impartial and definitive information about the file formats, software products, and other technical components required to support long-term access to electronic records and other digital objects of cultural, historical, or business value."[39] Besides being a technical registry of information about file formats, PRONOM also provides tools and services. The DROID (Digital Record Object Identification) software tool is a major service, automating the identification of file formats. PRONOM and other file format registries will be discussed in greater detail in chapter 8.

Once file formats are identified, the digital preservationist needs to determine whether the format is suitable for digital preservation. While this decision may often vary by project or repository, there are some common factors usually considered when determining a file format for digital preservation purposes. Typically file formats that are open and widely utilized are preferred. An example for images includes TIFF files (formerly Tagged Image File Format, TIFF, but as of version 6 in 1992 known only as TIFF), and for textual documents, PDF/A files. Chapter 8 discusses file formats used for digital preservation in much greater detail.

CONTENT

No matter how well thought-out your management policy and plans are or how good your technology is, without content there is nothing to preserve. Acquiring content to preserve should typically involve all areas of an organization. Digital content for preservation might come from collections the organization already possesses, such as a library's special collections or born digital records in an archive. Content may also come from other areas of the organization or from external organizations such as a local historical society or an enthusiasts group. When working to acquire external content, digital preservationists should attempt to include all relevant personnel in their outreach and other communication efforts. For example, it is important that subject librarians, archivists, and curators be knowledgeable enough about digital preservation that when a stakeholder comes to them with a question involving digital objects they can either answer the question or can direct the person to someone who can. People who serve as the public face of the institution for both content producers and content users do not necessarily need to become digital preservation experts, but they should be provided with enough information so as to effectively communicate with a variety of stakeholders. One major issue with content is access and reuse. This section looks at copyright issues both in the United States and internationally and briefly considers some kinds of content that might be included in digital preservation systems.

Copyright Issues

Providing usable content is one goal of maintaining a digital preservation system. Regardless of the source of content being digitally preserved, copyright issues should be investigated to make sure the proper intellectual property rights have been granted that are legally required to preform the actions necessary for long-term preservation. Copyright is designed to protect the creativity of content creators by protecting their creative works. Copyright is a difficult topic for digital preservationists, though, who need to balance the protection of the rights of the copyright holders with the rights of the digital preservation system's users. As Laura Gasaway pointed out in the *Journal of Entertainment & Technology Law*, "because the contents of [LAM] digital collections often consist of one-of-a-kind original works such as unpublished letters, documents, and manuscripts, the digitization of existing content can more broadly facilitate the creation of new knowledge by an even wider array of scholars and researchers than in the past."[40] Before content in a digital preservation system can go online, digital preservationists need to think through and document information relating to the rights of those content items and secure permissions as necessary or as possible.

Even the nature of accessibility and copies is different when talking about digital content. The digital item created and made accessible as part of a digital preservation system is fundamentally different from an analog item. Period. After looking at an artifact in a museum, there is no copy created anywhere. Yet when looking at a digital image online, the computer's cache will create and store a copy of that image long term, if not indefinitely.[41] The nature of digital content adds a layer of complexity to the question of ownership and rights. "Our copyright laws," says William Patry in *How to Fix Copyright*, "are based on the marketplace and technologies of the eighteenth century."[42] When institutions make digitized content available, what are their obligations to the owners of the original work? The creators of the digital file? Their users?

Before posting anything in a publicly accessible repository, institutions should have the permission to make that content available or should reasonably assume that the work is in the public domain or is an orphan work. Gasaway explains that most libraries post a disclaimer along with a work if they are unable to ascertain the copyright status of the work. If a copyright owner comes forth and objects, the library then no longer provides public access to the content.[43] Although it might seem counterintuitive at first, the very act of making a digital copy of an analog work or of another digital item does not grant the institution any kind of rights, even if the institution undertook considerable expense to have those copies made.[44] The intellectual property being housed in the collection and being made available is not the institution's simply because items were digitized in-house using staff hours, for example. Digital objects that an institution does not have the rights to make available may still be curated and preserved but will be housed in a *dark archive* where they are not accessible by unauthorized users.

Digital preservationists record all known rights information in the metadata for a digital object and, at the same time, have the obligation to keep protected content off the Web. As mentioned in the first chapter, digital preservation does not necessarily equate to open access. When protected content is in question, repositories should know their rights and responsibilities, making an informed choice about how to proceed.

International Aspects of Copyright

Copyright is a national issue that is addressed by national laws; laws on intellectual property enacted in the United States, for example, do not apply in other countries.[45] On a practical level, treaties and agreements govern the protection of rights internationally; those treaties include the Berne Convention and the World Trade Organization's Trade-Related Aspects of Intellectual Property Rights (TRIPS).[46] When digital preservation systems make content available on the Web, the potential exists for anyone, worldwide, to access and use that content. It is no surprise that the United States perceives itself as a major creator of copyrightable materials and that it has very strong intellectual property laws in effect. This may be different from developing countries, often seen as consumers of copyrighted materials, who may have less-stringent laws on the books.[47]

International users may have a very different approach to digital content and rights. Patry argues that the "copy" in the English word *copyright* derives from the noun "copy" in the 1710 Statute of Anne but is now equally applied to the verb "to copy" or to reproduce.[48] Other countries and traditions may not be as concerned with the product of the creative endeavor as they are with the creator herself. French law, for example, addresses the question of *droit d'auteurs*, or author rights, as opposed to copyrights.[49]

Content-Related Challenges

Digital preservationists, in carrying out their work, will need to collect, organize, make available, and preserve a variety of digital objects in a way that ensures authenticity. It is important to acquire preservation-worthy content and to make sure that the proper permissions have been granted for long-term preservation. This includes the right to migrate content to new formats and make it accessible. Specific challenges relating to Content may pertain to aspects of Management—that is, developing the collection, ensuring its usefulness, and providing for its long-term preservation. Other challenges might relate to Technology—that is, the usability of the digital preservation system, the metadata, and the files themselves. Content-related challenges might also relate to the kind of content being preserved in light of the fact that research data, for example, is vastly different in its use and retrieval than digital humanities data. Both of these kinds of content will be examined in greater detail in part IV of this book.

CONCLUSION

This chapter focused on the nuts and bolts of getting started with digital preservation using the Digital Preservation Triad as a framework. To begin a digital preservation initiative, it is helpful first to step back and take a look at the big picture. Because digital preservation is a long-term undertaking that requires both human and financial resources, understanding the Management issues will play a role in the success of the digital preservation project. Costs for digital preservation can also be a huge consideration, and cost models were described that will help institutions think about such expenses over the long term. Policies and documentation that lay out the necessary steps and tasks will need to be created and maintained. Technology is an important next consideration, as it allows digital objects to be stored, retrieved, and used and is an ever-changing bull's eye that digital preservationists must attempt to target. Finally, without Content digital preservation is meaningless.

The remainder of the book will be divided into three parts organized around the Digital Preservation Triad. Part II revolves around management issues. Chapters in this section will cover The OAIS Reference Model; education, and human resources; and sustainable digital preservation. Part III consists of three chapters related to the technology portion of the Digital Preservation Triad, which chapters include discussions of formalizing trust in the digital repository, metadata and metadata for digital preservation, and file formats and software for digital preservation. Finally, part IV of the book will cover content-related aspects of digital preservation, including discussions of collection development and the preservation of both research data and humanities content.

NOTES

1. Sarah Jones, "Small Steps and Lasting Impact: Making a Start with Preservation," (paper presented at Getting Started with Digital Preservation, Glasgow, February 28, 2011), slide 18, http://www.bl.uk/blpac/pdf/digitalstartglasjones.pdf.

2. Digital Preservation Management Workshop, "Where to Begin?" accessed September 29, 2013, http://www.dpworkshop.org/dpm-eng/conclusion.html.

3. Life Cycle Information for E-literature (LIFE), *LIFE: Glossary and Reference*, s.v. "Ingest," accessed July 15, 2013, http://www.life.ac.uk/glossary/.

4. Canadian Heritage Information Network, "Checklist for Creating a Preservation Policy," last modified February 15, 2013, http://www.pro.rcip-chin.gc.ca/contenu_numerique -digital_content/preservation_numerique-digital_preservation/annexeA-appendixA-eng.jsp.

5. Planets is an acronym for Preservation and Long-term Access through NETworked Services (http://www.planets-project.eu/). See Christoph Becker, Hannes Kulovits, Mark Guttenbrunner, Stephan Strodl, Andreas Rauber, and Hans Hofman, "Systematic Planning for Digital Preservation: Evaluating Potential Strategies and Building Preservation Plans," *International Journal of Digital Librarianship* 10 (2009): 133–57, especially p. 137.

6. Library of Congress (LOC), "Planets," accessed September 29, 2013, http://www.digital preservation.gov/series/edge/planets.html.

7. Becker et al., "Systematic Planning."

8. DH Curation Guide, *Glossary*, s.v. "Versioning, version control," accessed September 29, 2013, http://guide.dhcuration.org/glossary.html.

9. Becker et al., "Systematic Planning," 137–38.

10. William Kilbride, "Introducing Digital Preservation" (paper presented at Getting Started with Digital Preservation, Glasgow, February 28, 2011), http://www.bl.uk/blpac/pdf/ digitalstartglaskilbride.pdf.

11. Andrea Goethals, Jimi Jones, Carol Kussman, Kate Murry, and Meg Phillips. "Who's Minding the (Data) Store? Results of the NDSA Digital Preservation Staffing Survey" (poster presented at the iPRES 2012 Conference, Toronto, October 1–5, 2012), http://www.digi talpreservation.gov/ndsa/documents/NDSA-staff-survey-poster-ipres2012.pdf.

12. Edward M. Corrado, "Implementing Rosetta at Binghamton University Libraries," *SUNYergy* 14, no. 1 (2012): 1, http://www.sunyconnect.suny.edu/sunyergy/default52.htm.

13. Neil Beagrie, "Keeping Research Data Safe: Costs of Research Data Preservation" (paper presented at the Preservation and Archiving Special Interest Group [PASIG] Conference, Dublin, October 2012), http://lib.stanford.edu/files/pasig-oct2012/12-Beagrie -PASIG-1012_CB_costs2.pdf.

14. Neil Beagrie, Brian Lavoie, and Matthew Woolard. *Keeping Research Data Safe 2: Final Report* (Salisbury, Eng.: Charles Beagrie Limited, 2010), 80, http://www.jisc.ac.uk/media/ documents/publications/reports/2010/keepingresearchdatasafe2.pdf.

15. Richard Wright, Matthew Addis, and Ant Miller. "The Significance of Storage in the 'Cost of Risk' of Digital Preservation" (presentation at iPRES 2008, London, September 29–30, 2008), 5, http://www.bl.uk/ipres2008/presentations_day1/21_Wright.pdf.

16. Life Cycle Information for E-literature (LIFE), "LIFE: Life Cycle Information for E-literature," "What Is Life," para 1, accessed December 23, 2012, http://www.life.ac.uk/about/.

17. Paul Wheatley, "Costing the DP Lifecycle More Effectively" (paper presented at iPRES 2008, London, September 29–30, 2008), 1, http://www.bl.uk/ipres2008/presentations_ day1/19_Wheatley.pdf.

18. Brian Hole, "Understanding the True Costs of Digital Preservation: LIFE³" (presentation at Decoding the Digital, London, July 27, 2010), http://www.bl.uk/blpac/pdf/decoding hole.pdf.

19. The LIFE³ Web Tool prototype is available online at http://www.life.ac.uk/tool/. See Brian Hole, Li Lin, Patrick McCann, and Paul Wheatley, "LIFE³: A Predictive Costing Tool

for Digital Collections" (paper presented at the iPRES 2010 Conference, Vienna, September 19–24, 2010), 4, http://www.life.ac.uk/3/docs/Ipres2010_life3_submitted.pdf.

20. UC Curation Center and California Digital Library, "Total Cost of Preservation (TCP): Cost Modeling for Sustainable Services, Revision 2.0 (draft) 2012-11-09," U.C. Curation Center and California Digital Library, November 9, 2012, https://wiki.ucop.edu/download/attachments/163610649/TCP-cost-modeling-for-sustainable-services-v2.pdf.

21. Lewis J. Bellardo and Lynn Lady Bellardo, *A Glossary for Archivists, Manuscript Curators, and Records Managers* (Chicago: Society of American Archivists, 1992), 24.

22. BusinessDictionary.com, s.v. "Stakeholder," accessed September 29, 2013, http://www.businessdictionary.com/definition/stakeholder.html.

23. Carole Rosenstein, "When Is a Museum a Public Museum? Considerations from the Point of View of Public Finance," *International Journal of Cultural Policy* 16, no. 4 (Nov. 2010): 450.

24. Ruben Riestra, Xenia Beltran, Panos Georgiou, Giannis Tsakonas, Kirnn Kaur, Susan Reilly, and Karlheinz Schmitt, *Business Preparedness Report* (Dorset, Eng., and The Hague: APARSEN, 2013), 23, APARSEN-REP-D36_1-01-1_0, http://www.alliancepermanentaccess.org/wp-content/uploads/downloads/2013/03/APARSEN-REP-D36_1-01-1_0.pdf.

25. APARSEN stands for Alliance Permanent Access to the Records of Science in Euorpe Network. See Riestra, Beltran, Georgiou, Tsakonas, Kaur, Reilly, and Schmitt, *Business Preparedness Report*, 39.

26. Corrado, "Implementing Rosetta," 1.

27. Ex Libris/Rosetta, *The Ability to Preserve a Large Volume of Digital Assets: A Scaling Proof of Concept* (Jerusalem: Ex Libris, Ltd., 2010), 13, http://www.exlibrisgroup.com/files/Products/Preservation/RosettaScalingProofofConcept.pdf.

28. Tessella Digital Preservation, "Basic Repository," accessed June 15, 2014, http://www.digital preservation.com/solution/basic-repository/.

29. Tessella Digital Preservation, "Preservica," accessed June 15, 2014, http://www.digital preservation.com/solution/preservica/.

30. Priscilla Capalan, "DAITSS, an OAIS-Based Preservation Repository," in *Proceedings of the 2010 Roadmap for Digital Preservation Interoperability Framework Workshop*, Gaithersburg, Md., March 29-31, 2010, http://daitss.fcla.edu/sites/daitss.fcla.edu/files/DAITSS%20in%20ACM%20rev_0.pdf.

31. Ibid, 2.

32. Ibid.

33. Ibid.

34. Library of Congress (LOC), "Library Develops Bagit Specification for Transferring Digital Content," para 2, accessed July 31, 2013, http://www.digitalpreservation.gov/news/2008/20080602news_article_bagit.html.

35. Devika P. Madalli, Sunita Barve, and Saiful Amin, "Digital Preservation in Open source Digital Library Software," *The Journal of Academic Librarianship* 38, no. 3 (2012): 161–64.

36. Martha Anderson, "B Is for Bit Preservation," *The Signal*, September 7, 2011, http://blogs.loc.gov/digitalpreservation/2011/09/b-is-for-bit-preservation/.

37. International Organization for Standardization (ISO), "ISO 19005-1:2005: Document Management; Electronic Document File Format for Long-Term Preservation, Part 1: Use of PDF 1.4 (PDF/A-1)," http://www.iso.org/iso/iso_catalogue/catalogue_tc/catalogue_detail.htm?csnumber=38920, cited in Alexandra Oettler, *PDF/A in a Nutshell 2.0: PDF for Long-Term Archiving; The ISO Standard, from PDF/A-1 to PDF/A-3* (Berlin: Association for

Digital Document Standards, 2013), 5, accessed September 29, 2013, http://www.pdfa.org/wp-content/uploads/2013/05/PDFA_in_a_Nutshell_211.pdf.

38. For additional information about Microsoft Word file formats, see http://en.wikipedia.org/wiki/Microsoft_Word#File_extension.

39. National Archives, "Welcome to PRONOM," para 2, accessed November 25, 2012, http://www.nationalarchives.gov.uk/PRONOM/Default.aspx.

40. Laura N. Gasaway, "Libraries, Digital Content, and Copyright," *Vanderbilt Journal of Entertainment & Technology Law* 12, no. 4 (2010): 758–59.

41. Gretchen McCord Hoffmann, "Browsing and Caching," in *Copyright in Cyberspace 2*, edited by Gretchen McCord Hoffmann, especially 73 (New York: Neal-Schuman, 2005).

42. William Patry, *How to Fix Copyright* (Oxford: Oxford University Press, 2011), 37–38.

43. Gasaway, "Libraries, Digital Content, and Copyright," especially 763.

44. Gasaway, "Libraries, Digital Content, and Copyright," 760 and footnote 19.

45. Andreas P. Reindl, "Choosing Law in Cyberspace: Copyright Conflicts on Global Networks," *Michigan Journal of International Law* 19 (1998): 799, 800.

46. Michael Boardman, "Digital Copyright Protection and Graduated Response: A Global Perspective," *Loyola of Los Angeles International & Comparative Law Review* 33, no. 2 (2011): 223–54.

47. Susy Frankel, "Digital Copyright and Culture," *The Journal of Arts Management, Law, and Society* 40 (2010): 140–56.

48. Patry, *How to Fix Copyright.*

49. Heather Lea Moulaison and Sarah Wenzel, "Who Owns the Eiffel Tower? Issues Surrounding the Digitization of Cultural Heritage in Modern France," *Documents to the People* 39, no. 1 (2011): 21–25.

II

MANAGEMENT ASPECTS

3

The OAIS Reference Model

Management issues are the first issues raised in the Digital Preservation Triad. One way to begin thinking about management aspects of digital preservation is to examine established standards that focus on broad-strokes approaches. The Open Archival Information System (OAIS) Reference Model is a high-level model widely accepted by digital preservationists as a key standard for digital repositories; for this reason, we begin our look at Management issues here. The OAIS Reference Model describes how digital objects should be preserved for a certain group of users from the point when the objects are deposited into the system to the point when they are disseminated, including ongoing preservation and administrative activities in between. Because the OAIS Reference Model is meant to apply to a wide variety of situations, it is not specific in describing what the needs are of any one specific designated community. It is designed to be entirely context neutral. Instead, the task of determining the user group and its needs is left to the individual repository administrators. Likewise, the OAIS Reference Model stops short of "specifying the detail of formats or hardware required."[1] The OAIS Reference Model is an ISO (International Organization for Standards) Standard (ISO 14721).

Since the OAIS Reference Model is designed to be context neutral, it "deliberately avoids jargon from both the IT and archival professions; this is very useful, as it makes both groups speak the same language."[2] In an attempt to retain context neutrality, the OAIS Reference Model introduces its own vocabulary to define terms related to digital preservation; in this chapter, OAIS vocabulary terms begin with a capital letter as they do in the Reference Model. The model maintains context neutrality rather successfully through the terms it uses, but introducing a new vocabulary is not without some drawbacks. Because the OAIS vocabulary uses terms and phrases that might already be part of staff members' professional jargon, initial misunderstandings or miscommunication are possible. This pitfall can usually be avoided with a little bit of effort by those involved in digital preservation if they make themselves familiar with the OAIS terminology and use it consistently when talking about digital preservation.

It is important to understand that the OAIS Reference Model is not a specific implementation; rather, it is an abstract model for thinking about digital preservation repositories. While software developers may need to be familiar with all of the intricacies of the OAIS Reference Model, digital preservationists do not necessarily need to know all of the ins and outs. They should, however, become familiar with the model and the vocabulary. The following overview will be helpful in this respect. We begin with a look at the history of the OAIS Reference Model. After that, we examine the four components, especially in light of how they pertain to the management aspect of digital preservation.

HISTORY

The OAIS Reference Model was developed within the Consultative Committee for Space Data Systems (CCSDS). Development formally began on April 4, 1994, when a "new work item (NWI) related to 'archiving space data'" was proposed to an ISO technical subcommittee.[3] The development process was lead by Don Sawyer, the head of the U.S. National Aeronautics and Space Administration (NASA) Office of Standards and Technology (NOST).[4] Although the process of developing the OAIS Reference Model was undertaken to preserve data collected from outer space, the process was *open* to interested parties from other disciplines as well. The word *open* in Open Archival Information System refers to the openness of the process through which the standard was created. It does not mean the repository must be open in familiar terms such as open access, open data, or open source software. All told, over three hundred people participated in one or more workshops that were part of the development and review of the model.[5]

The appropriate ISO subcommittee approved a version of the OAIS Reference Model to be distributed as a draft international standard (DIS) in May 2000. This version is known as Red Book 1.[6] After being revised a few times, the OAIS Reference Model was published as an ISO standard (ISO 14721:2003) in February 2003. The September 2007 Blue Book is identical to the 2003 version of the ISO standard except for some editorial corrections. In August 2009, a Pink Book version that contained an updated "draft recommended standard" was released. In June 2012 a revision to the standard was approved. The new version of the OAIS Reference Model is known as Magenta Book 2. This text is identical to the updated ISO 14721 standard that was also approved in 2012 (ISO 14721:2012).[7]

OAIS REFERENCE MODEL COMPONENTS

The OAIS Reference Model provides four basic things: these are (1) a vocabulary intended to describe common applications (vocabulary terms are defined in section 1 of the OAIS Reference Model and briefly discussed in this chapter), (2) an information model (sometimes referred to as a *data model*), (3) a recommended functional model for "carrying out the archive's required responsibilities,"[8] and (4) a set of required responsibilities for an Archive. Below, we discuss each of the four basic aspects covered in the OAIS Reference Model.

Vocabulary

As mentioned above, the OAIS Reference Model includes a vocabulary for terms relating to digital preservation. Although there is a convergence in interest in digital preservation among members of the information professions and those working in cultural heritage institutions, the OAIS Reference Model assumes that digital preservationists will need their own language in order to communicate effectively between themselves and with IT. Terms in the OAIS Reference Model vocabulary are written with capital letters to distinguish them from less-formal uses. For example, the term *Archive* is defined as "an organization that intends to preserve information for access and use by a Designated Community."[9] An OAIS is defined as a specific type of "Archive, consisting of an organization, which may be part of a larger organization, of people and systems, that has accepted the responsibility to preserve information and make it available for a Designated Community."[10] Additionally, in order to be considered an OAIS, the Archive must meet specific requirements outlined in the OAIS Reference Model.

In providing the digital preservation community with a means to speak clearly and understand each other unambiguously, the OAIS Reference Model permits cross-disciplinary dialogue about preservation to be efficient and precise. Selected vocabulary terms from the OAIS Reference Model will appear throughout this chapter, in subsequent chapters as necessary, and in this book's glossary as well.

Information Model

The OAIS Reference Model describes a conceptual structure for supporting long-term preservation of information. This structure is known as an Information Package. "An Information Package is a container that contains two types of Information Objects, the Content Information and the Preservation Description Information (PDI)"[11] These Information Packages are used within an OAIS-compliant digital preservation system and are provided to, or submitted by, external users and systems. There are three variants of Information Packages described in the OAIS Reference Model: Archival Information Packages, Submission Information Packages, and Dissemination Information Packages.

An Archival Information Package (AIP) is an Information Package that is preserved within an OAIS-compliant digital preservation system. AIPs contain Content Information including descriptive metadata. Along with the Content Information, they also must contain Preservation Description Information (PDI), "information that will support the trust in, the access to, and context of the Content Information over an indefinite period of time."[12] The PDI must include the "information that is necessary to adequately preserve the particular Content Information with which it is associated. It is specifically focused on describing the past and present states of the Content Information, ensuring it is uniquely identifiable, and ensuring it has not been unknowingly altered."[13] For more information about the PDI, see chapter 7 in this book on metadata for digital preservation.

The OAIS Reference Model defines a Submission Information Package (SIP) as "an Information Package that is delivered by the Producer to the OAIS for use in the construction or update of one or more AIPs and/or the associated Descriptive Information."[14] A SIP contains data (digital objects) and any metadata that is supplied by the Producer.

A Dissemination Information Package (DIP) is defined by the OAIS Reference Model as "an Information Package, derived from one or more AIPs and sent by Archives to the Consumer in response to a request to the OAIS."[15]

OAIS Functional Model

The OAIS Functional Model is the portion of the OAIS Reference Model standard that typically receives the most attention. The OAIS Functional Model describes six main functional entities and how they interact with each other: (1) Ingest, (2) Archival Storage, (3) Data Management, (4) Administration, (5) Preservation Planning, and (6) Access. We give a brief description of each of these functional entities in table 3.1. Figure 3.1 shows the interaction of these functional entities.

Table 3.1. OAIS Functional Entities

Functional Entity	Brief Description
Ingest	The Ingest Functional Entity provides services and functions that allow digital objects to be deposited into the system. It accepts Submission Information Packages (SIPs) and prepares the contents of the SIP so that it can be managed and stored with the OAIS–compliant archive. A SIP usually includes some content information and some Preservation Description Information (PDI).
Archival Storage	The Archival Storage Functional Entity provides services and functions related to the storage, maintenance, and retrieval of Archival Information Packages (AIPs). Archival Storage services include placing AIPs in permanent storage, disaster recovery capabilities, error checking, and providing AIPs to the Access Functional Entity.
Data Management	The Data Management Functional Entity provides services and functions related to populating, maintaining, and accessing descriptive and administrative metadata. Functions include maintaining schemas and views, performing database updates, and performing queries and producing reports based on data management queries.

Functional Entity	Brief Description
Administration	The Administrative Functional Entity provides services and functions that support the overall operation of the system. "Administration functions include soliciting and negotiating submission agreements with Producers, auditing submissions to ensure that they meet Archive standards, and maintaining configuration management of system hardware and software."[1] Additionally it provides systems-engineering functions and is "responsible for establishing and maintaining Archive standards and policies, providing customer support, and activating stored requests."[2]
Preservation Planning	The Preservation Planning Functional Entity provides "services and functions for monitoring the environment of the OAIS, providing recommendations and preservation plans to ensure that the information stored in the OAIS remains accessible to, and understandable by, the Designated Community over the Long Term, even if the original computing environment becomes obsolete."[3] Functions include recommending archival information updates, migrating current archive holdings, and documenting Archive standards and policies. Other functions include providing risk analysis reports and monitoring technological changes and changes in the Designated Community's service requirements.
Access	The Access Functional Entity provides services and functions that support end users—or, in OAIS terms, *Consumers*—of information, including being able to determine "the existence, description, location, and availability of information stored in the OAIS and allowing Consumers to request and receive information products. Access functions include communicating with Consumers to receive requests, applying controls to limit access to specially protected information, coordinating the execution of requests to successful completion, generating responses (Dissemination Information Packages, query responses, reports), and delivering the responses to Consumers."[4]

1. Consultative Committee for Space Data Systems (CCSDS), *Reference Model for an Open Archival Information System (OAIS): Recommended Practice CCSDS 650.0-M-2; Recommendation for Space Data System Practices*, Magenta Book, Recommended Practice, issue 2 (Washington, D.C.: CCSDS Secretariat, June 2012), http://public.ccsds.org/publications/archive/650x0m2.pdf.

2. Ibid, 4-2.

3. Ibid, 4-2.

4. Ibid, 4-3.

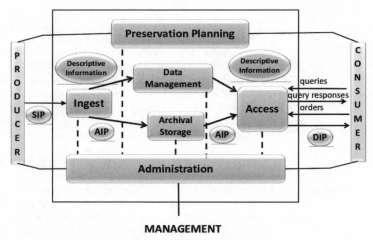

MANAGEMENT

Figure 3.1.   Interaction of OAIS Functional Entities
Reprinted with permission of the Consultative Committee for Space Data Systems.

There are also Common Services, which are assumed and usually not included in diagrams describing the OAIS Functional Model. Common Services can include operating system service, network services, backup and temporary storage services, and security-related services.[16]

OAIS Required Responsibilities

The OAIS Reference Model identifies six mandatory responsibilities that, at minimum, an *OAIS*, the digital preservation system and its staff, must undertake. An OAIS is responsible for (1) negotiating for and accepting information, (2) obtaining sufficient control for preservation, (3) determining the Designated Community, (4) ensuring information is independently understandable, (5) following established preservation policies and procedures, and (6) making the information available.[17] Each of these responsibilities will be discussed in the following.

Negotiates for and Accepts Information

When operating an OAIS, an organization should have criteria that help define the types of information that the Archive will or is required to accept. These criteria can often be in the form of a collection development policy. Factors that could be included in these criteria are subject matter, the source of the information, uniqueness of the material, and the format of the material (file format, physical media, etc.). See chapter 9 for more on collection development as a way of procuring content in digital preservation systems.

Digital preservationists working at an OAIS-compliant digital Archive also need to negotiate with the Producer of the information to ensure that they acquire appropriate information and that the Archive and the Producer agree on an acceptable format for the digital preservation system. This negotiation should include, whenever necessary, details such as acceptable file formats and digitization specifications for physical materials. Any necessary or relevant descriptive information should also be obtained in this process.

Obtains Sufficient Control for Preservation

Physical possession of content is separate from the ownership of intellectual property. It is important for digital preservationists to understand this and to make sure that they are granted the specific rights to fulfill their preservation duties. If the organization that maintains the OAIS is the same entity that created the intellectual content being preserved, it will usually already have this permission. If it was not responsible for the creation of the intellectual content, however, the OAIS will have to negotiate for the appropriate permissions. "In most cases, it will be preferable for the OAIS to negotiate an agreement that specifies the rightsholder(s)['] requirements and authorizes the OAIS to act in accordance with those requirements without active involvement of the rightsholder(s) in individual cases."[18] This is preferred because it may not be possible to contact the rightsholder(s) in the future when actions need to be taken in a timely fashion (or at all). The OAIS Reference Model identifies three related categories that should be considered—intellectual property and other legal issues, authority to modify content information, and agreements with external organizations. These three categories are described in greater detail in table 3.2.

Determines Designated Community

A Designated Community of Consumers of Content Information needs to be determined so that the OAIS can be sure the information deposited is useful for the intended end users. Not all communities will have the same needs or requirements. For some types of data, advanced domain-specific knowledge will be required of Consumers, while other types of data, such as a digitized portrait of Teddy Roosevelt, do not require the same level of domain knowledge to be useful. When defining a Designated Community, it is useful to remember that over time the Designated Community can broaden or narrow. When practical, "selecting a broader definition of the Designated Community (e.g., general public) when the information is first proposed for Long Term Preservation can reduce this concern and also improve the likelihood that the information will be understandable to all in the original community."[19]

Ensures Information Is Independently Understandable

Specialized knowledge or software is sometimes required to make use of data. The OAIS should be responsible for ensuring that the Designated Community

Table 3.2.   Categories Related to Having Sufficient Control of Content for Preservation

Category	Brief Description
Copyright implications, intellectual property, and other legal restrictions on use	An OAIS needs to honor all applicable laws and other legal restrictions. When discussing the preservation of digital content, Archives most commonly need to deal with copyright and other intellectual property issues. The OAIS should be familiar with the applicable laws and establish guidelines for content ingestion and dissemination as appropriate.
Authority to modify Content Information	At some point in the future it will likely become necessary for the OAIS to migrate some or all of the content it is preserving to new representative forms as file formats become obsolete. The OAIS should negotiate the permission to make these migrations when it is first accepting the content since it might not be able to easily contact the intellectual property rights holder(s) and/or secure these permissions in the future.
Agreements with external organizations	In some cases the OAIS will want to work with other organizations. For example, if two Archives house the same information, only one may need to undertake preservation activities. Arrangements with other organizations should be documented and monitored to ensure they are being followed and are still relevant.

can understand, and therefore make use of, the content in the Archive. Descriptive information including information about the purpose of a digital object, how it was created, its various pieces of data, and how it was obtained may need to be preserved along with the data itself. It may also be necessary to make sure that specialized software is available to users. One strategy that an OAIS may undertake is emulation (see Sidebar 3.1 on page 51), but this may not always be cost-effective. Migration to other formats is another strategy that may be utilized. If the OAIS does not have the skills necessary to evaluate the understandability of content, it may be necessary to consult outside members of the Designated Community to verify that the content is indeed understandable.

Follows Established Preservation Policies and Procedures

"It is essential for an OAIS to have documented policies and procedures for [preservation], and it should follow those procedures."[20] The nature of these policies and procedures will vary from Archive to Archive, but having strong polices and procedures in place will help prevent errors and add to the trustworthiness of an OAIS.

SIDEBAR 3.1. EMULATION

Computer emulation—or simply *emulation*—is when one computer system imitates, or emulates, the functions of another system. The goal of emulation is to provide an exact replication of the functionality of the system that is being emulated. In other words, it focuses on the technological environment instead of on specific digital objects or file formats. Emulation is one strategy that may be used for digital preservation and can be particularly effective for interactive computer programs including three-dimensional programs,[1] video games, and simulators. Some of the advantages of emulation identified by Michael Lesk include that "there are relatively few hardware platforms to emulate, compared with the number of software programs and software formats[;] . . . program behavior can be very hard to understand and imitate; running old code is easier[; and] when you improve the emulator for a device, every piece of software you are trying to save on it improves at once."[2]

Although emulation can be an effective digital preservation strategy in some situations, it is not without its drawbacks. Emulators can be complicated to implement and may require extensive staffing. Computer programmers might be needed to create and maintain emulators; digital preservationists and Consumers may need to learn and understand the antiquated or unfamiliar computer systems that are being emulated in order to take full advantage of digital objects presevered through this strategy. It is also important to remember that since emulators are digital technology, digital preservationists will also need to make sure that they digitally preserve any emulators they rely on for preservation purposes. Intellectual property rights can be another barrier to implementing an emulation digital preservation strategy. Various patents, licenses, and copyright restrictions may cover the systems being emulated. Digital preservationists will do well to make an effort to understand the potential risks involved before suggesting this strategy for software programs or platforms, especially.

---

1. Julie Doyle, Herna Viktor, and Eric Paquet, "Long-Term Digital Preservation: Preserving Authenticity and Usability of 3-D Data," *International Journal on Digital Libraries* 10 (2009): 33–47.

2. Michael Lesk, *Understanding Digital Libraries* (Boston: Elsevier, 2004), 259.

These documents should also be shared with the appropriate persons and communities. For example, "Producer and Consumer communities should be provided with submission and dissemination standards, policies, and procedures to support the preservation objectives of the OAIS."[21]

Policies and procedures should include monitoring the Designated Community to ensure that Content Information is still understandable (or even useful) for them. A long-term technology-use plan is also identified as being essential in the OAIS Reference Model. Additionally an "Archive should have a formal Succession Plan, contingency plans, and/or escrow arrangements in place in case the Archive ceases to operate or the governing or funding institution substantially changes its scope."[22]

Makes the Information Available

An OAIS makes Content Information visible and available to the Designated Community, by definition. This does not necessarily mean that the content must be available via open access terms or needs to otherwise be openly available to all. Some content will and can have restricted access policies due to copyright, patent, and other intellectual property issues, confidentially and privacy reasons (including Health Insurance Portability and Accountability Act of 1996 [HIPAA] and Family Educational Rights and Privacy Act [FERPA] regulations), embargo reasons, or any number of other factors. Regardless of the reason why an object is restricted, the OAIS needs to be able to provide the content to authorized users. "The OAIS should have published policies on access and restrictions so that the rights of all parties are protected."[23]

CONCLUSION

The OAIS Reference Model is the basis for many repository and digital repository and digital preservation system architectures, a solid approach to the Management aspects of the Digital Preservation Triad. The OAIS Reference Model is a high-level reference model, "at its heart a fairly generic, domain-independent model, largely concerned with preservation needs."[24] It is widely accepted and useful for the way it creates a shared understanding of what a long-term preservation system should do. For these reasons, digital preservationists should have a foundational understanding of the OAIS Reference Model and what it aims to accomplish before moving on to explore other aspects of digital preservation. Because the OAIS Reference Model is so widely accepted, many digital preservation system developers and repository developers design their systems with it in mind. Many also claim that their design is OAIS-compliant; however, the meaning of *compliance* is sometimes difficult to determine.[25] It is important for the digital preservationist to remember that even if the software used in the digital preservation system is indeed complaint with the OAIS Functional Model, the Archive itself, on a Management level, also needs to be compliant with the other portions of the OAIS Reference Model, most notably the OAIS Mandatory Responsibilities.

NOTES

1. Paul Laughton, "OAIS Functional Model Conformance Test: A Proposed Measurement," *Program: Electronic Library and Information Systems* 46 (2012): 308–20.

2. Paradigm, "Workbook on Digital Private Papers," accessed June 1, 2013, http://www.paradigm.ac.uk/workbook/index.html.

3. Christopher A. Lee, "Open Archival Information System (OAIS) Reference Model," in *Encyclopedia of Library and Information Sciences*, 3rd ed. (Boca Raton, Fla.: CRC Press, 2009), doi:10.1081/E-ELIS3-120044377.

4. For this reason, the OAIS Reference Model is sometimes incorrectly referred to as a standard developed by NASA.

5. Lee, "Open Archival Information System (OAIS) Reference Model."

6. There were also red books 1.1 (April 2001), 1.2 (June 2001), and 2 (July 2001) before the revised Blue Book was circulated for approval. The different revisions of the OAIS model are often referred to by the color of their cover. The color of a CCSDS book cover reflects the type of content or stage of development a standard is in. Blue books are recommended standards, red books are draft standards that are updates of a blue book, magenta books are best current practices, and pink books are draft recommendations for updates to blue books that have been released for formal review. For other book cover colors and additional information, see http://public.ccsds.org/about/FAQs.aspx.

7. Barbara Sierman, who works at the National Library of the Netherlands, provides a nice overview of the changes in the 2012 version on her personal blog at http://digitalpreservation.nl/seeds/oais-2012-update/. Many of the changes were meant to make the model more understandable. Other changes include a greater emphasis of emulation as a digital preservation strategy, the addition of Access Rights information to the Preservation Description Information, more interaction between the Administration and the Preservation Planning Functional Entities, and a few modified and additional definitions.

8. John Mark Ockerbloom, "What Repositories Do: The OAIS Model," *Everybody's Libraries Blog*, October 13, 2008, accessed September 29, 2013, http://everybodyslibraries.com/2008/10/13/what-repositories-do-the-oais-model/. See also Everybody's Libraries Blog, "What Repositories Do: The OAIS Model," specifically "What OAIS Is and Isn't," para. 2, October 13, 2008, accessed September 29, 2013, http://everybodyslibraries.com/2008/10/13/what-repositories-do-the-oais-model/.

9. Consultative Committee for Space Data Systems (CCSDS), *Reference Model for an Open Archival Information System (OAIS): Recommended Practice CCSDS 650.0-M-2; Recommendation for Space Data System Practices*, Magenta Book, Recommended Practice, issue 2 (Washington, D.C.: CCSDS Secretariat, June 2012), 1-9, http://public.ccsds.org/publications/archive/650x0m2.pdf.

10. Ibid, 1-1.

11. Ibid, 4-33.

12. Ibid, 4-29.

13. Ibid, 4-29.

14. Ibid, 1-15.
15. Ibid, 1-11.
16. Ibid.
17. Ibid.
18. Ibid, 3-2.
19. Ibid, 3-4.
20. Ibid, 3-5.
21. Ibid.
22. Ibid, 3-6.
23. Ibid, 3-6.
24. Ockerbloom, "What Repositories Do," "What Else You Need to Think about," para. 1.
25. Ibid.

4

Human Resources and Education

Management of digital preservation requires the hard work and skill of digital preservationists and specialized staff at the Archive. Human resources are some of the most valuable resources an OAIS can possess, since without digital preservationists there is no preservation! Being a digital preservationist is, like digital preservation, not an afterthought. Working with digital preservation requires actively learning new skills, researching and understanding trends, and being part of an open community that supports long-term accessibility for Consumers. As a large-scale and long-term undertaking where both technology and users are involved, digital preservation requires that information professionals constantly scan the information horizons to learn about what is new and noteworthy in digital preservation. Education, continuing education, and an understanding of the current research are an essential foundation for any digital preservationist. In this chapter, we begin by considering the most important aspects of human resources for digital preservation. We continue by looking at opportunities for education, continuing education, and the dissemination of digital preservation research in support of their work. We then consider the future of digital preservation (the field), concluding with encouragement for digital preservationists undertaking some very challenging and also fascinating tasks.

HUMAN RESOURCES

Digital preservation is a complex undertaking with many differing aspects that require different types of skills. Employees who are information professionals and who work in cultural heritage institutions have specialized skills and knowledge stemming from the tradition in which they were educated and trained. This knowledge and skill is refined on the job and is invaluable to them as they work. Unless an employee has been trained as a digital preservationist or has been taking care to pursue continuing education opportunities, however, it is unreasonable to expect that traditionally trained information professionals and cultural heritage employees will automatically be at ease at work on a digital preservation initiative without some additional management-level support.

In fact, many organizations that are considering implementing a digital preservation system may already have employees with the required digital preservation skills. It is unlikely, however, that they are already in a single department in a coherent way that enables them to work as a digital preservation unit or team. Additional human resources or the restructuring of existing areas of the organization may be required to support digital preservation. In many cases both restructuring and new human resources will be required.

Categories of Human Resources

The human resources required for digital preservation can be divided into three broad categories: technical (systems), metadata (cataloging), and collection specialists. There also needs to be administrative, or management, support. Depending on the content being presevered and the mission of the organization, additional skill sets may also be required. For instance, if an Archive wants to preserve digital copies of early wax sound recordings, it may need someone familiar with handling wax cylinders and digitizing audio content. These multiple roles are not necessarily mutually exclusive; for instance, in some cases the person with subject- or content-specific skills may also be the person with the necessary skills to create descriptive metadata. Each category of skill sets will be examined below.

The technical or information technology (IT) skills required will vary depending on the digital preservation system used. Besides having the necessary IT skills to run a complex digital preservation system, an organization may also need to have human resources available with software application development skills. Personnel who can create metadata crosswalks using programming languages or XSLT (eXtensible Stylesheet Language) style sheets may also be required. Metadata crosswalks and XSLT are discussed in greater detail in chapter 7.

In order for a digital object to be truly preserved, it needs to be accessible and usable by the Designated Community. Accessibility depends on being able to find or discover a digital object. This requires descriptive metadata that includes information about the digital object such as title, subject, and creator. Although the amount of descriptive metadata may vary based on collection, object, or Archive, it is still necessary to have adequate descriptive metadata. Some of this metadata may be generated automatically; in many cases, someone with the requisite skills and knowledge of descriptive metadata will need to be consulted. Even when descriptive metadata can be automatically generated or extracted from digital objects, someone needs to decide into which metadata field that information should be placed. Metadata specialists may also be called on to train subject specialists more familiar with the content being preserved on the proper ways to create descriptive metadata.

The third area of human resources necessary for digital preservation is subject and content specialists. Because it is impossible to preserve every digital object ever produced, decisions need to be made as to what to preserve and why. Subject specialists who are knowledgeable about the field will know what content is more likely to be of value now and into the future. It is also helpful to have people who are familiar with disciplinary norms in the content areas that are being collected and with copyright and other intellectual property concerns.

In order to tie this all together, there needs to be sufficient administrative structure and support. It is management that oversees and enables the work of the digital preservation staff.

Regardless of the role any particular staff member plays in digital preservation, one of the most important attributes required is passion for digital preservation. Digital preservation is a new and growing field, so one cannot just learn it once. Digital preservationists need to be willing to keep learning new technology, new techniques, and new theories relevant to the field and be willing and able to put their new knowledge into practice at their local institutions with proper planning and support. It is also important that the people involved with digital preservation be advocates for digital preservation and services that the Archive provides. Digital preservation systems are not a case of "build it and they will come." Many researchers, scholars, and other content producers do not understand digital preservation and how it is important for future access. Digital preservationists, therefore, can help spread the word about the reasons for and importance of digital preservation.

EDUCATION FOR DIGITAL PRESERVATION

Education for digital preservation is, quite understandably, slightly different from standard education in the three libraries, archives, and museums (LAMs) traditions. Researchers are increasingly noting a convergence in the requirements for digital preservation education, with LIS and Archives requiring similar if not identical work of students. Museum studies remains slightly different in the kind of requirements it makes of its students.[1] The three disciplines, however, are seen to have converged on the question of digital preservation in terms of educational needs.[2]

Fortunately for future information professionals working in libraries and archives, the study of digital preservation methods and tools "is now becoming a mainstream part of an information science education."[3] Unfortunately, there are fewer indicators that museum studies education offers identical opportunities,[4] requiring museum professionals to focus instead on continuing education opportunities. Below, we compare the terms *digital preservation* and *digital curation* and describe some education opportunities in digital preservation. Next, we look at continuing education options available to those who have a basic knowledge of or experience in a LAM environment, followed by a look at outlets for research in digital preservation.

Digital Preservation and Digital Curation: What's in a Name?

Before beginning to consider education in digital preservation, it is worth giving thought to the terms that might be used to describe such programs. Confusingly, the terms *digital curation* and *digital preservation* may be used interchangeably, depending on the speaker. "In the United States *digital preservation* tends to be interpreted as the life-cycle management of materials from the point of their creation, while in the United Kingdom the term *digital curation* is used for life-cycle management while *digital preservation* is reserved for those activities specifically geared towards future accessibility."[5] This book, for example, is about the all-encompassing, North American sense of the term, but we acknowledge that not everyone in North America uses the term *digital preservation* in the same way. Some programs may use the term *digital curation* to denote the overarching concept, reserving the term *digital preservation* for the management and technical aspects of preserving designated digital content for future use in a very limited sense. Part of the confusion between the two terms stems quite simply from their newness. As researchers have pointed out, the field of digital preservation is, itself, a new field.[6]

As explained in the preface, this book takes the broader, life cycle approach to the discussion of digital preservation. Therefore, where others in their program of study, their research, or their practice may refer to *digital curation*, we use the term *digital preservation* to describe their work in a way that is consistent with the term's use throughout this book.

University-Level Education for Digital Preservation

Focusing on programs in North America, the convergence noted by researchers can be seen in LIS and archives education in the field of digital preservation.[7] Six universities and some of their relevant programs are discussed briefly in the following as a way of understanding the kinds of higher education programs available in the North American context; this is not a comprehensive list but, rather, a sampling to give an idea of the breadth and depth of possibilities.

University of Maine (http://digitalcuration.umaine.edu/)

The University of Maine is offering an online certificate in digital curation. The two-year program first began in the fall of 2012 and includes faculty from the departments of New Media, Computer Sciences, History, Art, and Spatial Information Science and Engineering. It also includes professionals from the Folger Library, the Hudson Museum, and the Maine Folklife Center.

New York University (http://www.nyu.edu/tisch/preservation/)

New York University's Tisch School of the Arts offers a master of art program focused on Moving Image Archive and Preservation (MIAP), and much of the curriculum relates to digitized and born digital media. More specifically, the program is designed to train future collection managers and archivists to "manage preservation-level collections of film, video, new media, and other types of digital works."[8] The program aims to have an international and comprehensive approach and provides theoretical, methodological, and practical education in this area. Unlike many of the other North American master's degree programs, the NYU's MIAP degree is not accredited by the American Library Association (ALA).

Simmons (http://www.simmons.edu/gslis/)

The Graduate School of Library and Information Science (GSLIS) at Simmons offers courses and programs that very closely align LIS and archives. Simmons offers a master of science in Library and Information Science with an option for students to follow the Preservation Management track. There is also an online master of science in Library and Information Science/Archives Concentration and a dual degree in Library and Information Science Archives (MS)/History (MA), demonstrating the convergence of LIS and Archives outside of the realm of digital preservation. The master's degrees are accredited by ALA, meaning that graduates have the credentials to work as professional librarians upon successful completion of the program. Lastly, Simmons also offers a post-master's Digital Stewardship Certificate (DSC) program that awards an Archives Certificate - Digital Stewardship for online students taking the required classes.

University of California–Los Angeles (UCLA) (http://is.gseis.ucla.edu/)

UCLA also offers several degree programs and options that could be of interest to those wishing to study digital preservation in a LAM context. The Department of Information Studies offers degrees of interest to potential digital preservationists including a master of library and information science with an Archival Studies specialization. There is also a Moving Image Archive Studies (MIAS), which is a degree through the Department of Information Studies and the Department of Film, TV, and Digital Media jointly with UCLA's Film and Television Archive. UCLA's master's program is, like Simmons's, accredited by the American Library Association.

Université de Montréal (http://www.ebsi.umontreal.ca/)

The French-speaking Université de Montréal's *École de bibliothéconomie et des sciences de l'information* (School of Library Science and Information Science) in Montréal, Canada, offers a *Maîtrise en sciences de l'information* (M.S.I.), a master's degree in Information Science accredited by ALA. The program also offers an un-dergraduate certificate in archival studies and one in records management. Neither undergraduate certificate is a part of the ALA-accredited program, but each bears testimony to the faculty's interests and to the convergence of archives education with the information professions' education.

University of Illinois, Urbana-Champaign (http://www.lis.illinois.edu/)

The Graduate School of Library and Information Science (GSLIS) at the University of Illinois, Urbana-Champaign (UIUC), offers a series of courses to support its Data Curation Concentration for its graduate degrees. Additionally, graduate certificate in Special Collections is available as a post-master's certificate, a Certificate of Advanced Study (CAS). The Data Curation Education Program (DCEP), a specialization through GSLIS's Center for Informatics Research in Science and Scholarship (http://cirss .lis.illinois.edu/CollMeta/dcep.html), supports data curation education in both the hard sciences and the human sciences. The GSLIS master of science in Library and Information Science is ALA-accredited.

University of North Carolina at Chapel Hill (https://sils.unc.edu/)

Similar to the UIUC GSLIS, the University of North Carolina (UNC)–Chapel Hill's School of Information and Library Science (SILS) offers a post-master's certifi-cate (PMC) with a Data Curation emphasis. SILS also offers a certificate in Digital Curation at the master's level. Additionally, an active research group composed of both faculty and students is devoted to the study of preserving digital objects.

Other Formal Instruction Relating to Digital Preservation

Two major online directories list programs that, if chosen carefully, can put stu-dents of digital preservation onto their chosen career paths. Those directories are the *Preservation Education Directory* 9th ed. rev. 2012 (http://www.ala.org/alcts/ resources/preservation/educationdirectory) and the Society of American Archivists' *Directory of Archival Education* (http://www2.archivists.org/dae). Many of the above degree and certificate programs at North American universities are listed in both of these resources due to the converged nature of the programs of study. Specifically in the SAA directory, "over 70 percent of the listed graduate programs were affiliated with ALA–accredited programs. A Certificate of Advanced Studies in Digital Librar-ies was often listed as an option for Archivists in this directory."[9] Archival education is clearly overlapping with education for the library profession and other information professions. A third directory, the *National Council for Preservation Education's Guide to Academic Programs* (http://www.ncpe.us/academic-programs/), might assist those looking to specialize in traditional preservation and (artifact) conservation, although digital preservation is not a major focus of the programs listed.

Continuing Education for Digital Preservation

Continuing education assumes that participants have some basic foundational knowledge, and it works to build on that prior knowledge or, in some cases, experience. Opportunities for continuing education in digital preservation run the gamut, varying from short online webinar sessions to intensive in-person workshops, from conferences with keynotes and breakout sessions to entire online certificate programs offered through universities.

The ultimate continuing education experience might be the certificates and programs of advanced study that give current professionals an opportunity to learn new skills and new approaches. An idea of some of the certificate programs was given above. Not all institutions or employees can envision a leave of absence, even for a short time, to participate in continuing education initiatives. For many, time may be of the essence. Candace Sall, associate museum curator at the Museum of Anthropology at the University of Missouri, notes that with webinars "we can get several of our staff around a computer and learn new things in an hour or two."[10] This section of this book, therefore, supplies information about both ongoing short-term and ongoing long-term workshops as continuing education opportunities. Additional conferences potentially of interest for those wanting to sharpen their digital preservation skills and learn about scholarship in the field are listed in the next section on research.

Self-Guided Continuing Education in Digital Preservation

For the motivated digital preservationist willing to work alone at his or her own pace, there are quite a few options for consulting high-quality online resources. One of the most comprehensive are the training materials at the Digital Curation Centre (DCC) (http://www.dcc.ac.uk/training). *Digital Curation 101: How to Manage Research Data*, for example, includes free access to online content. Although any self-guided experience will be solitary, the information will be just as immediately applicable once learned.

University-Sponsored Continuing Education Workshops in Digital Preservation

Institutes and workshops provide additional knowledge and skills for information professionals working in digital preservation. One well-known institute is the DigCurr Professional Institute (http://ils.unc.edu/digccurr/institute.html) at the School of Information and Library Science (SILS) at the University of North Carolina at Chapel Hill. The program of study lasts one week, with follow-up expectations. The DigCCurr project evolved from the International Digital Curation Education and Action (IDEA) Working Group, "an international alliance examining and advising on curriculum needs to continue building the skill base."[11] Another well-known workshop, the week-long Digital Preservation Management Workshop (http://www.dpworkshop.org/workshops/fiveday.html), is currently hosted by the Massachusetts

Institute of Technology (MIT). According to its website, the workshop was begun in 2003 at Cornell University and had been further developed at the University of Michigan's Inter-university Consortium for Political and Social Research (ICPSR) for three years before moving to MIT. These are just a few of many short-term workshops in which digital preservationists or aspiring digital preservationists can learn the latest about digital preservation from leading experts.

Institute-Sponsored Continuing Education in Digital Preservation

The Society of American Archivists (SAA) offers a Digital Archives Specialist (DAS) curriculum and certificate program (http://www2.archivists.org/prof-education/das). Available to members, this program includes four tiers of study, in-person and distance learning opportunities, and assessment quizzes to help with placement. Additionally, the Image Permanence Institute (IPI), Rochester Institute of Technology, Rochester, New York, hosts Digital Print Workshops (https://www.imageperma nenceinstitute.org/imaging-information-media/digital-print-workshops-ipi), a series of workshops relevant to the preservation of digitally printed materials.

Research in Digital Preservation

Because it is new, digital preservation draws from other fields, creating an interdisciplinary environment that includes researchers and practitioners from LIS, Archival Studies, Computer Science, Engineering, and other disciplines.[12] Research supporting digital preservation tends to be carried out in interdisciplinary institutes affiliated with universities, to be published as papers in a variety of journals that can be interdisciplinary, and to be presented as papers in conferences that might also be interdisciplinary. Below, a few examples of each are given as a starting point for future research into the field of digital preservation. The appendix and the bibliography found at the end of this book may also be helpful for digital preservationists wishing to delve more deeply into topics broached in this book.

Institutes for Research into Digital Preservation

As the concepts and practices behind digital preservation have begun to mature, support organizations and research institutes have been created. These institutes can have a variety of functions, including supporting internal research or promoting international digital preservation initiatives.[13] The following centers support research into digital preservation; although the work they do is mainly for their own institutions, the projects they undertake may be of interest to digital preservationists wishing to learn about cutting-edge research being done by peer groups.

The University of California Curation Center (UC3) (http://www.cdlib.org/services/uc3/), according to its website, "helps researchers and the UC libraries manage, preserve, and provide access to their important digital assets."[14] The CDL timeline on the "About CDL" page indicates that UC3 was established in 2009[15] "as a partnership supporting the ten University of California campuses."[16] Despite these inward-looking beginnings, the UC3 is doing work that is of interest to digital preservationists writ large, including supporting projects like the EZID, which "makes it easy to create and manage unique, long-term identifiers."[17] Purdue University Library's Distributed Data Curation Center (D2C2) (http://d2c2.lib.purdue.edu/), according to their website, "investigates issues and problems related to making research data available and collaborates to develop solutions for research data curation, management, dissemination, and preservation in distributed environments." Four core researchers work in conjunction with librarians to address problems related to data curation.[18]

Venues for Publishing on Digital Preservation (Journals)

Perhaps one of the most important venues for reading scholarly, peer-reviewed articles about topics in digital preservation is the online *International Journal of Digital Curation* (IJDC) (http://www.ijdc.net/). As articles published in the journal assert, "the IJDC is published by UKOLN at the University of Bath and is a publication of the Digital Curation Centre."[19] The IJDC is published online and is open access. In its section on digital preservation journals, the DCC lists roughly ten additional peer-reviewed journals that may be of interest to those doing research in digital preservation; it also lists two Web magazines.[20] Scholarly, peer-reviewed journals on the list include: *CODATA Data Science Journal, First Monday, International Free and Open Source Software Law Review, International Journal of Internet Research Ethics, International Journal on Digital Libraries, Journal of the American Society for Information Science and Technology, Journal of Digital Information, Journal of Electronic Publishing, Journal of Librarianship and Scholarly Communication, Journal of Web Semantics*, and *World Digital Libraries*. The Web magazines are *Ariadne* (http://www.ariadne.ac.uk/) and *D-Lib Magazine* (http://www.dlib.org/). Although not every article published in these journals and magazines pertains directly to digital preservation, many of the articles may touch on technology, on the process of working with digital content, or on the management of digital items through their life cycles. There are also articles in various other archives, libraries, museums, and technology-focused journals that discuss digital preservation and related topics as well.

Venues for Presenting on Digital Preservation (Conferences)

Some ongoing conferences are specifically dedicated to the field of digital preservation. Other conferences include information specific to digital preservation, but digital preservation is not the sole focus of the conference. These related conferences may be of interest to those active in digital preservation even if they do not have tracks focusing on digital preservation. We will look at examples of both kinds of conferences in turn.

Four major conferences that specifically are in the field of digital preservation are the International Conference on Preservation of Digital Objects (iPRES), the International Digital Curation Conference (IDCC), the Preservation and Archiving Special Interest Group (PASIG) International Meeting, and the Archiving Conference. The iPRES conference is held in December/January of each year and has met in China, Germany, the United Sates, Great Britain, Austria, and Canada. The 2013 conference was in Portugal. Information about each conference is maintained by the host institution, with the result that there is not a central website with information about the conference as an annual event. Many authors have made their contributions freely available to the scholarly community, however, and conference papers are easily retrieved through scholarly search engines and scholarly communications portals. Like the iPRES conferences, the IDCC conferences are also held internationally in December/January. Conferences have been held in Europe and the United States in Bath, Glasgow, Washington, D.C., Edinburgh, London, Chicago, Bristol, and Amsterdam. The IDCC conferences are sponsored by the Digital Curation Centre (DCC) and include keynotes, papers and posters, and workshops. Information about the conference, held since 2005, is available on the DCC website in the Events section.[21] The third, PASIG, is a vendor-neutral forum open to both practitioners and commercial organizations. For the last few years, PASIG has had two conferences a year, one in North America and one in Europe. Presentations tend to cover comparisons of OAIS architectures as well as topics relating to storage architectures and trends. A fourth related conference focusing on digital preservation is the Society for Imaging Science & Technology (IS&T)'s Archiving Conference, a venue "to discuss the most pressing issues related to the digital preservation and stewardship of hardcopy, audio, and video."[22] Held annually, the conference alternates between venues in North America and Europe. The Archiving Conference was first held in 2004, and proceedings from each of the conferences are available on the main conference page.[23]

Also, because of the interdisciplinary nature of digital preservation, a lot of current research can be relevant without being specifically presented in a digital preservation forum. A number of supporting fields do research into complementary areas of interest to digital preservationists that are relevant to their work. To study this, Alex H. Poole and his colleagues and mentor at UNC–Chapel Hill's SILS queried researchers in digital preservation. Of the researchers identified, 180 completed the survey for a nearly 30 percent response rate. Poole et al. found that respondents reported regularly attending conferences on digital preservation, but they also reported regularly attending conferences in related areas of specialization. Of the conferences regularly attended, according to Poole et al., respondents in their study regularly attended two digital preservation conferences: iPRES (27.4 percent) and IDCC (9.6 percent). The conference of the Society of American Archivists (SAA) was the next-most frequently attended conference among respondents, with 8.9 percent mentioning it. Fourth was the conference of the International Association for Social Science Information Services & Technology (IASSIST) (6.8 percent). Tied for fifth were the conference of the erstwhile American Society for Information Science & Technology (ASIST) (now known as the Association for Information Science and Technology) and the

Open Repositories conference (6.2 percent each). Additional conferences that may be of interest are listed in the appendix to this book.[24]

Future Directions in Digital Preservation

The field of digital preservation, although known by many names and approached from the vantage point of a variety of disciplinary backgrounds, is actively being researched. Part of that work involves researchers who are working at the same time to train the next generation of digital preservation researchers.[25] As the field matures, issues with terminology will likely be resolved over time. The pioneering work of the OAIS Reference Model led the way (see chapter 3), and such work to normalize the use of terms can only continue.

Given the current state of the field and the perceived need among LAM professionals, a large number of university programs and continuing education programs exist. This trend will surely continue with more sophisticated options for cross-training between members of the various LAM professions in both education and continuing education opportunities.

With the continued sophistication of technology and the increasing creation of digital and online resources, the need for digital preservation and digital preservationists will continue to increase in the coming years. To support them and their work, research presented as scholarly publications and at conferences will continue to focus on the needs of digital preservationists as they work toward preserving content into what is, technologically speaking, a still-uncertain future.

CONCLUSION

Digital preservation is an exciting and mesmerizing new prospect that depends on the talent, dedication, and hard work of the people involved. At its core, digital preservation represents a recently emerged interdisciplinary approach to providing long-term access to digital content. Digital preservation is challenging and represents a new field whose tools are changing constantly, whose education is converging and becoming formalized, and whose research agenda is taking shape and expanding. As digital preservation matures as a discipline, it will be in a position to realize its full potential. Today, however, Archives are busily putting to work talented and competent digital preservationists who understand the importance of Management, Technology, and Content to the digital preservation initiative.

NOTES

1. Terry Weech, "Convergence of Education for Information Professionals in Libraries, Archives, Museums, and Other Institutions in LIS Schools in Research and Curriculum Offerings: The U.S. and Canadian Experience" (PowerPoint presented at the Convergence of

Education for Information Professionals workshop, iConference 2013, Fort Worth, Texas, February 2013), https://ideals.illinois.edu/handle/2142/42574.

2. Anna Maria Tammaro and Melody Madrid, "Digital Curator Education: Professional Identity vs. Convergence of LAM (Libraries, Archives, Museums)" (unpublished manuscript, 2012), 6.

3. Sarah Higgins, "Digital Curation: The Emergence of a New Discipline," *International Journal of Digital Curation* 6, no. 2 (2011): 84, http://www.ijdc.net/index.php/ijdc/article/download/184/251.

4. Weech, "Convergence of Education," slide 11.

5. Priscilla Caplan, "Digital Preservation," *Library Technology Reports* 44, no. 2 (Feb./Mar. 2008), 7.

6. Alex H. Poole, Christopher A. Lee, Heather L. Barnes, and Angela P. Murillo, "Digital Curation Preparation: A Survey of Contributors to International Professional, Educational, and Research Venues: UNC SILS Technical Report 2013-01," April 15, 2013; accessed September 29, 2013, http://sils.unc.edu/sites/default/files/news/SILS%20Report%20TR-2013-01-final.pdf.

7. Weech, "Convergence of Education."

8. New York University, "Moving Image Archive Program," accessed September 29, 2013, http://www.nyu.edu/tisch/preservation/.

9. Weech, "Convergence of Education."

10. Candace Sall, personal communication, May 29, 2013.

11. Higgins, "Digital Curation," 84.

12. Poole et al., "Digital Curation Preparation."

13. Higgins, "Digital Curation."

14. University of California: California Digital Library, "University of California Curation Center," accessed September 29, 2013, http://www.cdlib.org/services/uc3/.

15. University of California: California Digital Library, "About CDL," accessed September 29, 2013, http://www.cdlib.org/about/.

16. Higgins, "Digital Curation."

17. EZID, "EZID Homepage," accessed September 29, 2013, http://n2t.net/ezid.

18. Distributed Data Curation Center, "About Us," accessed September 29, 2013, http://d2c2.lib.purdue.edu/about.

19. Higgins, "Digital Curation," is the example article consulted.

20. Digital Curation Centre, "Curation Journals," accessed September 29, 2013, http://www.dcc.ac.uk/resources/curation-journals.

21. Digital Curation Centre, "Events," accessed September 29, 2013, http://www.dcc.ac.uk/events.

22. Imaging.org, "Archiving," accessed September 29, 2013, http://www.imaging.org/ist/conferences/archiving/index.cfm.

23. Ibid.

24. Poole et al., "Digital Curation Preparation."

25. Ibid.

5

Sustainable Digital Preservation

Managing digital preservation initiatives requires a bird's-eye view of the task at hand, the resources for attaining the established goals, and the ability to implement the process over the long term. Sustainability is the ultimate goal of a digital preservation initiative and, for this reason, is the third aspect of Management we will discuss in part II of the book.

The United States Environmental Protection Agency (EPA) describes sustainability as an idea that "creates and maintains the conditions under which humans and nature can exist in productive harmony that permit fulfilling the social, economic, and other requirements of present and future generations."[1] Although the concept of sustainability often refers to environmental sustainability as it does in this definition, it is frequently applied to other domains as well. Digital preservation is one such area, and how to implement sustainable digital preservation is a common topic discussed by those in the field. In digital preservation terms, economic sustainability can be defined as "the set of business, social, technological, and policy mechanisms that encourage the gathering of important information assets into digital preservation systems and [that] support the indefinite persistence of digital preservation systems, enabling access to and use of the information assets into the long-term future."[2] Another way of looking at this is to say that sustainable digital preservation is meant to ensure the "continuity of digital resources within resource levels over the required period of time."[3] Sustainability is a key Management issue in digital preservation and affects every aspect of it. Because of this, every aspect of digital preservation should be performed with sustainability in mind. This chapter will cover some of the key factors that influence digital preservation sustainability, but it is not comprehensive. Likewise, since sustainability is related to every area of digital preservation, some content in this chapter will serve to reinforce and expand on topics relating to digital preservation that appear throughout this book.

As one can imagine, making digital preservation sustainable comes with many challenges. Unlike some other projects that libraries, archives, and museums (LAMs) might undertake, such as putting on an art exhibition, there is almost never an end in sight when undertaking long-term digital preservation. One of the biggest challenges is that while funding streams need to be secured indefinitely, the value of such expenditures is often not immediately apparent. Digital preservation is a more abstract, but no less important, good. Decision makers and funders need to see evidence of the benefit of digital preservation in order to commit to adequate funding levels over time. This chapter on sustainability takes a broad approach to sustainability, looking not only at economic sustainability but also at other issues like an Archive's sustained access to content. We begin by looking closely at risk management in the context of digital preservation sustainability. Then, we examine the five conditions necessary for sustainable digital preservation put forth by the Blue Ribbon Task Force on Sustainable Digital Preservation and Access. Four factors affecting digital preservation sustainability are subsequently identified and discussed, and the chapter ends with a discussion of Memorandums of Understanding (MOUs) and their role in ensuring content and in promoting access.

DIGITAL PRESERVATION AS RISK MANAGEMENT

Ultimately, digital preservation is an exercise in risk management. *Risk* is defined by the United States National Aeronautics and Space Administration (NASA) as "the scenario(s) leading to degraded performance in one or more performance measures" along with considerations of the likelihood and the consequences.[4] Performance measures in digital preservation generally focus on end users' ability to use preserved content over time. Risk management can be defined as the "identification, assessment, and prioritization of these risks followed by the coordinated and economical application of resources to minimize, monitor, and control the probability and/or impact of unfortunate events."[5] Therefore, in LAMs, risk management decisions are often driven by an institution's limited resources. It is impossible to preserve everything, so decisions have to be made regarding which risks are acceptable and what the potential benefits of any action will be. Making these decisions can be a complicated process and may be more of an art than a science, as it may not be possible to imagine all of the potential uses of digital objects into the future. Digital preservationists need to look at ways in which they can lower risk, ensuring long-term access and use to the right content, while staying within budget.

Risk management is an essential aspect of digital preservation, and we identify the following key strategies for insuring access across the long-term: (1) starting early in the creation process, (2) using open and well-documented standards and systems, (3) documenting decisions, (4) using accepted metadata schemas, (5) understanding user expectations, (6) having an exit strategy, and (7) planning for succession.

We discuss each of these below in the context of Management in general and of risk management in particular.

Involvement in the Creation Process

Digital preservationists should be involved as early in the creation of digital content as possible. Ideally, this may even mean involving them before the content is created. If content is created with long-term preservation in mind it will be less complicated and therefore less expensive to preserve the content over time. Best practices including creating documentation, using meaningful filenames, using open file formats, and discussing intellectual property issues like copyright in the beginning to make sure that these aspects do not derail or complicate the digital preservation process down the road. Digital objects are fragile, and people with the intimate knowledge of these digital objects may leave the institution for any number of reasons. This means that there can often be a short window of opportunity to act to preserve files. If digital preservation does not start early enough it may be less effective, too costly, or potentially impossible in cases where data is lost. The earlier an Archive can start preparing for digital preservation of an object, the easier it will be.

Open and/or Well-Documented Standards and Systems

Digital preservationists should plan to use open and/or well-documented standards for file formats and within digital preservation systems and software. Open file formats are typically easier to preserve and migrate to new formats than are closed, proprietary formats. See chapter 8 for specifics about file formats.

Documentation of Decisions

Those working to mitigate risk should take care to make documentation a priority. Digital preservation policies, procedures, and process should be documented. The "organization's processes in relevance to digital preservation must be evident for their sustainability."[6] As discussed next in chapter 6, documentation is one of the key requirements to receiving the Data Seal of Approval, Trustworthy Digital Repository certification, and other trusted repository certifications.

Accepted Standards for Metadata Schemas

Digital preservationists should use widely accepted standards for technical and descriptive metadata schemas. Technical metadata is necessary to ensure that the files do not suffer from bit rot or other technological failures. It also helps identify specific file format versions, which are important to know when trying to determine file format obsolesces. Descriptive metadata is important for making digital objects discoverable. If a digital object is not retrievable due to lack of metadata, is it truly preserved? Chapter 7 will discuss metadata for digital preservation in detail.

Needs of the User

Be aware of current and anticipated needs of the user for preservation. The user in this context can be the creator of the content or the consumer of the content. If the needs of the user are not met, the user will be unlikely to provide her support. While it is sometimes difficult to predict what the users will want in the future, digital preservationists should try their best to predict just that. Digital preservationists also will need to try to predict what will be necessary for preservation purposes in the future. If, for example, a file format is likely to become obsolete, digital preservationists may want to suggest migrating the digital objects into a more sustainable file format before they are *ingested*, or uploaded, into the digital preservation system.

One of the most important end-user needs is access to the materials being preserved. As the name implies, digital preservation is deeply entrenched in both the modern technologies allowing for digital access and consumption of content and the preservation work traditionally carried out in archives and other cultural heritage institutions. Access, at least at some level, is almost always required for digital preservation to be sustainable.[7] Digital preservation is not an inexpensive proposition, so there needs to be either immediate demand for the material being preserved or a reasonable and mission-derived long-term perceived value. Not only can implementing a digital preservation system be an expensive proposition, a long-term digital preservation strategy, by definition, requires a long-term commitment by the institution, in part ensuring content consumers over the long term.

Exit Strategy

Having an exit strategy from any digital preservation solution upfront will reduce risk in the long run. No matter how good the digital preservation system an Archive is using today, it is unreasonable to think the digital preservation system will always be around and that it will still be the best system for the Archive's environment in five, fifty, or one hundred years. One of the technological factors that will help support an exit strategy is the use of open standards for software. The Open Source Initiative lists the following five criteria as the Open Standards Requirement (OSR) for Software:

1. No intentional secrets: The standard *must not* withhold any detail necessary for interoperable implementation. As flaws are inevitable, the standard *must* define a process for fixing flaws identified during implementation and interoperability testing and to incorporate said changes into a revised version or superseding version of the standard to be released under terms that do not violate the OSR.
2. Availability: the standard *must* be freely and publicly available (e.g., from a stable website) under royalty-free terms at reasonable and nondiscriminatory cost.

3. Patents: All patents essential to implementation of the standard *must*
   - be licensed under royalty-free terms for unrestricted use or
   - be covered by a promise of nonassertion when practiced by open source software.
4. No agreements: there *must not* be any requirement for execution of a license agreement, NDA, grant, click-through, or any other form of paperwork to deploy conforming implementations of the standard.
5. No OSR-incompatible dependencies: implementation of the standard *must not* require any other technology that fails to meet the criteria of this requirement.[8]

If the digital preservation software being used supports open standards and stores the digital objects and all of the metadata in such a way that allows system administrators easy access using standard operating system tools, it will be easier to migrate to another system in the future. Counterintuitively, perhaps, this does not necessarily equate to open source software. Although there can be some exit strategy-related benefits to the use of open source systems—and many open source programs support open standards and this type of access to content—not all open source programs will. Conversely, proprietary systems may also allow for effective exit strategies to be enabled, especially if the digital objects are saved using open file formats. See the section on technological factors below for further discussion of benefits and drawbacks to the kinds of digital preservation systems in use.

Succession Planning

Succession planning is important in risk management. Making sure that the digital preservation process does not rely on any one person is necessary for the good health of a digital preservation initiative. Succession planning can be described as "a process for identifying and developing internal people with the potential to fill key business-leadership positions."[9] Effective succession planning should not be limited to upper-management positions. There is a need for people who can be prepared to step into positions throughout the Archive, either temporarily or permanently. For digital preservation, this might mean that there is a need for people who can maintain the technology, ingest materials, create descriptive metadata, and so on. Organizational knowledge should be openly shared and documented whenever possible. Having written guidelines, policies, and procedures can also be an important factor in successful succession planning.

Other Considerations for Risk Management

To mitigate risk and encourage sustainability, digital preservation should begin as early as possible in the data life cycle process. This is one of the reasons the United States' National Science Foundation (NSF) requires data management plans to be submitted with grant-funding applications. If preservation is treated as a key part of the data life cycle and researchers use open file formats, document along the way (including any custom code), use professional-quality digitization methods and standards, and do not use customized software or browser plugins, the outputs of the project will be easier to preserve and subsequently to access and use in the long run.

An additional risk that needs to be investigated early in a digital preservation project is copyright and other intellectual property rights. It may be costly, if it is even possible, to contact and clear rights with all of the people involved with a project after the fact. Take, for example, a digital recording of a performance of Sophocles' classic Greek tragedy *Antigone*. There will be directors, choeographers, costume and set designers, actors, and many others involved, each of whom will have some degree of intellectual property rights to a recording of the performance. Due to the public domain status of the play, the only person involved who does not have any intellectual property rights would be Sophocles![10] Yet all of the performance's participants have intellectual property rights that must be respected by digital preservationists.

SUSTAINABLE DIGITAL RESOURCES

There have been a limited number of case studies investigating the sustainability of digital projects, and more are needed. However, a November 2009 report, *Sustaining Digital Resources: An On-the-Ground View of Projects Today*, produced by the "Ithaka Case Studies in Sustainability project, closely examined the business models of twelve digital projects resulting in a set of twelve detailed case studies."[11] This report offers some insight into how sustainability planning is incorporated into different organizations and projects. The key findings of this report include the following:

1. There was "no clear consensus . . . on what sustainability is or how to achieve it."[12]
2. There were tensions between wanting to share content widely and the need to generate revenue.
3. Projects were experimenting with multiple ways to create revenue. None of the nonprofit organizations profiled in the report earned enough money to operate independently, however.
4. "Cost control strategies were at least as important as revenue models in the sustainability plans."[13]
5. "The role of in-kind contributions from the host institution was often significant. . . . In many cases, neither project nor host institution [was] fully aware of the value of these 'hidden costs,' which could lead to inefficiencies at scale."[14]

Digital preservationists will want to bear these findings in mind as they begin work on their digital preservation initiatives.

The report over these case studies also identified five key factors that influence the sustainability of digital projects: (1) leadership, (2) a clear value proposition, (3) the problem of direct costs, (4) developing revenue streams, and (5) goals and their assessment. We discuss each in turn below.

1. Dedicated and entrepreneurial leadership: While not every organization can have someone devoted to this full time, "a certain passion and tireless attention to setting and achieving goals is critical to success. A willingness to experiment in this fast-moving digital space"[15] is also important.
2. A clear value proposition: organizations "with the greatest impact are the ones whose leaders have a deep understanding [of] and respect for the value their resource contributes to those who use it."[16]
3. Minimizing direct costs: It is important that Archives minimize the direct costs. Part of doing this will involve quantifying the contributions of the host institution.
4. Developing diverse sources of revenue: Although many programs receive generous contributions from a host institution, "leaders of digital projects often turn to revenue generation as a means to fund ongoing operations as well as upgrades needed to keep the resource vital to its users."[17]
5. Clear accountability and metrics for success: "While all of the above is important, without clearly established goals and the means to assess progress toward those goals, sustainability may be difficult to achieve. And not all measures of success need be financial; [the report's authors] observed many digital resource projects with mission-related goals. By establishing these targets, reaching them, and communicating this to stakeholders, leaders of digital projects are better able to secure the support they require."[18]

Given the issues that arise with providing for the sustainability of a standard digital project, digital preservationists will be wise to think about how these factors may be amplified in working to store and manage digital objects over the long term, if not indefinitely. For these reasons, sustainability must be a central focus of any digital preservation management initiative.

BLUE RIBBON TASK FORCE ON SUSTAINABLE DIGITAL PRESERVATION AND ACCESS

A Blue Ribbon Task Force on Sustainable Digital Preservation and Access (BRTF-SDPA) was formed in 2007 with funding from the NSF and the Andrew W. Mellon Foundation. BRTF-SDPA partners included the Library of Congress, Jisc (formerly the Joint Information Systems Committee [JISC]), the Council on Library and Information Resources (CLIR), and the United States' National Archives and Records Administration. The BRTF-SDPA had three goals. They were to:

- Conduct an analysis of previous and current models for sustainable digital preservation and identify current best practices among existing collections, repositories, and analogous enterprises.

- Develop a set of economically viable recommendations to catalyze the development of reliable strategies for the preservation of digital information.
- Provide a research agenda to organize and motivate future work in the specific area of economic sustainability of digital information.[19]

The BRTF-SDPA's final report, *Sustainable Economics for a Digital Planet: Ensuring Long-Term Access to Digital Information*, identified issues intrinsic to all digital objects and proposed action items that could be taken to meet the challenges of digital preservation sustainability. The BRTF-SDPA specifically looked at four types of content they believed were in the public interest—scholarly discourse (journal articles, books, etc.), research data, commercially owned copyrighted cultural content, and collectively produced Web content.

Based on their investigations, the BRTF-SDPA came up with three imperatives for sustainable digital preservation: (1) articulating a compelling value proposition, (2) providing clear incentives to preserve in the public interest, and (3) defining roles and responsibilities among stakeholders to ensure an ongoing and efficient flow of resources to preservation throughout the digital life cycle. These imperatives are implicit in the remaining discussion of sustainability in the digital preservation context, especially for the four kinds of content that were enumerated.

Five Conditions Necessary for Digital Preservation Sustainability

The BRTF-SDPA also identified five conditions necessary for digital preservation sustainability in their final report: (1) having decision makers recognize the benefits of digital preservation, (2) selecting digital objects that have long-term value, (3) having incentives for digital preservation, (4) having appropriate organization and governance of digital preservation activities, and (5) ensuring financial sustainability.[20] We will discuss each of these in turn.

The first condition is having decision makers recognize the benefits of digital preservation. Decision makers can include anyone from university presidents, provosts and deans, research foundations, granting agencies, and faculty members to anyone that has created any form of digital object with potential cultural or scientific value. Decision makers need to understand that their decisions can bring either positive benefits or negative benefits." Positive benefits of digital preservation include access to content over time, and the opportunity of reuse of the content for new and in different ways. Negative benefits are what may be potentially lost if no action to preserve digital objects is taken.

The second condition identified by the BRTF-SDPA is the selection of digital objects that have long-term value. This is necessary because digital preservationists are unable to preserve everything. Collection development policies and procedures can help prioritize the selection of materials that are of the greatest use both now and into the future. The selection process should reach across the organization as far as necessary. For example, an academic library may want to get subject librarians involved in collection development from a content perspective, information technology staff involved for a technological perspective, and metadata librarians involved for creating descriptive metadata. Having all of these people coming from different points of view involved early in the selection process will help the Archive determine what the effort will be to preserve the digital objects, to judge the value of preserving the digital object's value, and to create the opportunity to predict the potential return on investment.

The BRTF-SDPA's third condition is that there need to be incentives for decision makers to preserve digital content in the public interest. Incentives can be financial (such as requiring digital preservation as a requirement for grant funding), legal, or social. Besides creating or strengthening positive incentives, negative incentives that are barriers to digital preservation should be removed wherever possible. Barriers can include copyright law and other intellectual property–related issues, time constraints, and costs of preservation.

Appropriate organization and governance of digital preservation activities is the fourth condition the BRTF-SDPA identified. To satisfy this condition, digital preservation organizations need to be transparent and accountable. Organizations "should have clear policies that specify roles, responsibilities, and procedures."[21] When multiple organizations are involved in preserving a digital object or a collection of digital objects, a memorandum of understanding or similar document should be created that clearly identifies which organization will be responsible for what. For example, if a group of museums wants to preserve a collaboratively curated collection of slides, and if digital copies do not already exist, it must be determined who will be responsible for creating the digital objects, what specifications the resulting digital images should have, who will create the descriptive metadata, and so on.

The last condition identified by the BRTF-SDPA is to have mechanisms in place "to secure an ongoing, efficient allocation of resources to digital preservation activities."[22] In other words, in order for digital preservation to be sustainable, there needs to be financial sustainability. Funding models need to be created that are sufficient to meeting user exceptions and are within community norms. Because digital preservation may be costly, it might mean that different levels of digital preservation services will be offered in different situations. Financial sustainability issues will be discussed in more detail later in this chapter.

FACTORS AFFECTING
DIGITAL PRESERVATION SUSTAINABILITY

There are different ways to break down the challenges of digital preservation and the factors that can lead to, or prevent, sustainable digital preservation. For example, the BRTF-SDPA identified the five conditions for sustainable preservation discussed above. It is likewise possible to look at the *factors* that affect digital preservation sustainability. As there are more ways than one to skin a cat, there are multiple ways to divide the factors affecting digital preservation sustainability. For our purposes, we identify four factors affecting digital preservation sustainability: (1) organizational factors, (2) financial factors, (3) social and societal factors, and (4) technological factors.

Organizational Factors

There are many different organizational factors that can influence the sustainability of digital preservation initiatives. The following will highlight a few of these factors that digital preservationists will want to keep in mind when preparing an overall digital preservation plan or strategy. These factors include the alignment of digital preservation initiatives with organizational goals and mission, the business needs of the organization, the clarity of the communication plans of the project, and the potential for partnering with other organizations to help ensure digital preservation sustainability.

In order to sustain digital preservation initiatives, it is important to align these initiatives with the organization's goals and mission. Sometimes digital preservation is seen as a technological solution to a technological problem. However, unless an organization's purpose is to create or implement new technological solutions, implementing any technology, let alone a digital preservation system, is probably not a core part of the organization's mission. Digital preservation "technology is not the solution, only part of it."[23] Digital preservationists need to be able to convince management and other decision makers that digital preservation is important to the overall mission of the organization and not just an experimental technology project. As Clive Billenness described it, "digital preservation is a long-term project, so service provision must also be long-term."[24] In other words, a long-term commitment is necessary to have an effective long-term digital preservation program.

Digital preservation sustainability goals should be based on an institution's business needs and aligned with organizational mission and priorities. Ideally, where appropriate, digital preservation should also be integrated "within governance policies [to provide] the opportunity to migrate [digital preservation] activities from short-lived projects to being part of the core activity of the organisation."[25]

There are many benefits to digital preservation that align well with the organizational mission and goals of cultural heritage institutions. However, many of the benefits of long term digital preservation are not appreciated straightaway, since, by definition, digital preservation is meant to ensure materials are accessible in the future. The good news is that in a recent survey of 101 research libraries located across forty-nine countries "most of the participant libraries (65 percent) rated [digital preservation] as 'extremely important' or 'very important' for their activities. Another 34 percent rated [digital preservation] as 'important' or 'slightly important'; and only one rated [digital preservation] as 'not important at all.'"[26] Despite the recognition by decision makers of the benefits of digital preservation, decision makers still "need to strengthen their support to DP [digital preservation] by inserting DP in organisational governance practices."[27]

One of the keys to getting sufficient management buy-in for sustainable digital preservation is to have a communication plan that clearly describes the benefits of digital preservation to management and other key stakeholders in the organization. A successful communication plan should not only explain the benefits of digital preservation but also create digital preservation advocates throughout the organization. Tyler Walters and Katherine Skinner predict cultural heritage organizations "that build and care for collections now, through digital acquisition, Web archiving, digitization, and content creation, will be the leading organizations of the future."[28] If Walters and Skinner's prediction proves to be correct, those institutions that do not engage in these activities risk being marginalized in the future. If the case that digital preservation is important to the overall mission of an organization can be made effectively, then it will be more likely that the necessary organizational commitment necessary to sustaining digital preservation over the long term will be received.

In some situations the sustainability of the organization itself and/or its future ability to honor commitments to long-term digital preservation is a concern. For this reason, some digital preservationists suggest partnering with other organizations to provide digital preservation services. Agreements can be made that allow for a second institution to continue to preserve the digital objects of an institution should that initial institution fail. Agreements can be established in different ways. Institutions could implement a simple reciprocal agreement, a private LOCKSS (Lots of Copies Keep Stuff Safe) network could be formed, or a larger cooperative partnership could be constructed. However these agreements are fashioned, it is worth looking into them, especially for smaller institutions or those on shakier financial footing.

Financial Factors

One of the most important components of institutional commitment to any project is financial support, and digital preservation is no different. Unlike some shorter-term projects proposed to management, digital preservation is a long-term commitment with no end in sight. Not only does sustainable digital preservation require financial resources, it requires that those resources be ongoing. "From a financial point of view, good [digital preservation] practice and planning can support processes to maintain digital content collections and ensure they remain accessible and trustworthy over the required lifespan in a cost-efficient way."[29]

In 2008, Brian Lavoie wrote that, although there has been much discussion about the problem of ensuring access to files over time, "there has been relatively little discussion of how we can ensure that digital preservation activities survive beyond the current availability of soft-money funding."[30] While the discussion about the financial and economic sustainability of long-term digital preservation has increased significantly since Lavoie voiced this concern, the problem still remains and only a limited number of studies have been published in the literature that review real-world economically sustainable digital preservation models.[31] Below, we look more closely at cost models, return on investment, and revenue streams.

Cost Models

In order to do any long-range financial planning for digital preservation, it is important to have reasonable estimates of the costs. Unfortunately, there are a limited number of long-term digital preservation cost models "for ongoing storage of digital content."[32] This may be due to the unpredictable changes involved with technology and the potentially unlimited length of time digital preservation services will be needed. Also, since digital preservation is still a relatively new and ever-evolving field, few real-world cost analyses of digital preservation have been undertaken. "In order to increase the opportunity for key decision makers to buy in and support [digital preservation], there has been recorded a need to develop models that support economically sustainable preservation, as well a need to evaluate similar business cases that reflect the multiple value dimensions of [digital preservation]."[33]

Not only are there limited real-world cost analyses for institutions to use when trying to estimate digital preservation costs, many institutions also do not have procedures in place that allow them to document how much they spend on digital preservation. According to a recent survey of research libraries, "many organisations estimate [their digital preservation] budget by experience or cannot estimate budget at this level. Only 5 percent of the organisations claim to have estimated budget and costs through cost models."[34] It is unfortunately true that "little is known about the costs academic libraries incur to implement and manage institutional repositories"[35] (that may or may not offer digital preservation capabilities) as well.

In order to do any long-range financial planning for digital preservation, however, it is important to have reasonable estimates of costs. This may be difficult to do, since digital preservation is a relatively new field and there is limited practice and research in this area to build on. However, as was discussed in chapter 2, there has been some work on cost models, including that done in the LIFE Project. Two other cost-modeling projects of interest include the Netherland's Data Archiving and Networked Service (DANS) Cost of Digital Archiving (parts 1 and 2) projects and the Danish National Archives and the Danish Royal Library's Cost Model for Digital Preservation (CMDP). DANS's Cost of Digital Archiving project aimed to clarify cost structures and create a model for digital preservation costs.[36] Additional information about the Costs of Digital Archiving project, including details about the cost model, is provided in Anna Palaiologk and colleagues' article "An Activity-Based Costing Model for Long-Term Preservation and Dissemination of Digital Research Data: The Case of DANS," which appeared in the *International Journal on Digital Libraries*.[37] CMDP was a three-phase project that created models to estimate the costs of preservation planning and digital migrations, ingest, and archival storage. CMDP resulted in a Microsoft Excel–based tool that estimates the costs of ingest, preservation planning, archival storage, and some administrative costs.[38] Additional studies and models of interest can be found on the "Digital Preservation and Data Curation Costing and Cost Modelling" wiki page[39] and Butch Lazorchak's blog, The Signal, under "A Digital Asset Sustainability and Preservation Cost Bibliography."[40]

Return on Investment

While knowing how much digital preservation costs is important, it is also important to know what the return on investment (ROI) in digital preservation is. If a positive ROI can be demonstrated, financial and other types of support are more likely to follow. Digital preservation may require a substantial investment in time and money. However, by undertaking digital preservation, an institution can protect its, often significant, investment of time and money in born-digital and digitized content. Additionally, many "organisations have valuable intellectual assets and important collections now in digital format and need to ensure that they are available in the future."[41] Therefore institutions that "choose not to preserve [their] digital resources . . . incur real costs that are associated with that choice. These costs come in multiple forms: cultural, political, scientific, and institutional."[42]

Revenue Streams

The creation of digital objects, be they born-digital or digitized, is often funded by soft money such as grants, one-time donations, or other one-time expenditures. The same is true of many current and past digital preservation initiatives. While these short-term infusions of money are appreciated, they cannot be counted on into the future and thus cannot by themselves support sustained long-term digital preservation. Grants are usually short-term, but in some cases it might be possible for organizations to put some portion of the money that they receive from grants into an ongoing endowments for digital preservation. Likewise, LAMs should consider soliciting donations that are earmarked specifically for digital preservation–related endowments.

Some organizations that have undertaken digital preservation initiatives have looked at providing digital preservation services for a fee to other organizations. These services can include storage, software platforms, and consulting services. For example, the Chronopolis digital preservation network, headquartered at the San Diego Supercomputer Center (SDSC) at University of California–San Diego (with partners University of California–San Diego Libraries, the National Center for Atmospheric Research, and the University of Maryland Institute for Advanced Computer Studies), provides digital preservation storage services for a fee. The charge for University of California customers is less than it is for other customers, because an overhead fee is applied to non–University of California customers. The overhead fee increases the total cost of storage by just over 45 percent.[43] Although this model may work for organizations like Chronopolis, and while 40 percent of university libraries "reported that [they] might try providing [digital preservation] services in the future,"[44] only a small number of LAM institutions are currently attempting this strategy of providing digital preservation services to others for a fee.

LAM organizations can provide digitization-on-demand services. When someone wishes to access a document that is currently only available in physical form, that person is charged a fee to cover the costs of scanning the document and depositing it into a digital archive. Often this fee is only large enough to cover the costs of scanning the document. While digitization-on-demand services will be unlikely to provide significant revenue to most LAMs, it can help offset the costs of creating digital materials.

Some cultural heritage organizations attempt to offset their costs by charging users a fee for digital access. This can be a one-time fee or can be done by subscription. For some Archives that have culturally significant materials in high demand, this can be a money maker; however it may not scale well. First, the Archive needs to have materials that people are willing to pay for, and it also needs to have the resources available to support this activity.

Organizations that are contemplating charging for digitization need to determine if a fee-based model is appropriate, since such a model may not align well with their mission. There is also the risk of backlash from scholars about the costs, even if they are small. A blog post on the *Guardian* website said that "the costs and difficulties in accessing archival documents is having an impact on history researchers who may feel that it is too hard to access these documents and instead rely on more limited sources. . . . In doing so, they miss out on a wealth of information, and the quality of research suffers."[45]

Social and Societal Factors

Social and societal factors can influence the long-term sustainability of digital preservation initiatives. Some of these factors could make sustainable digital preservation more difficult. Other factors, conversely, may help make the argument for long-term digital preservation. For example, one societal factor that may lead to an organization having almost no choice but to implement a digital preservation strategy is a legal mandate to do so. National, state, and other archives are often legally required to maintain and preserve records, and since these records are now coming in digital form, these institutions have no choice but to preserve the digital objects.

Not all legal issues help make the case for sustainable digital preservation. Copyright, patent, and other intellectual property laws can significantly increase the difficulty of digitally preserving objects. In fact, many digital preservation strategies are borderline illegal in some countries if the LAM has not been granted the rights to carry out digital preservation by those holding the intellectual property rights. For example, in some countries it may be illegal to circumvent Digital Rights Management (DRM) technologies, while in others it may be illegal to make a copy of a digital object, effectively preventing a digital preservationist from legally migrating the digital object into a new, sustainable file format.

Increasingly, citizens are clamoring for transparency in government. This includes the transparency of (and access to) government-funded research. Early in President Barack Obama's second term, his director of the Office of Science and Technology Policy, John Holdren, issued a memorandum that called for federal agencies "with over $100 million in annual conduct of research and development expenditures to develop a plan to support increased public access to the results of research funded by the federal government."[46] In this memorandum, long-term preservation objectives are specifically mentioned. The memorandum also calls for researchers applying for federal grants to describe "how they will provide for long-term preservation of, and access to, scientific data in digital formats resulting from federally funded research, or explaining why long-term preservation and access cannot be justified."[47] Similar initiatives that are designed to help ensure public access to research over time are underway in other countries as well. Two examples are the Research Councils UK (RCUK)'s open access policy and the Australian government's funding of the Australian National Data Service.

User expectations can play an important role in digital preservation sustainability. Many users of libraries, archives, and museums want access to information in digital format. Digital objects, unlike physical ones, are accessible from a distance, and it can be easier to manipulate content stored in a digital format than a physical one. This is especially true if the physical format is rare or fragile. This demand for digital content "supports the case for [digital preservation] engagement and interaction among users and [LAM] organisations."[48]

In addition to making content available digitally, LAMs can undertake content enrichment and create value-added applications for end users. Consider e-learning applications, which very well could "make digital preservation truly sustainable."[49]

User demand for digital objects can help increase the demand for long-term digital preservation. Indeed, much of the value of a digital repository may "be derived by its acceptance and by its use."[50] This in turn can help support sustainability. Managing user demand, however, is not without its challenges. As technology and delivery methods evolve, users will want the LAM institutions to evolve as well. They will ask for a modern look and feel, support for new platforms (mobile, tablets, etc.), and additional features that commercial websites might employ. Keeping up with these changes will be important to maintaining user support but will also be a challenge to many Archives, especially those with limited staff and budget.

Technological Factors

Digital preservation involves digital technology, and the proper technology, when used correctly, can be an important piece of the digital sustainability puzzle. While technology is an important part of digital preservation, it can also work against long-term digital preservation. This is because technology is always changing. Digital preservation software as well as the software that creates digital content needing to be persevered are both constantly evolving. Because of ever-changing technology and the fact that digital storage media are not very stable compared to most traditional physical storage containers, such as books, letters, and sculptures, "preservation in the digital terrain is always and already an act of will, and one that takes ongoing work for every asset."[51]

New file formats and new software programs are constantly being released, and creators of digital objects will use them. Digital preservation systems need to have "the capacity to interact with new formats with minimum difficulty."[52] In order to respond to change, digital preservation technology and Archives providing digital preservation need to remain flexible. This is challenging because an important aspect of digital preservation involves documentation, policies, and procedures. Ultimately digital preservation is unpredictable because technology is unpredictable over time. Digital preservationists can only make their best-educated guess and carry out due diligence over time. By making informed decisions and following digital preservation best practices, such as taking advantage of trustworthy file formats and creating descriptive metadata that will help ensure that the meaning of digital objects is not lost over the course of time, digital preservationists can greatly increase the chances of successful access to digital content long into the future. On the contrary, if nothing is done, it is rather likely that at some point digital objects will become unusable, either due to physical deterioration of the media or due to obsolescence. Technological obsolescence is when hardware or software is no longer viable even if it is still in working order. One obsolete technology is the eight-track audio cartridge. A good example of obsolescence related to computer technology is punched cards. As Michael Lesk describes, "punched cards were made from quite strong paper. . . . Stored under reasonable humidity, [they] would certainly last for decades. But today you would only find a card reader in the Smithsonian or companies specializing in rescuing old data."[53]

When selecting technology to be used for digital preservation it is important to ask some questions about the sustainability of the technology being considered. One of the first areas to look at is the user community. Organizations should inquire as to the number of organizations using the system. They also should look to see if the user community has similar goals to their own.

HOMEGROWN, OPEN SOURCE, AND PROPRIETARY SOFTWARE DEVELOPMENT MODELS

The digital preservation system can either increase or decrease how sustainable a digital preservation initiative is. The software itself needs to be sustainable. In general, there are three different types of software development models that can be used for digital preservation: (1) homegrown software, (2) free and open source software (FOSS), and (3) commercial/proprietary software.[54] Each of these types of software has its positives and negatives and needs to be evaluated carefully. When discussing digital preservation software tools, one should be "mindful that any software tool, including a FOSS tool, is itself a digital artifact with its own preservation challenges."[55] Each of these three types of software for digital preservation is discussed below.

A homegrown software solution makes it possible for a software developer to customize the software for the needs of the organization, and, since it is developed in-house, at least one person on the staff should have intimate knowledge of the software. Digital preservation software, however, can be complicated technology, and most LAMs do not have large programming staffs. Even if an institution does have a fleet of programmers, it can be a challenge if one of the key developers leaves. Will the organization be able to hire a replacement, and, if so, how long will it take the replacement to learn the system? Additionally, if there are budget cuts or new organizational priorities, programming staff may be affected. Will developers be taken off the digital preservation project if the department is forced to downsize?

FOSS, or free and open source software, can help alleviate many of the problems of homegrown solutions, because there is, ideally, a community of users that helps create and maintain the software. Some benefits of open source (along with open standards) "include lower costs, great accessibility, and better prospects for long-term preservation of scholarly works."[56] It is sometimes tempting to look at open source systems as a way to save money because "open source software is generally available for free (or at a minimal cost)," which can lead to lower initial costs.[57] However, it is important to remember that, even though initial costs may be lower, it is not necessarily true that open source will be cheaper overall. C. Sean Burns, Amy Lana, and John M. Budd surveyed academic libraries that operated institutional repositories and found "near equal median expenses between annual operating costs for institutions that use open source software and institutions that use proprietary solutions."[58] Whether an organization is choosing a homegrown, open source, or proprietary system, all of the costs involved with running the software should be considered. This includes any licensing fees, support costs, and the staff necessary to operate the system.

Another reason digital preservationists may lean toward FOSS tools is the "tool's openness itself," since transparency is "a virtue in many aspects of digital preservation."[59] However, institutions evaluating FOSS for digital preservation need to be careful to evaluate the sustainability of the software. Is the user community of sufficient size to provide support? Is commercial support from the developer or another source that is familiar with the program available? Likewise, the sustainability of the core development team needs to be evaluated. Is the development pattern truly open source, or is the project developed by one organization that is closed off? In other words, is the software open source in name only? If the development community is small, a FOSS solution may still be the best option for an Archive, but before selecting the software, the Archive will need to consider the appropriate course of action if the FOSS development team breaks down. Looking at the viability of the user and developer community is a key factor in evaluating the sustainability of free and open source software, and the same principle could be said to apply to proprietary software, except in that situation the question to ask is whether the company is viable. The advantage with FOSS is that the code can still be used and invested in by another group of people unrelated to the original group. "An engaged community of use is the best guarantor of [the vitality of and FOSS tool."[60] If the Archive evaluating a FOSS solution has a small user and developer community and believes that it will be able to continue development of the project should the organization(s) leading the project loses interest, the FOSS may still be the best choice.

Commercial, proprietary solutions for digital preservation are also available. Some digital preservationists will tout the benefits of using open source software for long-term preservation, but it might not be for everyone. A proprietary software suite developed, marketed, and supported by a commercial entity might be a better choice than an open source solution for an institution without a large information technology staff. Proprietary software may seem even more appealing if the vendor has a proven track record of providing software solutions and has a solid customer base. Of course, there are drawbacks with proprietary systems, as well. As mentioned earlier, these drawbacks can include vendor lock-in if the vendor is not using open standards. Drawbacks can also potentially include high licensing and maintenance fees. It is important to consider the viability of the vendor and the product being offered. If the vendor goes out of business, what happens to the software? Likewise, if the vendor determines that the product is not profitable, the vendor may choose to discontinue the product, leaving the Archive without support.

Regardless of the type of software development model used, it is important when selecting a digital preservation system to make sure it is sustainable in the environment for which it is being selected. One digital preservation solution may work well at one organization but not another. Each organization should do its own evaluation to make sure the system meets its needs and is a sustainable solution. As part of this sustainability analysis, organizations should consider exit strategies. Since it is likely that long-term digital preservation initiatives will outlast the current technology, it is important to be able to migrate from one system to another in the future.

MEMORANDUMS OF UNDERSTANDING (MOUS)

The best digital preservation systems in the world are worth nothing without Content. One way to encourage sustainability is through formal agreements with content providers. Securing ongoing access to new, relevant, and valuable content is one strategy for pleasing Consumers. Content providers can be identified from among a variety of stakeholders and for the reasons mentioned above have the potential to provide content that will be desirable to maintain over the long term. When working with partners toward the goal of sustainability, a few key ideas need to be kept in mind so that all parties will be pleased with the outcome.

When accepting digital content from partners, it is a good idea to get all of the expectations in writing. In many, if not most cases, the objects being deposited into a digital preservation system were not created by the entity operating the system. Transparency, therefore, is important for all concerned. For this reason, the institution responsible for digital preservation will typically want to have a written agreement with the researcher, people, departments, or other organizations providing content to the repository. Often these agreements take the form of a *memorandum of understanding*, or MOU. While there is no one agreed-upon definition of a memorandum of understanding as a matter of law, it is generally considered "more formal than a 'gentleman's agreement' but 'less than a contract.'"[61] Memorandums (or *memoranda*, if using a Latin version of the plural) of understanding can be useful tools to explain what the roles and expectations of both parties are.

Whenever possible, the MOU should be between responsible organizations and not individuals, since individuals affiliated with organizations can change over time. A well-thought-out MOU will help answer the question of who is responsible for what and how to proceed when the roles and responsibilities of stakeholders are unclear. The contents of MOUs will often vary depending on individual circumstances, although there will usually be many things in common. It is also not unusual to see a generic MOU used for one-off deposits, deposits that are not expected to repeat. For example, a university library might have a generic MOU or similar document that is completed by a student when he deposits his electronic thesis or dissertation. Likewise, there may be a generic agreement or license used when a faculty member deposits a copy of a scholarly article or conference presentation she created. Before writing an MOU for digital objects created locally, one should check to make sure that the institution does not have existing policies and agreements in place that already sufficiently address these issues.

While the topics covered in an MOU may differ from Archive to Archive and from digital collection to digital collection, there are some items that managers of digital preservation systems should consider including in the MOU. Digital preservationists involved in writing MOUs may wish to identify explicitly the parties involved, the content in question, pre-ingestion work to be done, the length of time content will be preserved, the terms and conditions for the preservation, the rights of the Archive, and information about funding. Each will be explored below in greater detail, even though not all of the items described here will apply to every digital collection being preserved. Furthermore, there might be additional items that some digital repositories may wish to include. Some institutions may address some of these items in other agreements or policies. In those situations, the memorandum may include references to these other policies.

The first, and perhaps most obvious, thing to delineate in an MOU is who the parties are that are involved with the project. From the institution's point of view, this could be the LAM as well as its particular department or specific employee responsible for the digital collection to be preserved. From the submitter's point of view, it could be the individual, the leaders of a project, or the institution responsible for the creation of the digital content. It is recommended that the MOU specify an individual (or specific position) to be a liaison for the collection. This is true both for the LAM and for the entity that is providing the materials. From the LAM's standpoint, this may be the digital preservation manager, a metadata or subject librarian, or a project manager. A logical contact should likewise be designated to represent the submitter of content. Some LAMs may decide to include language in the agreement that the collection liaison information be confirmed or updated on a regular, perhaps yearly, basis.

A description of the objects that are to be preserved should be included in the MOU. This does not need to be an in-depth description but should at least define the scope of the collection. The MOU could also include information about the size of the digital collection and if the collection is going to continue to grow. If the collection is an ongoing collection, how often new content will be added to the collection can be included as well. If the objects are already in electronic format, the acceptable formats of the digital objects should be described or a pointer to an overarching policy of the digital preservation system provided.

In almost all cases, a collection will need some level of pre-ingestion processing. In cases involving papers, print photographs, or other physical objects, the objects will need to be digitized first. In the case of born digital objects, in some situations the digital objects may need to be migrated to a more preservation-friendly format. Both born digital and digitized objects will need metadata. Although much of the technical metadata can be created automatically, descriptive and administrative metadata will need to be created by one or more individuals. The MOU should outline who will be responsible for this pre-ingestion work. If the LAM is providing training, such as how to create descriptive metadata or how to format digital objects, this might be included in the MOU as well. In some cases, time frames and other metrics may also be defined.

Often LAMs will aim to preserve digital content indefinitely; however, this is not always the case, especially in Archives where there may be legal requirements and other legal or regulatory concerns about the length of time information is kept. The length of time a digital object is to be preserved is something to consider including in a MOU. Related to this is what will happen to the digital content should the researcher or group responsible for the collection leave the university (or other organization) that the digital preservation system is for. For example, it is not uncommon for an academic journal to change the place of publication, and institutes of advanced studies have been known to change their affiliation to a different university. If the academic journal's content or the institute's scholarly output were to be placed into the university's digital preservation system, what would happen to the content should these types of changes take place? In many cases, the content created while the person or group was affiliated with the institution would remain in the digital preservation system, but this should be spelled out, if possible. Likewise, if, how, when, and in what format the researchers or organizations will receive a "dump" of their content should they change their affiliation or status is worth considering including in the MOU.

The terms and conditions under which digital objects will be accessed and displayed is another topic for a MOU. In many cases, items will be available openly, but in other cases they will be restricted to on-campus or password-protected use or perhaps placed in a dark archive. A *dark archive* is primarily concerned with long-term preservation and does not provide public access to the objects in the archive. Usually these terms will be nonexclusive, meaning the person depositing the material retains the rights to publish or display the content elsewhere. If there are any special copyright, intellectual property, privacy, or confidentiality issues related to the collection, they could be mentioned here as well. Another issue that may be referenced is the steps the repository will take if someone objects for legal or other reasons to something that has been deposited into the digital preservation system. Most likely this will not be specific to individual collections, so it might not be explicitly defined in the MOU. However, the memorandum could point to the policy where the appropriate procedure is described for the digital preservation system as a whole.

In order to perform long-term digital preservation, it may be necessary to migrate digital objects into new or alternative formats. The agreement should outline the rights of the repository to do perform these actions. Cardiff University's Electronic Theses and Dissertations agreement says that the depositor agrees that the university "may electronically store, copy, or translate the Work to any approved medium or format for the purpose of future preservation and accessibility. Cardiff University is not under any obligation to reproduce or display the Work in the same formats or resolutions in which it was originally deposited."[62] In addition to this, an MOU may include or refer to what type of reasonable steps a repository will take in order to preserve digital objects. Often this may vary based on file format and will change over the course of time, so when describing this it might be more appropriate to refer to a policy external to the MOU that can be updated as needed instead of including it directly in the memorandum.

In some situations there may be a grant or other external funding related to the collection and to the collection's preservation. When appropriate, the memorandum can address how such funding will be distributed. If in order to process the collection the LAM or the owner of the collection needs to hire additional personnel (even if the staff doing the work are interns or student workers in an academic setting), this might be something to include as part of an MOU as well.

As mentioned previously, not all of these topics ought necessarily be included in every MOU. This could be because they are not needed for a particular collection or the topics are addressed in other agreements or policies. There may be additional items that should be included that are not mentioned here. Each LAM performing digital preservation needs to decide what is important to include in its MOUs given its unique set of circumstances. An example worksheet for a library photo collection is provided in table 5.1 to help identify the sections of an MOU.

Table 5.1. Example MOU Worksheet

Category	Example in a Library Photo Collection
Who are the parties involved?	The University Libraries and the Office of Public Relations.
Describe the objects and the size of the collection.	There is a collection of 50,000 photographs in TIFF format, averaging 4.7 MB each. The collection is expected to grow by 5,000 photographs annually. The Office of Public Relations will provide new photographs semiannually on portable hard drives.
What steps need to be performed before the objects are ingested into the digital preservation system? Who will carry them out (descriptive metadata creation, file format conversion, digitization, etc.)?	The Libraries will create Dublin Core descriptive metadata from the keywords and other metadata that were embedded by the University Photographer into the photos.
What is the length and level of preservation?	The Libraries aim to provide "Full" digital preservation for these photographs as defined in the "Digital Preservation Levels" document. The length of preservation will be indefinite.
What type of access will be provided?	A version of the photographs will be made available to the general public via the Libraries' discovery layer in a low-definition, watermarked format. Anyone requesting access to the original high-quality version will be directed to the Office of Public Relations for approval.
What steps will be taken to preserve the digital objects (migration, normalization, emulation, etc.)?	The Libraries may copy or migrate the photographs into any format necessary for the purposes of long-term preservation.
Are there any specific staffing or funding needs related to this collection?	N/A
Is there anything else that should be included in the MOU?	The Libraries will ingest the photographs when time permits with the goal of ingesting the original digital photographs by the end of the 2014–2015 academic year.

CONCLUSION

The Management of digital preservation initiatives requires oversight. "Digital preservation costs money and requires active and ongoing attention."[63] If the organizational commitment and financial resources are not available to support digital preservation over the long term, the preservation effort is likely to fail. It is important that digital preservationists and administrators work to create sustainable conditions for digital preservation. If an Archive is going to solicit digital objects to preserve, be they research data, e-records, or works of arts, the Archive needs to be able to commit to making the resources available for long-term preservation. A key factor in getting resources for long-term digital preservation is communication. Digital preservationists not only need to create plans and polices and implement technology suited for sustainable digital preservation, but they also must communicate why it is important for the long-term goals and mission of the institution, securing content and pleasing stakeholders, like Consumers, in the process.

This chapter ends the discussion of the Management portion of the Digital Preservation Triad. Management issues will continue to surface throughout the next chapters, however, as no digital preservation initiative can take place without oversight, planning, and resources. Next, in part III, we look at the Technology necessary to supporting sustainable and well-managed digital preservation initiatives.

NOTES

1. U.S. Environmental Protection Agency, "Sustainability: Basic Information," para 1, accessed May 15, 2013, http://www.epa.gov/sustainability/basicinfo.htm.

2. Brian Lavoie, Lorraine Eakin, Amy Friedlander, Francine Berman, Paul Courant, Clifford Lynch, and Daniel Rubinfeld, "Sustaining the Digital Investment: Issues and Challenges of Economically Sustainable Digital Preservation," 19, Blue Ribbon Task Force on Sustainable Digital Preservation and Access (BRTF-SDPA), December 2008, http://brtf.sdsc.edu/biblio/BRTF_Interim_Report.pdf.

3. David Pearson, "Sustainable Models for Digital Preservation," slide 5 (paper presented at the Sustainable Data from Digital Fieldwork International Conference, Sydney, December 4–6, 2006), http://www.nla.gov.au/openpublish/index.php/nlasp/article/viewArticle/920.

4. National Aeronautics and Space Administration (NASA), *NASA Risk Management Handbook*, version 1.0, NASA/SP-2011-3422 (Washington, D.C.: NASA Headquarters, 2011), 202, http://permanent.access.gpo.gov/gpo24492/20120000033-2011025561.pdf.

5. Douglas W. Hubbard, *The Failure of Risk Management: Why It's Broken and How to Fix It* (Hoboken: John Wiley and Sons, 2009), 10.

6. Su-Shung Chen, "Digital Preservation: Organizational Commitment, Archival Stability, and Technological Continuity," *Journal of Organizational Computing and Electronic Commerce* 17 (2007): 207.

7. This sentiment is described in some detail in *Sustainable Economics for a Digital Planet: Ensuring Long Term Access to Digital Information*, the final report issued by the Blue Ribbon Task Force on Sustainable Digital Preservation and Access (BRTF-SDPA) (San Diego: San

Diego Supercomputer Center, 2010), http://brtf.sdsc.edu/biblio/BRTF_Final_Report.pdf. Some aspects of this report will be discussed in more detail later in the chapter.

8. Open Source Initiative, "Open Standards Requirement for Software," accessed September 29, 2013, http://opensource.org/osr.

9. Wikipedia, s.v. "Succession Planning," accessed March 21, 2013, http://em.wikipedia.org/wiki/Succession_planning.

10. A survey respondent made a similar statement, except in that case Shakespeare was used as the example. The survey was described in Tom Evens and Laurence Hauttekeete, "Challenges of Digital Preservation for Cultural Heritage Institutions," *Journal of Librarianship and Information Science* 43 (2011): 157–65.

11. Nancy L. Maron, K. Kirby Smith, and Matthew Loy, *Sustaining Digital Resources: An On-the-Ground View of Projects Today*, 9 (report prepared by Ithaka with support from U.K. Joint Information Systems Committee [JISC], the U.S. National Endowment for the Humanities, and the U.S. National Science Foundation, April 2009), http://www.jisc.ac.uk/media/documents/publications/general/2009/scaithakaprojectstodayfundersedition.pdf.

12. Ibid, 9.

13. Ibid, 10.

14. Ibid, 10.

15. Ibid, 10.

16. Ibid, 10.

17. Ibid, 10.

18. Ibid, 11.

19. Blue Ribbon Task Force on Sustainable Digital Preservation and Access, "Blue Ribbon Task Force on Sustainable Digital Preservation and Access Homepage," accessed May 26, 2013, http://brtf.sdsc.edu/index.html.

20. Blue Ribbon Task Force on Sustainable Digital Preservation and Access (BRTF-SDPA), *Sustainable Economics for a Digital Planet*.

21. Ibid, 84.

22. Ibid, 12.

23. Anne R. Kenney and Nancy Y. McGovern, "The Five Organizational Stages of Digital Preservation." In *Digital Libraries: A Vision for the 21st Century; A Festschrift in Honor of Wendy Lougee on the Occasion of her Departure from the University of Michigan*, edited by Patricia Hodges, Mark Sandler, Maria Bonn, and John Price Wilkin, "Introduction, para 6 (Ann Arbor: Scholarly Publishing Office, University of Michigan, University Library, 2003), http://quod.lib.umich.edu/s/spobooks/bbv9812.0001.001/1:11?rgn=div1;view=fulltext.

24. Clive Billenness, "Building a Sustainable Model for Digital Preservation Services," slide 2 (paper presented at the third annual WePreserve Conference, Nice, October 28–30, 2008), http://www.digitalpreservationeurope.eu/preservation-training-materials/files/WEP RESERVEsustainability.pdf.

25. Ruben Riestra, Xenia Beltran, Panos Georgiou, Giannis Tsakonas, Kirnn Kaur, Susan Reilly, and Karlheinz Schmitt, *Business Preparedness Report* (Dorset, Eng., and The Hague: APARSEN, 2013), 41, APARSEN-REP-D36_1-01-1_0, http://www.alliancepermanentaccess.org/wp-content/uploads/downloads/2013/03/APARSEN-REP-D36_1-01-1_0.pdf.

26. Ibid, 18.

27. Ibid, 40.

28. Tyler O. Walters and Katherine Skinner, "Economics, Sustainability, and the Cooperation Model in Digital Preservation," *Library Hi Tech* 28 (2010): 261–62.

29. Riestra et al., *Business Preparedness Report*, 25.

30. Brian F. Lavoie, "The Fifth Blackbird: Some Thoughts on Economically Sustainable Digital Preservation," *D-Lib Magazine* (March/April 2008): "Blackbird Revisited," para 3, http://www.dlib.org/dlib/march08/lavoie/03lavoie.html.

31. Walters and Skinner, "Economics, Sustainability." Walters and Skinner review the economic-sustainability model of the MetaArchive Cooperative.

32. National Digital Stewardship Alliance, *National Agenda for Digital Stewardship 2014* (Washington, D.C.: Library of Congress, 2014), 18, http://www.digitalpreservation.gov/ndsa/documents/2014NationalAgenda.pdf.

33. Riestra et al., *Business Preparedness Report*, 5.

34. Ibid, 40.

35. C. Sean Burns, Amy Lana, and John M. Budd, "Institutional Repositories: Exploration of Costs and Value," *D-Lib Magazine* 19, no. 1–2 (2013), http://dlib.org/dlib/january13/burns/01burns.html.

36. More information about "Costs of Digital Archiving, vol. 2" can be found on the DANS website at http://www.dans.knaw.nl/en/content/categorieen/projecten/costs-digital-archiving-vol-2.

37. Anna Palaiologk, Anastasios A. Economides, Heiko D. Tjalsma, and Laurents B. Sesink. "An Activity-Based Costing Model for Long-Term Preservation and Dissemination of Digital Research Data: The Case of DANS." *International Journal on Digital Libraries* 12 (2012): 195–214. doi:10.1007/s00799-012-0092-1.

38. More information about the Cost Model for Digital Preservation, including how to download and use the costing tool, is available on the project's website at http://costmodelfordigitalpreservation.dk/.

39. OPF Knowledge Base Wiki, "Digital Preservation and Data Curation Costing and Cost Modelling," last modified April 22, 2013, http://wiki.opf-labs.org/display/CDP/Home.

40. Butch Lazorchak, "A Digital Asset Sustainability and Preservation Cost Bibliography," *The Signal: Digital Preservation Blog*, June 26, 2012, accessed September 29, 2013, http://blogs.loc.gov/digitalpreservation/2012/06/a-digital-asset-sustainability-and-preservation-cost-bibliography/.

41. Riestra, et al., *Business Preparedness Report*, 5.

42. Walters and Skinner, "Economics, Sustainability," 261.

43. As of November 11, 2013, the Chronopolis usage fee for UC customers was $1500 per terabyte, while non–UC customers were charged $2200 per terabyte. Pricing and other information about this service, and Chronopolis in general, is available on the Chronopolis website at http://chronopolis.sdsc.edu/.

44. Riestra, et al., *Business Preparedness Report*, 31.

45. Nell Darby, "The Cost of Historical Research: Why Archives Need to Move with the Times," *Higher Education Network Blog*, May 23, 2013, para 4, accessed September 29, 2013, http://www.guardian.co.uk/higher-education-network/blog/2013/may/23/history-research-costs-archive-fees.

46. John P. Holdren, "Memorandum for the Heads of Executive Departments and Agencies: Increasing Access to the Results of Federally Funded Scientific Research," February 22, 2013, 2, http://www.whitehouse.gov/sites/default/files/microsites/ostp/ostp_public_access_memo_2013.pdf.

47. Ibid, 5.

48. Riestra, et al., *Business Preparedness Report*, 21.

49. Dinesh Katre, "Ecosystems for Digital Preservation in Indian Context: A Proposal for Sustainable and Iterative Lifecycle Model," 152 (paper presented at the Indo–U.S. Workshop on International Trends in Digital Preservation, Prune, India, March 24–25, 2009), http://www.scribd.com/doc/36284662/Indo-US-DP-Proceedings-C-DAC-2009.

50. Burns, Lama, and Budd, "Institutional Repositories," para. 2.

51. Walters and Skinner, "Economics, Sustainability," 260.

52. Billenness, "Building a Sustainable Model," slide 3.

53. Michael Lesk, *Practical Digital Libraries: Books, Bytes, and Bucks* (San Francisco: Morgan Kaufmann, 1997), 190.

54. It is worth mentioning that some software programs fall somewhere between the three different models. For example, there can be collaborative projects that are somewhere between homegrown and open source or open source projects that are supported by a commercial organization whose model (and potential benefits) in reality falls somewhere between open source and a commercial/proprietary model.

55. Sheila Morrissey, "The Economy of Free and Open Source Software in the Preservation of Digital Artefacts," *Library Hi Tech* 28 (2010): 212.

56. Edward M. Corrado, "The Importance of Open Access, Open Source, and Open Standards for Libraries," *Issues in Science and Technology Librarianship* (Spring 2005): "Conclusion," para 1, http://www.istl.org/05-spring/article2.html.

57. Ibid, "Open Source," para 2.

58. Burns, Lama, and Budd, "Institutional Repositories," "Discussion," para 2.

59. Morrissey, "Economy of Free and Open Source Software," 212.

60. Ibid, 220.

61. Frank Lyall and Paul B. Larsen, *Space Law: A Treatise* (Surrey, Eng.: Ashgate Publishing, 2009), 37.

62. The agreement can be found at Cardiff University's website: "Cardiff University Electronic Theses and Dissertations Publication Form," http://www.cf.ac.uk/regis/resources/Electronic%20Theses%20and%20Dissertations%20Publication%20Form.pdf.

63. Martin Gibbs and Sarah Colley, "Digital Preservation, Online Access and Historical Archaeology 'Grey Literature' from New South Wales, Australia," *Australian Archaeology* 75 (2012): 95.

III

TECHNOLOGY ASPECTS

6

The Digital Preservation
Repository and Trust

Technology is one of the most unnerving aspects of digital preservation, and it certainly is one that gets a great deal of attention. The technologies needed, according to the Digital Preservation Triad presented in chapter 2, include but are not limited to the repositories themselves, the metadata, and the digital objects being preserved. This first chapter in part III on Technology covers the notion of the digital preservation system first and foremost as a system that can document adherence to standards to demonstrate its trustworthiness. In doing so, broad issues of documentation, self-assessment, and transparency are raised in relationship to Technology. Subsequent chapters in part III focus on the metadata being used (chapter 7) and the file formats in which the digital objects are stored (chapter 8).

Heightening the anxiety about digital preservation is the fact that the ability to perform long-term digital preservation is not something that can be proven until years into the future. Primarily, digital preservation is something that must be accepted on the basis of trust. Trust is a crucial aspect of a well-functioning society, and this is particularly true "when it comes to unfamiliar digitally encoded information, especially when it has passed through several hands over a long period of time,"[1] which is likely to happen to content deposited into a digital repository. How can an Archive operating a digital preservation system or repository establish trust? Some digital preservationists believe one way to answer this question is for repository administrators to establish procedures based on current best practices that have been agreed on by experts within the digital preservation community and then to document that they are following them rigorously. Increased levels of trust from outsiders may be gained by performing self- and external audits designed to demonstrate that the digital preservationists are, in fact, following these best practices as they have been documented.

Not all Archives that operate digital preservation systems will opt to review their documentation in order to become certified. Demonstrating trustworthiness through certification is, however, one way to show that an Archive is serious about its commitment to long-term preservation through planning and transparency. It is important to remember that any type of audit or certification, including those designed for digital preservation, should not be viewed as a one-time endeavor but, rather, as an ongoing commitment. A trusted digital repository that has a mission to provide long-term access and preservation should expect to perform constant monitoring and be perpetually engaged in planning. In order for a digital preservation system to remain trustworthy, a regular cycle of audit and certification is recommended.

TRUST

Trust can be defined as "reliance on the integrity, strength, ability, surety, etc., of a person or thing; confidence."[2] There are a number of initiatives that try to provide evidence to show that a digital repository and a digital preservation system can be trusted. These include audit and certification standards, such as the Data Seal of Approval, DIN 31644, and ISO 16363. These three will be described later in this chapter. Repository administrators and staff may wonder whether the audit process is worth the effort. Many organizations that have gone through a formal or trial audit process have said that the process was indeed worthwhile, not only in helping to establish trust with people outside of their organizations but also, if not more so, in helping to identify the strengths and weaknesses of the digital repository and in identifying opportunities where the digital preservation process could be improved.

In terms of digital preservation, what does it mean to be trustworthy? The Alliance Permanent Access to the Records of Science in Europe Network (APARSEN) produced a *Brochure on Trust* to help answer this question. In the brochure, APARSEN identifies four key questions related to trust that need to be addressed.

1. Has the data been preserved properly?
2. Is it of high quality?
3. Has it been changed in some way?
4. Does the pointer get me to the right object?[3]

It is worthwhile to reflect on these four questions in turn when thinking about the importance of demonstrating the trustworthiness of the preservation repository.

The first question, whether or not the data's been preserved correctly,[4] encourages all levels of employees, from administrators to practitioners, to reflect on the ongoing process of preserving digital content in a rapidly changing technological environment. Preservation strategies need to be constantly revisited as users, standards, technology, and collections change. When starting a repository a considerable amount of work is involved, yet that work, if trust is to be ensured, is never fully completed;

preserving content in a manner that is trustworthy is an ongoing process requiring constant professional vigilance.

APARSEN's second question asks whether the data quality is high.[5] While reviewing the quality of the data inside of a repository is usually the domain of scientists or domain experts instead of repository administrators, "quality assurance of scientific information is an integral component of digital long-term archiving."[6] Future and indeed current users will not be well served by accessing inaccurate content; trust requires that the resources presented are of the highest quality and that the metadata be equally accurate to ensure seamless access and use.

ARSPEN then asks whether the data has changed in any way.[7] This question gets at the concept of authenticity, which is a complex topic when it comes to digital objects and to preservation in general. The more evidence that a user has to judge the authenticity of a digital object, the better. Repositories can help establish authenticity by collecting and preserving the proper evidence. The evidence then needs to be dealt with intelligently and securely. One goal of the preservation system, depending on technical strategies for keeping data accessible, is to demonstrate that content has *not* been modified and that a digital object in the digital preservation system is identical to the original. With analog items, it can be straightforward to notice whether, for example, a page has been removed or text has been altered. In the realm of electronic media, however, the integrity of the electronic document has to be ensured in other ways.

And finally APARSEN asks whether the pointer gets the user to the right object.[8] This question gets to the challenges of persistent identifiers and interoperability issues as they relate to trustworthiness. Since URLs serve as a means of identifying both a resource and its location, they cannot always be considered reliable tools for assuring that the appropriate document is being accessed. For this reason, various persistent identifiers for objects have been created. These include digital object identifiers (DOI) and Persistent URL (PURL). There are also persistent identifiers for authors such as ORCID (Open Researcher and Contributor ID) and Researcher ID. However, because there are multiple persistent identifier schemes available, and since this is unlikely to change any time soon, interoperability becomes a challenge. To help confront the identifier challenge, ARPESN is working on an interoperability framework for persistent identifiers.

TRUSTED REPOSITORY CRITERIA AND CHECKLISTS

In 1996, the Task Force on Archiving Digital Information, convened by the Commission on Preservation and Access and by Research Libraries Group (RLG), identified the need for trusted organizations capable of providing long-term digital preservation.[9] However, the task force did not believe that organizations could simply identify themselves as trusted. As Robin Dale explains, in the absence of a decades-long track record, organizations "have to prove capable stewardship of digital certification of their digital archives and repositories."[10] With this concept in mind, the task force called for a certification process to be created, although they "stopped short of articulating the details of such a certification process."[11]

In 2003, RLG and the U.S. National Archives and Records Administration (NARA)'s Task Force on Digital Repository Certification took on the challenge of creating one of the first sets of criteria and checklists for long-term digital preservation. The document created by this task force is known as the *Trustworthy Repositories Audit and Certification: Criteria and Checklist*, or TRAC for short.[12] TRAC Version 1.0 was published in February of 2007. At that time, the Center for Research Libraries (CRL) agreed to take on the task of performing audit and assessment activities, work that CRL continues to be involved with today. TRAC is the basis of the current ISO 16363:2012 (Audit and Certification of Trustworthy Digital Repositories) international standard that has now superseded it.

Besides TRAC and ISO 16363:2012, there have been other efforts to establish criteria and checklists that can be used as tools when auditing digital preservation systems. Two of the most notable of these efforts are the Data Seal of Approval and Deutsches Institut für Normung (DIN; in English, it's known as the German Institute for Standardization) standard #31644, a German standard that was started by Nestor (Network of Expertise in Long-Term STOrage of Digital Resources), "the German competence network for digital preservation," and is currently maintained by the DIN Trusted Archives–Certification Working Group.[13] Digital Repository Audit Method Based on Risk Assessment (DRAMBORA) is yet another initiative that will be discussed below.

European Framework for Audit and Certification of Digital Repositories

On July 8, 2010, the chairs of the Consultative Committee for Space Data Systems (CCSDS)/ISO Repository Audit and Certification Working Group (RAC), the Data Seal of Approval (DSA) Board, and the DIN Trusted Archives–Certification Working Group signed a memorandum of understanding stating that they would work together to create standards for trusted digital repository certification. This effort is known as the European Framework for Audit and Certification of Digital Repositories. The framework designates three levels to represent increasing degrees of trustworthiness[14]—basic certification, extended certification, and formal certification. The concept behind the different levels is that some repositories may not be able to or may not desire to perform a full external audit and certification of their digital preservation system due to the time, expense, or other considerations. Formal certification, therefore, should not be the only option but, rather, should be the most advanced of a suite of options for certification.

In order for a digital repository, both in Europe and abroad, to be granted the European Framework's basic certification, the repository needs to obtain the Data Seal of Approval certification. Extended certification is given to repositories that, in addition to receiving basic certification, "perform a structured, externally reviewed, and publicly available self-audit based on ISO 16363 or DIN 31644."[15] Formal certification requires basic certification as well as a complete external audit and certification based on either DIN 31644 or ISO 16363 (i.e., extended certification), which will be described in the following.

Basic Certification: Data Seal of Approval

The Data Seal of Approval was originally developed by Data Archiving and Networked Services (DANS), located in the Netherlands. In 2009, control of the administration of the Data Seal of Approval was given to an international board, members of which are now located both inside and outside of Europe. The guidelines for the seal "can be seen as a minimum set distilled from" national and international guidelines, including Kriterienkatalog vertrauenswürdige digitale Langzeitarchive (developed by Nestor), Digital Repository Audit Method Based on Risk Assessment (DRAMBORA), and TRAC's criteria and checklist.[16]

There are three major steps in the process of obtaining a Data Seal of Approval. The first is to perform a self-assessment. Afterward, an external expert from an organization that has already been awarded a Data Seal of Approval performs a review of the assessment and provides feedback. The organization applying for a seal for its repository then takes that feedback and makes any necessary adjustments, then submits the assessment for a second round of review.

The Data Seal of Approval self-assessment requires only a few days' effort if the documentation is already in place.[17] At the Data Seal of Approval 2012 Conference in Florence, Italy, Archeology Data Service's Catherine Hardman mentioned that it took about four days for her organization to prepare the information for their Data Seal of Approval application with only one day actually spent doing the self-study.[18] The Archeology Data Service had already had many procedures and documents in place when starting the process, so other organizations that don't already have required procedures and documentation in place may require more time to prepare. Still, the Archeology Data Service experience demonstrates that an organization can perform this self-study without dedicating an exorbitant amount of time or other resources to the process.

The Data Seal of Approval is awarded to a specific repository rather than to a specific organization, and the repository can choose to display the seal (see figure 6.1) on its website. If an organization has multiple repositories that it wishes to certify, it will have to go through the self-assessment process for each repository that it operates. The guidelines for the seal consist of sixteen different criteria that a repository is to be assessed against. For each guideline, a repository assigns itself a compliance level. The compliance levels range from 0 to 4. Table 6.1 shows the compliance levels and provides a short description for each.[19] Beginning with the July 2013 release of the Data Seal of Approval 2014-2015 (version 2) guidelines, organizations applying for the seal are asked to supply information about the context of the repository so that the reviewers can understand the applicant.[20]

Figure 6.1. The Data Seal of Approval
Reprinted with permission of the Data Seal of Approval Board.

Table 6.1.   Data Seal of Approval Compliance Levels

Compliance Level	Description
0	Not Applicable
1	The repository has not considered this yet
2	The repository has a theoretical concept
3	The repository is in the implementation phase
4	This guideline has been fully implemented for the needs of the repository

http://www.datasealofapproval.org

For all but one of the sixteen criteria, a compliance level of at least 3 is required in order to meet the guidelines for the 2014–2015 version of the Data Seal of Approval. It is expected that by 2015 the requirements will call for level-4 compliance for all guidelines.[21] The sixteen guidelines are divided into three different categories based on various types of stakeholders involved. These categories are for (1) Data Producers, (2) Data Repositories, and (3) Data Consumers. Table 6.2 shows the 2014–2015 Guidelines (also referred to as version 2 of the guidelines) and minimal compliance level requirements.[22] Requirements 1 through 3 are for data producers, 4 through 13 for data repositories, and 14 through 16 for data consumers. Besides the sixteen guidelines with which the repository must be in compliance, Data Seal of Approval applications are expected to also include "repository context" information.

One of the guiding principles of the Data Seal of Approval is transparency. The board behind the seal believes strongly that transparency assists in establishing trust. For example, one of the reasons the Archeology Data Service was attracted to the Data Seal of Approval is because "the spirit of openness an[d] trust on which it is built, we hope, reflects the nature of our own relationship with depositors."[23] Therefore, in order to be awarded the Data Seal of Approval, the documentation that demonstrates the compliance levels must be publicly available via the Internet (although personal or confidential information, such as phone numbers and passwords, may be withheld). This also applies to the self-assessment and the reviewer's comments.[24]

As mentioned previously, an international board now controls the Data Seal of Approval. All organizations that have received a Data Seal of Approval are automatically part of the Data Seal of Approval community and are welcome to participate in the governance process. People from organizations that are part of the governance process are eligible to become board members, leading to the addition of board members from beyond Europe's borders.

The Data Seal of Approval is awarded for a period of two years, during which time the seal's logo can be displayed on the repository's website. At the end of the two-year period, organizations can apply for a new seal, using any updated guidelines, or they may continue to display the older, outdated seal if they so choose.

Extended Certification: DIN 31644 and Nestor Certification

DIN standard 31644 is a "criteri[on] for trustworthy digital archives" developed in Germany.[25] It was published in 2012, but its origins can be traced back to at least 2004 when Nestor, the German competence network for digital preservation, formed a working group focused on trustworthy digital archives.[26] In contrast to the Data Seal of Approval, which started with a focus on research data, this working group began with all types of digital repositories in mind. Early on, this working group decided to create criteria "to support two activities: the certification of a digital archive as well as the self-evaluation of such a newly founded archive."[27] Two versions of these criteria were published in both German and English. The first was published

Table 6.2.   Data Seal of Approval 2014–2015 Guidelines (Version 2)

Guideline Number	Description	Minimum Compliance Level
0	Repository context (This is a new requirement in version 2 of the guidelines. Its purpose is to help reviewers understand the applicant).	N/A
1	The *data producer* deposits the research data in a data repository with sufficient information for others to assess the scientific and scholarly quality of the research data and compliance with disciplinary and ethical norms.	3
2	The *data producer* provides the research data in formats recommended by the data repository.	3
3	The *data producer* provides the research data together with the metadata requested by the data repository.	4
4	The *data repository* has an explicit mission in the area of digital archiving and promulgates it.	4
5	The *data repository* uses due diligence to ensure compliance with legal regulations and contracts.	4
6	The data repository applies documented processes and procedures for managing data storage.	4
7	The *data repository* has a plan for long-term preservation of its digital assets.	3
8	Archiving takes place according to explicit work flows across the data life cycle.	3
9	The *data repository* assumes responsibility from the data producers for access and availability of the digital objects.	4
10	The *data repository* enables the users to utilize the research data and refer to them.	3
11	The *data repository* ensures the integrity of the digital objects and the metadata.	3
12	The *data repository* ensures the authenticity of the digital objects and the metadata.	3
13	The technical infrastructure explicitly supports the tasks and functions described in internationally accepted archival standards like OAIS.	3
14	The *data consumer* complies with access regulations set by the data repository.	4
15	The *data consumer* conforms to and agrees with any codes of conduct that are generally accepted in higher education and scientific research for the exchange and proper use of knowledge and information.	4
16	The *data consumer* respects the applicable licenses of the data repository regarding the use of the research data.	4

Available online at https://assessment.datasealofapproval.org/guidelines_52/html/.

in 2006, and, after receiving feedback a second version was published in 2008. Also in 2008, the Nestor working group decided that this set of criteria should become a DIN standard. In order for this to happen, a new group, containing many of the same people, was formed under the auspices of DIN. Additionally, a separate Nestor group was subsequently formed in order to offer certification.[28]

The DIN 31644 standard consists of thirty-four different criteria that are divided into three separate parts. "The first twelve criteria are connected with the organisation of the digital archive. The next 22 are related to the single objects, which should be preserved. The last two criteria are describing infrastructure and security."[29] As with the Data Seal of Approval, the DIN 31644 standard emphasizes transparency. Other guiding principles include documentation, adequateness, and measurability. Utilizing DIN 31644, a test audit of the Deutsche Nationalbibliothek (DNB; in English, the German National Library) was performed by the Nestor working group. The main motivation for DNB to undergo the test audit "was to have their own processes and documentation reviewed, scrutinized, and ideally approved by some external professionals."[30] DNB reports that the process has been valuable because it revealed the strengths of their repository as well as identifying some gaps that they now will be able to address. Extended certification under DIN 31644 by Nestor was planned to begin some time in 2013. Nestor extended certification will require that most of the criteria be fulfilled completely, although it is recognized that for some institutions certain criteria may not be applicable for various reasons. As of this writing, DIN 31644 is only available in German, but an English translation and guidelines for applying DIN 31644 is expected to be published in English in the near future.

There are two additional DIN standards that digital preservationists may wish to research further on their own. DIN 31645 is a standard related to ingesting digital files, and DIN 31646 is a standard that describes requirements for the long-term management of persistent identifiers.

Formal Certification

As mentioned above, formal certification requires basic certification as well as extended certification based on either DIN 31644 or ISO 16363. Formal certification also includes a complete external audit. Readers of this book will likely not be considering an external audit for their digital preservation systems at this time, but it is a possibility for certification that well-established Archives may wish to pursue.

TRAC, TRD, and ISO 16363

The Europeans are not the only ones devising standards and processes to demonstrate trustworthiness. In early 2000 the U.S.-based RLG and OCLC began collaborating on a project designed to describe the attributes of a digital preservation system based on the OAIS Reference Model, which was on its way to becoming an international standard. This collaboration resulted in the May 2002 report, *Trusted Digital*

Repositories: Attributes and Responsibility, which defined what a trusted digital repository is and also identified seven attributes that a trusted digital repository should have. The attributes follow.

1. compliance with the Reference Model for an Open Archival Information System (OAIS)
2. administrative responsibility
3. organizational viability
4. financial sustainability
5. technological and procedural suitability
6. system security
7. procedural accountability[31]

Some of these trusted digital repository attributes are obviously more technology-related and fit within the Technology portion of the Digital Preservation Triad, while others are more administration and policy oriented and fit into the Management portion.

In January 2002 the first *Reference Model for an Open Archival Information System (OAIS)* was released. This version is also known as the Blue Book. One of the sections of the Blue Book is a call for related standards including "standard(s) for accreditation of archives."[32] Perhaps with this call in mind, the following year "RLG and the National Archives and Records Administration (NARA) created a joint task force to specifically address digital repository certification."[33] The RLG–NARA task force built on the RLG–OCLC's *Trusted Digital Repositories: Attributes and Responsibility* report and other documents to create version 1.0 of the *Trusted Repository Audit and Certification: Criteria and Checklist (TRAC)*, which was published in February 2007. In September 2011, *Audit for Certification of Trustworthy Digital Repositories: Recommended Practice (TDR)* was published. TDR, also known as the Magenta Book, "follows on from TRAC in order to create an ISO Standard."[34] In March 2012 this standard was approved for publication as ISO 16363. While there are some differences between TRAC and TDR/ISO16363, they have many similarities, and TDR can be viewed as an updated version of TRAC.

The TDR checklist has more than eighty items on it, grouped into three sections: (1) organizational infrastructure, (2) Digital Object Management, and (3) technologies, technical infrastructure, and security. The RLG–NARA task force adopted the work of Nestor for articulating the principles of documentation, transparency, adequacy, and measurability that should be used when applying any criteria to trusted digital repositories. These same concepts were guiding principles in DIN 31644.

The first section of the TDR checklist, organizational infrastructure, focuses on organization attributes, not so much on technology, because while adequate technology "underpin[s] a trusted digital repository, . . . organizational attributes of digital repositories are equally critical."[35] The checklist is broken down into five groups of criteria to be used when auditing organizational infrastructure.[36]

1. governance and organizational viability
2. organizational structure and staffing
3. procedural accountability and policy framework
4. financial sustainability
5. contracts, licenses, and liabilities

If Archives do not have the appropriate organizational infrastructure in place, then they will not be able to meet the other requirements of the checklist over the long-term.

The TDR checklist's section on Digital Object Management includes both organizational and technological responsibilities, whose requirements are broken down into six groups based an OAIS functional entities.[37]

1. ingest: acquisition of content
2. ingest: creation of the Archival Information Package (AIP)
3. preservation planning
4. AIP preservation
5. information management (which includes, but is not limited to, discovery metadata and other descriptive and location information)
6. access management ("the repository's ability to produce and disseminate accurate, authentic versions of the digital objects"[38])

The technology aspects of the Digital Object Management section of the checklist should be met with a software system that is designed to be OAIS–compliant. However, in order to be fully compliant with this portion of the checklist, organizational issues also need to be addressed.

The last section of the TDR checklist addresses technologies, technical infrastructure, and security. Though focused on technology, this section does not prescribe any particular hardware or software programs. Instead, it describes security and data management best practices. This section is divided into two groups.[39]

1. technical infrastructure
2. security risk management

If an organization has undergone an information technology security certification process, such as the ISO 27000 series of standards for information security, it is likely that the certification process will satisfy most of the criteria in this section.

Center for Research Libraries TRAC Audits

The Center for Research Libraries (CRL) conducts preservation audits of digital repositories using TRAC.[40] As of March 2013 CRL has certified four North American digital repositories. They are, in the order they received certification,

Portico, HathiTrust, Chronopolis, and Scholar's Portal.[41] The process of being certified by CRL involves three broad steps. The first step is for a repository to perform a self-audit, which involves answering all of the questions on the TRAC checklist. Once the self-audit is complete, a team from CRL analyzes the self-audit and performs a site visit. During this visit, CRL talks to repository administrators and stakeholders. Based on the self-assessment and site visit, CRL and the repository discuss and recommend changes. Finally, in the third stage, CRL releases a final audit report.[42] Certification expires after four years, and there is a required consultation between the repository and CRL auditors within eighteen to twenty-four months after certification.

DRAMBORA

The DRAMBORA serves a different purpose than the Data Seal of Approval, DIN 31644, ISO 16363, TRAC, or others. Though it is not a set of criteria or a checklist designed for certification, it remains a useful tool for those interested in demonstrating the trustworthiness of a digital repository. DRAMBORA is a methodology and an online interactive toolkit developed jointly by DigitalPreservationEurope and the Digital Curation Centre (DCC).[43] DRAMBORA is designed to facilitate internal audits that assist organizations in identifying their capabilities and the strengths and weakness of their digital repository. Additionally, once these weaknesses, or risks, are identified, DRAMBORA can be used to help plan effective ways for repository administrations to minimize these risks.

The benefits that organizations can expect following a self-assessment using the DRAMBORA toolkit include:

- a well-established and documented organizational profile
- clearly identified and documented repository assets, roles, and activities
- a catalogue of pertinent risks and interrisk relationships
- a shared understanding of the successes and shortcomings of the repository's management and structure
- alerts for repository managers to the likelihood of a specific risk occurring
- and the implementation of contingency mechanisms to alleviate the effects of risks that cannot be avoided.[44]

There are multiple stages involved in successfully utilizing DRAMBORA. The first stage is for repository administrators using the toolkit to define the reason and the scope of what they hope to achieve. Once this preliminary stage is completed, the self-assessment process can begin.

The DRAMBORA self-assessment is divided into two phases. In the first, the focus is "on attaining a comprehensive overview of the objectives and activities of the organisation supported by adequate documentation."[45] The second phase focuses on identifying and assessing risks. When using DRAMBORA, risks are assessed using three characteristics: (1) impact, (2) impact expression, and (3) probability. *Impact* is defined by the potential impact of a realized risk. *Impact expression* is how "the negative effects of the risks occurrence manifest themselves."[46] Finally, *probability* is the likelihood and frequency that the risk will occur.

The final stage of DRAMBORA is to describe risk management measures. For each risk identified, "details of treatment, avoidance measures, and anticipated outcomes should be recorded and monitored over time."[47] Repository administrators should also create a time frame for regular reassessment so that any new risks that may occur can be identified and mitigated in the future.

CONCLUSION

As Jason Speck reminds us, "when it comes to trust, there is no magic potion or silver bullet."[48] That said, there are a number of ways digital repositories can help build trust—using self-assessments, certification, and audit tools such as those described here. By their very nature, assessments like the Data Seal of Approval, DIN 31644, or ISO 16363 open digital repositories to outside scrutiny. This scrutiny can be seen as intrusive. Extended and full certification can also be expensive and time consuming. Regardless, Archives that have performed these types of assessments have found them worthwhile. Digital preservation systems wishing to be seen as trustworthy by data producers and data users should consider self-assessments and even full audits. In part because of the newness of these certifications, there is limited evidence that they will build trust with users. By going through the process of being certified as a trusted digital repository, however, digital preservation system administrators can feel more confident about their abilities while at the same time learning how to improve their digital preservation activities, joining a community of like-minded administrators who are seeking to do the same, and, ultimately, making the preservation process as transparent as possible as a way of encouraging both use and users. Digital preservationists can feel more confident about the technology they are using, the decisions they are making, and the standards they are implementing and can make strides toward offering a trusted and trustworthy environment for sustainable digital preservation initiatives.

In the next two chapters we will move from a discussion of the trustworthiness of the Archive to the specifics of the Technology it houses. Technology, after all, is not only about the Archive but about the digital objects as well. First, in chapter 7, we will discuss the metadata that allows us to organize, retrieve, and use digital objects in the digital preservation system. And in chapter 8 we will cover the file formats used to make those digital objects available.

NOTES

1. Alliance Permanent Access to the Records of Science in Europe Network (APARSEN), *Trust Is Fundamental to the Working of Society* (Dorset, Eng., and The Hague: APARSEN, 2012), 2, http://www.alliancepermanentaccess.org/wp-content/uploads/downloads/2012/09/APARSEN-Trust-Brochure-Low-Res-Web-Version.pdf.

2. Dictionary.com, s.v. "Trust," accessed September 29, 2013, http://dictionary.reference.com/browse/trust.

3. APARSEN, *Trust Is Fundamental*, 2.

4. Ibid, 3.

5. Ibid, 4.

6. Ibid, 5.

7. Ibid, 6.

8. Ibid, 8.

9. Task Force on Archiving of Digital Information, "Preserving Digital Information: Report of the Task Force on Archiving of Digital Information" (commissioned by the Commission on Preservation and Access and the Research Libraries Group, May 1, 1996), http://www.oclc.org/content/dam/research/activities/digpresstudy/final-report.pdf.

10. Robin L. Dale, "Making Certification Real: Developing Methodology for Evaluating Trustworthiness," *RLG DigiNews* 9, no. 5 (2005): "Introduction, para 1, http://www.worldcat.org/arcviewer/1/OCC/2007/08/08/0000070511/viewer/file3025.html#article2.

11. CRL, *Trustworthy Repositories Audit and Certification: Criteria and Checklist (TRAC), Version 1.0* (Chicago and Dublin, Ohio: CRL and OCLC, 2007), 1, http://www.crl.edu/sites/default/files/attachments/pages/trac_0.pdf.

12. Center for Research Libraries (CRL), *Trustworthy Repositories Audit and Certification: Criteria and Checklist (TRAC), Version 1.0* (Chicago and Dublin, Ohio: CRL and OCLC, 2007), http://www.crl.edu/sites/default/files/attachments/pages/trac_0.pdf.

13. Nestor, "Nestor Homepage," accessed September 29, 2013, http://www.langzeitarchivierung.de/Subsites/nestor/EN/Home/home_node.html. For more information in English about nestor, see Susanne Dobratz and Heike Neuroth, "Nestor: Network of Expertise in Long-Term STOrage of Digital Resources; A Digital Preservation Initiative for Germany," *D-Lib Magazine* 10, no. 4 (April 2004), http://www.dlib.org/dlib/april04/dobratz/04dobratz.html.

14. TrustedDigitalRepository.eu, "Trusted Digital Repository Homepage," accessed September 29, 2013, http://www.trusteddigitalrepository.eu/Site/Trusted%20Digital%20Repository.html.

15. Ibid.

16. Data Seal of Approval, "Guidelines, Version 1," June 1, 2010, https://assessment.datasealofapproval.org/guidelines_1/pdf/.

17. APARSEN, *Trust Is Fundamental*, 2.

18. Catherine Hardman, "Case Study ADS: Presentation 4" (presentation at the Data Seal of Approval Conference 2012, Florence, December 10, 2013), http://www.datasealofapproval.org/sites/default/files/4_ADS_DSA_Florence2012-Cathrine_Hardman.ppt. The information about the length of time was part of the presentation's discussion and is not documented on the presentations slides.

19. For more information about the Data Seal of Approval, see their website at http://www.datasealofapproval.org/.

20. Data Seal of Approval, "DSA Guidelines for 2014–2015 Now Available," July 31, 2013, http://datasealofapproval.org/?q=node/95.

21. Data Seal of Approval, "Guidelines, Version 1."

22. Description and compliance levels retrieved from Data Seal of Approval, "Guidelines, Version 1."

23. Hardman, "Case Study ADS," slide 9.

24. Current seals and assessments can be found at https://assessment.datasealofapproval.org/seals/.

25. The DIN 31644 standard is currently only available in German, but an English translation and guidance on how to apply it is expected to be released shortly. An earlier draft version can be downloaded in English or German from Nestor, "Standardisation," last modified March 30, 2012, http://www.langzeitarchivierung.de/Subsites/nestor/EN/Standardisation/standardisation.html.

26. More information about Nestor can be found in English at Nestor, "About Us," last modified March 30, 2012, http://www.langzeitarchivierung.de/Subsites/nestor/EN/Header/AboutUs/ueberuns_node.html.

27. Christian Ketal, "DIN Standard 31644 and Nestor Certification" (paper presented at the Fondazione Rinascimento Digitale 2012, Florence, December 11–12, 2013), 2, http://www.rinascimento-digitale.it/conference2012/paper_ic_2012/keitel_paper.pdf.

28. More details about the history of DIN 31644 can be found in Ketal, "DIN Standard 31644."

29. Ketal, "DIN Standard 31644," 4.

30. APARSEN, *Trust Is Fundamental*, 3.

31. Research Libraries Group–Online Computer Library Center (RLG-OCLC), *Trusted Digital Repositories: Attributes and Responsibilities; An RLG-OCLC Report* (Mountain View, Calif.: RLG, 2002), 13, http://www.oclc.org/content/dam/research/activities/trustedrep/repositories.pdf.

32. Consultative Committee for Space Data Systems (CCSDS), *Audit and Certification of Trustworthy Digital Repositories: Recommended Practice CCSDS 652.0-M-1; Recommendation for Space Data System Practices*, Magenta Book, Recommended Practice, issue 1 (Washington, D.C.: CCSDS Secretariat, 2011), 1-4, http://public.ccsds.org/publications/archive/652x0m1.pdf.

33. CRL, *Trustworthy Repositories*, 2.

34. CCSDS, *Audit and Certification*, 1-2.

35. CRL, *Trustworthy Repositories*, 9.

36. CCSDS, *Audit and Certification*, 3-1–15.

37. Ibid, 4-1–27.

38. CRL, *Trustworthy Repositories*, 21.

39. CCSDS, *Audit and Certification*, 5-1–15.

40. It is reasonable to assume that in the future they will use TDR, but as of this writing there was no information to that effect on the CRL's Certification and Assessment of Digital Repositories website. Additionally, audits in process, including the FDsys audit, whose postponement was announced on January 24, 2013, were still utilizing the TRAC document.

41. Current certifications and documentation relating to the certifications can be found on the Certification and Assessment of Digital Repositories website: Center for Research Libraries (CRL), "Certification and Assessment," accessed September 29, 2013, http://www.crl.edu/archiving-preservation/digital-archives/certification-and-assessment-digital-repositories.

42. For details about how the certification process went at Chronopolis, see Chronopolis, "TRAC," accessed September 29, 2013, http://chronopolis.sdsc.edu/trac/index.html.

43. Digital Repository Audio Method Based on Risk Assessment (DRAMBORA), "A Risk-Aware Path to Self-Assurance and Partner Confidence for Digital Repositories" (flyer), accessed June 8, 2013, http://www.repositoryaudit.eu/img/drambora_flyer.pdf.

44. Ibid.

45. Ibid, 3.

46. Ibid, 3.

47. Ibid, 3.

48. Jason G. Speck, "Protecting Public Trust: An Archival Wake-Up Call," *Journal of Archival Organization* 8 (2010): 36.

7

Metadata and Metadata for Digital Preservation

Metadata is one of the fundamental Technologies that digital preservationists use to organize and retrieve content in the digital preservation system. Like digital preservation systems, metadata is a complex topic, and decisions about metadata can drastically affect access in the long term. Metadata does not have to be intimidating, however, and even misguided metadata decisions are reversible if good documentation has been kept and the metadata has been consistently applied. In some respects, then, the best bet is to become as informed as possible and then simply to dive in. This chapter is designed to help you understand the basics of metadata and to see how metadata applies to digital preservation.

It may be obvious that without metadata there is no access, since our digital preservation systems will not be able to retrieve digital content that is not described. But what is metadata really? A traditional and somewhat basic definition of *metadata* is "data about other data."[1] Although this definition at first seems blissfully simple and possibly even catchy, it does not further our understanding of metadata as it applies to libraries, archives, and museums (LAMs) and the items they curate and make available. The definition could also be somewhat misleading given the variety of definitions that *data* can have. Some digital preservationists might employ an archival definition of data like "facts, ideas, or discrete pieces of information, especially when in the form originally collected and unanalyzed."[2] If *metadata* is discrete pieces of information about discrete pieces of information, then traditional resources like finding aids and card catalog cards are obviously metadata. The "data about other data" definition is more troubling when *data* are considered to be facts or ideas in the data-information-knowledge-wisdom (DIKW) hierarchy. Here, *data* are potentially the components actually making up information. A definition of metadata where it is "components of information about other components of information" is fairly meaningless. To make sense of what metadata is and more specifically what it does

111

for digital preservation, a more-complex definition is required. Like other concepts having to do with the complex world of technology, however, finding a one-size-fits-all definition may be easier said than done.

There are a number of reasons that *metadata* evades an easy definition. "Metadata is difficult to define as an activity for two primary reasons. First, unlike library cataloging, metadata development involves a large number of stakeholders. . . . Second, metadata evolved from several different communities, each with its own disciplinary background and objectives."[3] To complicate things further, connotations of the term *metadata* are evolving at present. Increasingly, information professionals assume that metadata must be electronic; there is also a sense that metadata describes electronic resources. LAM metadata for digital libraries can be defined as "structured, encoded data that describes characteristics of information-bearing entities (including individual objects, collections, or systems) to aid in the identification, discovery, assessment, management, and preservation of the described entities."[4] Metadata is more than data, then; it allows the digital preservationist to organize and access items in the collection. Digital library metadata is poised to support not only end-user and information-professional access and use but also digital preservation, as we will see below.

Metadata can be kept in one of two ways. First, an entire metadata record can be created to describe an item (this works equally well for physical items and digital items). An example of this is a library cataloging record that contains information about a physical book. Second, metadata can also be embedded directly inside electronic items like Web pages. The header in a Hyperatext Markup Language (HTML) document, for example, gives metadata about that document's creation and potential uses. In retrieval systems, metadata permits users to discover the electronic item itself or an electronic surrogate of a physical or electronic item. "Surrogates can be metadata records, a scanned image of a document, digital photographs, transcription of a textual source, or any kind of extract or transformation (e.g., the spectral analysis of a recorded speech signal) of existing data."[5] When queries are launched in a digital library system, the list of hits is compiled based on the metadata in the system. In this chapter, we first look at metadata in general before moving on to focus on special needs and considerations for metadata in digital preservation.

METADATA IN DIGITAL LIBRARIANSHIP

In order to understand digital preservation metadata, it is necessary to look first at metadata that supports digital librarianship in general. This section gives a broad overview of the important concepts in metadata, concepts that are foundational to digital preservation. Digital preservation cannot take place without the metadata described in this section. We begin by looking at the four kinds of metadata used in digital librarianship. Next, we look at markup languages, metadata files and schemas, and how metadata schemas can be mixed and matched. We end this section on metadata in digital librarianship by looking at how schemas can be converted, how metadata is created, and the role of documentation.

Generally speaking, there are four principle kinds of metadata used in standard digital libraries to support their functions: (1) descriptive metadata, (2) administrative metadata, (3) technical metadata, and (4) structural metadata. Not everyone seems to agree on the exact types of metadata that fit into each category, and some even say there are five categories of metadata. This breakdown of the different kinds of metadata used in digital libraries is one approach (see table 7.1 as well). In truth, it

Table 7.1.   Four Basic Kinds of Metadata

Kinds of metadata used in LAM	Information about	Purpose	Examples
Descriptive metadata	Content item	Provide attributes of the item being described	Title, author/creator name, etc.
Administrative metadata	Use and uses of content item, files, and administrative metadata	Record information on rights, provenance; provide information necessary for preservation; record information about the creation of the surrogate	Copyright holder, access rights, etc.
Technical metadata	Electronic file	Record information necessary for accessing the item being described if it is electronic; provide information about accessibility for people with disabilities	File size, file format, etc.
Structural metadata	Set of electronic files	Record information about an electronic item's relationship to other related electronic items	Relationship to other files, etc.

really does not matter which category metadata is assigned as long as necessary metadata is provided, consistently created and input, and accessible through the system. In the following we look at each of the four kinds of metadata in turn.

Descriptive Metadata

In the LAM community, institutions use descriptive metadata to record information about an item's attributes. The physical and intellectual description of an item tends to be considered *descriptive metadata* across the board: its title, author, and subject are all considered descriptive metadata. In recording descriptive metadata, institutions record information about characteristics that might distinguish items from each other and permit users to select the item(s) that work best for them. Descriptive metadata in a digital library system is not unlike the information stored on traditional library cataloging cards. Charles Cutter's *Rules for a Dictionary Catalog* indicated that the information recorded (i.e., metadata) should permit the finding function, the collocation function, and the selection function in the catalog.[6] In the electronic environment, the IFLA Study Group on the Functional Requirements for Bibliographic Records (FRBR[7]) identified four user tasks: (1) find, (2) identify, (3) select, and (4) obtain. Descriptive metadata can provide a foundation for users to find, identify, and select documents in a system, with the potential for links or direct access so that an item can be obtained.

Administrative Metadata

Administrative metadata is necessary for recording information relative to the use of the item and has been perfected over the years in the information professions. Some disagreement exists as to the exact nature of administrative metadata. Marcia Lei Zeng and Jian Qin see administrative metadata writ large as "data used in managing and administering information resources, especially concerning acquisition, intellectual property, rights and access restrictions, technical characteristics related to history of processing, provenance, and preservation."[8] Not all of these functions are represented in all digital libraries' metadata, but the more that can be addressed, the better the understanding of where the item came from and the ways the item can be used. Examples of administrative metadata include information about the original object (in the case of a digitized object), file number, and copyright information, as well as information about the digitization of the object, the creation of the metadata record, the standards and schema used, and other information to help interpret the metadata and make use of the item. Granted, the same piece of metadata may serve multiple functions. In the case of a file number, this metadata may serve both administrative and descriptive purposes.

Technical Metadata

Technical metadata in digital libraries is necessary for accessing the item being described if that item is electronic. What is the file format? How big is the file? Is special software or hardware necessary to access the content? Zeng and Qin include accessibility metadata, "the degree to which the institution allows access to people with disabilities,"[9] as an additional kind of technical metadata. The National Information Standards Organization (NISO), instead, groups some technical elements with administrative metadata.[10] Text files have technical information about their fonts, and audio-visual files like digital photographs might also have technical metadata embedded. Automatically generated technical metadata in digital photographs can include the camera make and model, camera firmware version, shutter speed, and location where the photo was taken. Technical metadata from photographs can be automatically extracted from the image file and used in the digital library system. Figure 7.1 displays a sample of the metadata automatically captured by a digital camera and stored within a digital photograph. Note that the metadata includes the type of camera, date and time the photo was taken, resolution, and even GPS coordinates, since, in this case, the photo was taken using a GPS–enabled smartphone. All of this metadata was automatically captured and did not require the photographer's intervention.

Structural Metadata

Structural metadata provides information about an electronic item's relationship to other related electronic items. NISO defines it as one of three kinds of metadata, the one that "indicates how compound objects are put together, for example, how pages are ordered to form chapters."[11] It is distinct from the kinds of technical metadata that describes the file's internal composition, allowing a file to be connected within the system to related documents to create an intellectual whole. Metadata Encoding and Transmission Standard (METS), which will be described later in this chapter, is one example of a standard used to describe structural metadata.

Markup Languages

With markup languages, text-based digital objects (primarily) are marked up based on the content itself, the use the digital object will have, the mission of the institution, and the needs of potential users. Markup languages have Document Type Definitions (DTDs) that allow the records to be validated. "XML with correct syntax is 'Well Formed' XML. XML validated against a DTD is 'Valid' XML."[12] There are also other alternatives to DTDs. Two of the most prominent of these are XML schema languages known as XML Schema Definitions (XSDs, or sometimes somewhat confusingly known as *XML Schema* for short) and RELAX NG (REgular LAnguage for XML Next Generation). DTDs, XSD (XML Schema), and RELAX NG all have their strengths and weaknesses when compared to each other. In general XML schema languages have a much richer language and are more powerful than DTDs. However since the official definition of valid XML requires DTD, when using XML schema languages one may often have to be content with schema-aware validation. Another advantage of DTD is that it is the only of the three options

Properties	EXIF	ExifTool	GPS	Categories

▾ Camera

Camera Manufacturer	Apple
Camera Model	iPhone 4S
Orientation	top-left (1)
X Resolution	72
Y Resolution	72
Resolution unit	Inch
Software	6.1.3
Date modified	7/27/13 6:48 PM
YCbCr Positioning	centered (1)

▾ Image

Exposure time [s]	1/123
F-Number	2.4
Exposure program	Normal (2)
ISO speed ratings	50
EXIF version	02.21
Date taken	7/27/13 6:48 PM
Date digitized	7/27/13 6:48 PM
Components configuration	1000000
Shutter speed [s]	1/123
Aperture	F2.4
Brightness	3925/657
Metering mode	Multi-segment (5)
Flash	No flash
Focal length [mm]	4.3
FlashPix Version	01.00
Colour space	sRGB
EXIF image width	3264
EXIF image length	2448
Sensing method	One-chip color area sensor (2)
Exposure mode	Auto (0)
White balance	Auto (0)
Digital zoom	5
Focal length (35mm)	35
Scene capture type	Standard (0)

▾ GPS

Latitude Ref	North
Latitude	40° 48.50' 0.00"
Longitude Ref	West
Longitude	75° 45.34' 0.00"
Altitude Ref	Sea Level
Altitude	172.0000
TimeStamp	22
Img Direction Ref	T
Img Direction	36535/109

Figure 7.1. Automatically Generated Digital Photography Metadata

mentioned that can be embedded into the actual document.[13] Validated metadata records ensure a certain degree of quality and the ability to be shared with and be integrated in other repositories. Decisions need to be made ahead of time to mark up certain kinds of content in a digital object, and adopting best practices is essential to providing uniformity within a system (see sidebar 7.1). Employees will need to be trained to work with the electronic document, supplying markup based on the file's unique text and the best practices documentation. These files have a lot going on, with both content and markup being treated in the body of the document. They will also contain additional metadata in the headers, possibly from a combination of possible schema in use in cultural heritage institutions today.

Structure of Metadata Files

Metadata files in digital library systems generally have a header and a body and increasingly use Extensible Markup Language (XML) as an encoding language. According to the World Wide Web Consortium (W3C), XML is derived from Standard Generalized Markup Language (SGML) (ISO 8879). "Originally designed to meet the challenges of large-scale electronic publishing, XML is also playing an increasingly important role in the exchange of a wide variety of data on the Web and

SIDEBAR 7.1 BEST PRACTICES

In order to be consistent with their metadata creation, institutions and communities document their approaches to metadata creation, known as *best practices*. According to the Dublin Core Metadata Glossary, a best practice is a "guide and documentation to describe and standardize the use of metadata elements that best support a community's needs."[1] This can include information on the input standards and repeatability of elements in an Archive and will be the guide used by staff inputting metadata in the system. Many institutions will make their metadata best practices freely available on the Web or are willing to share them with other professionals when requested. Digital preservationists will want to consult best practices documents created by the community or by other institutions before finalizing their own documentation.

---

1. S.V. "Best practices," accessed September 18, 2013, http://dublincore.org/documents/2001/04/12/usageguide/glossary.shtml.

elsewhere."[14] XML's ability to exchange data on the Web and store that data in digital library and digital preservation systems makes XML–based languages an appealing choice for metadata formats in the LAM communities. Content in the body of the file is meant to be displayed to the user. Depending on the kind of file, embedded encoding may accompany that content to indicate to the computer how the display should look. No matter what, the user will see the displayed content, but the system will be able to read and store much, much more in a given metadata record.

Information recorded in the header is not meant for users to see; it is not content but metadata describing the creation of the file, the content of the file, and parameters for use, topic, author, and so on. Information in the header of a file is metadata for the system (against which it can run queries) and for the information professional. One non–XML example of a markup language used in libraries is MARC (MAchine-Readable Cataloging) (ISO 2709). MARC bibliographic records serve as surrogates for the information resource. Their header permits users to limit search results by date, language, format, and the like. Some digital library metadata, like MARC, is stored as separate files as a digital surrogate; in other instances, external metadata may be stored in a companion or sidecar file as text, XML, XMP, as a spreadsheet, etc., where it can easily be edited in bulk.[15]

Metadata for electronic documents, unlike metadata for physical items, can be stored inside the electronic document itself. In electronic file creation, much of the technical metadata generated by the software will be embedded in the file itself. Metadata can also be stored in separate files. Consider the example of crowdsourced social tags. Tags might be useful for retrieval within a system at a given period of time, but an institution might not choose to add them to the actual electronic file for the digital object until they can be vetted or fact checked. It is generally advisable that metadata created for digital library content be embedded in the file whenever practical, especially metadata for preservation since this helps establish the chain of custody necessary to ensure authenticity of the item. By storing metadata in the file itself, the process of preservation is streamlined since only one file (the target file) needs to remain readable and uncorrupted and the metadata is less likely to get separated from the file it describes. Naturally, each situation is different, and exceptions to this include instances where privacy or secrecy might be breached if metadata relating to corporate secrets, personal information, or perhaps even location information were made available as part of the file.[16] In these cases, sensitive information can either be stored separately or stripped from the file when it is shared.

Metadata Schema

Metadata schema "are sets of metadata elements designed for a specific purpose, such as describing a particular type of information resource."[17] Rules govern the use of the elements in the schema. Each schema will have a focus and will be maintained by and developed for certain groups. Some metadata schema are incredibly broad, like the Dublin Core Metadata Initiative (DCMI)'s Dublin Core Metadata Element

Set (DCMES). Other schemas are for specific kinds of digital items or record specific kinds of metadata.

As mentioned, metadata schema are composed of element sets, possible *elements* or information that can be recorded. Each element set has instructions for how elements should be used. Specifications also tell if certain elements are required in a metadata record and provide information about whether elements can be repeated. Metadata schema "may specify content rules for how content must be formulated (for example, how to identify the main title), representation rules for content (for example, capitalization rules), and allowable content values (for example, terms must be used from a specified controlled vocabulary)."[18] Certain elements or tags can be filled in with values from *value vocabularies*. Value vocabularies are controlled vocabularies, and terms from the Getty's Art & Architecture Thesaurus (ATT) or Library of Congress Subject Headings (LCSH) can be used to provide information in a structured way. The values of the elements can also be supplied without the use of value vocabularies, depending on the element. Information like date of publication, date of record creation, and other data-rich fields might not require the use of terms. Element sets, once formalized by their creators, can be submitted to the Open Metadata Registry as a way of explaining their mechanics in an effort to support interoperability.[19] Institutions can combine the uses of elements from a variety of metadata schema and DTDs in a single metadata record. Best practices documentation explaining to metadata creators which schema and DTD/XSD are in use and how they are used help ensure uniformity and, in the long term, interoperability.

Dublin Core Metadata Element Set (DCMES)

The Dublin Core Metadata Initiative (DCMI) maintains the fifteen-element Dublin Core Metadata Element Set (DCMES).[20] DCMES (ISO Standard 15836:2009), often referred to just as Dublin Core, is perhaps the quintessential element set. It is composed of the following fifteen elements used to describe resources: title, creator, subject, description, publisher, contributor, date, type, format, identifier, source, language, relation, coverage, and rights. These elements are designed to be "broad and generic, usable for describing a wide range of resources."[21] "All Dublin Core elements are optional, and all are repeatable."[22] DCMES elements can be divided into three categories: content (description), intellectual property (administrative), and instantiation (technical or structural).[23]

As noted, the Dublin Core elements are very generic. Additional, more-specific terms that can be used in metadata records are also maintained by DCMI in the *terms* namespace. There are over fifty terms in the terms namespace, and they can be used to refine the meaning of the properties identified in the fifteen elements of the DCMES.[24] Dates can be refined to clarify whether the date listed is a date accepted, date copyrighted, or date submitted. Previously, Dublin Core used qualifiers as refinements of the fifteen elements to create Qualified Dublin Core records. Those qualifiers have now been superseded by the terms, which are the only lists of refinements currently maintained by the DCMI.[25]

Metadata Schemas Used by Special Communities

The cultural heritage community is able to use the schema described above, especially Dublin Core, as a way of encoding their metadata records. Other, specialized schemas may be more applicable to certain kinds of unique, image, or non-text-based artifacts preserved by the institution. A few of these schema and standards include Categories for the Description of Works of Art (CDWA), Cataloging Cultural Objects (CCO), VRA Core, Metadata for Images in XML Standard (MIX), PBCore, and Describing Archives: A Content Standard (DACS), which will be discussed briefly in chapter 11. The scientific community's content and uses differ from those of the humanities or social sciences communities, which may be more closely linked to some cultural heritage institutions. Specific schema and standards have grown around the specialized needs of the scientific community and the content it needs to access and make available. A few examples of these schema—Directory Interchange Format (DIF), Content Standard for Digital Geospatial Metadata (CSDGM), and Darwin Core—are also discussed briefly in chapter 10. Although the need for differing metadata standards for different communities is acknowledged, there is a limit to the need for the number of schemas. To avoid situations like the one presented in the comic (see figure 7.2), Archives are strongly encouraged to adopt pre-existing metadata standards instead of creating their own new and unique standards.

Figure 7.2.   How Standards Proliferate (http://xkcd.com/927/)

Schemas for Administrative and Technical Metadata

No matter the community of users and the kind of item, metadata that records information relevant to the administrative function plays an important role in the management of all kinds of digital content. Information about digital provenance and rights is essential across the board. This kind of information can be recorded in metadata records. A few examples of very common and highly compatible administrative and technical metadata schema are provided below, focusing on digital provenance metadata schema and rights metadata schema, as well as a schema that describes technical aspects of digital text.

Digital Provenance Schemas

Provenance, as we saw, is an essential part of the authenticity of digital objects, both analog and digital. The DigiProv (Digital Provenance) Extension Schema is maintained by the Library of Congress for use in digital preservation initiatives and, because of its focus on provenance, is used to document information about "physical preparation of source materials" as well as information about how a file was made.[26] DigiProvMD (Digital Provenance MetaData) is "used to document a digital production process. The *digital production process* is defined as the people, methods, activities, and infrastructure involved in the conservation treatments and the digitization of the archival object."[27] Elements are available to document information about all of these actors in the digital production process. The data dictionary for DigiProv identifies elements and subelements for configuration file (configfile), instance, process, settings, task, and tool.[28]

Efforts from outside of the cultural heritage community also exist to create schema for documenting provenance. The Open Provenance Model (OPM) is an abstract model developed by the OPM community in 2007.[29] The resulting vocabulary, the Open Provenance Model Vocabulary (OPMV), "aims to assist the interoperability between provenance information on the Semantic Web" and can be used with other "vocabularies/ontologies such as Dublin Core and FOAF."[30] W3C's Provenance Working Group has developed the PROV Data Model (PROV-DM) to facilitate the "interoperable interchange of provenance information in heterogeneous environments such as the Web."[31] PROV-XML defines attributes and elements to be used in describing provenance in XML.[32] Although the PROV-DM is, to our knowledge, too new to have seen any implementations in the LAM environment, the potential is very interesting.

Rights Metadata Schemas

Information about intellectual property rights is discussed in the Access Rights Information section as Preservation Description Information (PDI) necessary for digital preservation according to the OAIS model. Two rights schema used currently in cultural heritage institutions are rightsMD and copyrightMD. RightsMD is an

XML–based metadata schema that can be used with METS (see below for more information on METS) and that features fourteen elements.[33] Information encoded in this schema includes licensing and restrictions and names, addresses, e-mails, and telephone numbers of rights holders.[34] CopyrightMD, created and maintained by the California Digital Library (CDL), is also compatible with METS. Only the top-level <copyright> element is required in a valid copyrightMD record; there are seven blocks of sub-elements that can optionally be used.[35]

Technical Metadata for Text (textMD)

The Library of Congress currently maintains textMD, Technical Metadata for Text, a metadata schema "originally created by the New York University Digital Library Team (NYU) . . . [that] had been maintained by NYU through the current version (2.2)."[36] Properties such as encoding information, character information, languages, and fonts, etc., can be recorded using textMD and can be used with PREMIS or METS, digital preservation metadata that will be discussed below.[37]

Preservation Vocabularies

Preservation metadata, metadata supporting preservation of physical and digital items, is being included in Library of Congress linked data initiatives available through its website.[38] For example, preservation vocabularies, such as Preservation Events, Preservation Level Role, and Cryptographic Hash Functions, have been published and are available as linked data.

Application Profiles

No one metadata schema is meant to do everything, and information professionals will find it necessary to mix and match their schemas depending on their collections, their users, and their purpose. Not creating a new schema might mean using two, three, four, or more existing schemas together creatively. Institutions need to document which metadata schemas they have decided to use and how they have decided to use them. This kind of documentation is called a *profile*. NISO defines profiles as "subsets of a scheme that are implemented by a particular interest group. Profiles can constrain the number of elements that will be used, refine element definitions to describe the specific types of resources more accurately, and specify values that an element can take."[39]

Converting Records and Data to a New Format

Instances may occur where metadata in one schema need to be converted to another schema. This might happen if data is harvested and subsequently needs to be ingested in a local system, if a local system is making changes or if one digitized collection is being added to another that uses different schema, vocabularies, etc.

Instead of recoding everything by hand, file-by-file, existing data that is encoded in a particular schema can automatically be crosswalked or mapped to another schema. eXtensible Stylesheet Language Transformations (XSLT) is one way of generating new files from ones that already exist. XSLT is a computer language "used to transform an XML document into another XML document, or another type of document that is recognized by a browser, like HTML and XHTML."[40] An example of using XSLT to create a new document format would be to take an XML document from a digital repository and transform it to HTML for viewing on the Web. An example of converting between schemes includes using XSLT converting a MARC record from a library catalog into a Dublin Core record for use in an institutional repository system. While crosswalks of metadata schemes are extremely useful and often necessary, they do not always come without a price. For example, converting a MARC record to Dublin Core, which is a less complex schema, usually results in a loss of granularity. While there are some software programs such as MARCedit that use XSLT behind the scenes to do transformations, frequently XSLT files require local customization to adequately meet the goals of a project.

Metadata Generation and Creation

As Karen Coyle points out, metadata is not a natural phenomenon; it must be created.[41] There are two primary ways to create metadata: it can be generated automatically by a system or created by a person through a deliberate action. Humans supply information that computers cannot, but humans are expensive to employ and are prone to error. As a result, there is a place for both kinds of metadata creation in digital preservation. Some metadata can be created automatically through the use of certain kinds of software or processes. As we saw above in figure 7.1, some technical elements of an electronic file can be recorded at the time of its creation without the intervention of the creator. Other examples of automatically generated metadata are the indexes created by search engines that have crawled the Web.[42] Additionally, checksums created to document a file's fixity are further examples of automatically generated metadata.

In digital preservation, with scanning or digital-editing software such as Adobe Photoshop or GIMP (Gnu Image Manipulation Program), it is possible to supply information automatically about the date of creation, the collection, the library, and other information that assists with understanding the chain of custody relating to the content object at the time of the scan's creation. This metadata is often embedded within a file. The support of and even the mandated use of embedded metadata in file formats such as the Digital Negative (.DNG) image format for digital photographs is considered a positive asset for a file format by digital preservationists.

Inferring a digital object's topic automatically has been more difficult than generating factual data about a file or checking to see whether its bits have rotted. In recent years, advances in technology have permitted machines to estimate more accurately the *aboutness* of a text-based digital resource based on the words it uses and other clues. Keywords, sometimes shown *in context*, can be automatically generated and used in retrieval. If automatically processing text was a challenge for many years, images were nearly impossible to handle automatically. Search engines like Google and Bing are now able to retrieve images based on creator-supplied text and inherent properties like color, shape of the main item being depicted, and type of image (photograph, drawing, etc.). These search engines seem to take advantage of human-supplied metadata along with aspects inherent in the image.

Although it is by no means automatic, the crowdsourcing of social tags for electronic documents also provides useful metadata that assists with retrieval but does not require the information professional to act on, as an intermediary. Crowdsourcing allows Internet users to supply metadata to electronic documents in a digital library. In cases of social bookmarking sites like CiteULike,[43] this might be for the convenience of the user. Other projects actively seek assistance from Web users in the identification of digitized content. Australia's Trove digital library is an example of a system that seeks user input as a way of providing organization for digitized content including newspaper articles and photos (see figure 7.3 for an image of the Trove homepage). Although crowdsourced metadata will likely remain in the realm of descriptive metadata, it is distinctly possible that crowdsourcing participants will supply meaningful data that will augment the digital preservationist's understanding of the item and will even, potentially, supply additional evidence for authenticity or ownership that will also assist with use in the long term.

When it comes to metadata for digital preservation, information professionals do a fair amount of the heavy lifting. Once they have identified the standards and schemas they will use, information professionals have to input information about the item that cannot be created otherwise, including a good deal of the descriptive and some of the administrative metadata. Automating the creation of metadata can be a good idea; asking creators for information to be included is also a strategy for

Figure 7.3. Trove Homepage (http://trove.nla.gov.au/). Trove shows statistics for user contributions (accessed June 3, 2013)
© 2013 National Library of Australia; used with permission.

saving the time of the professional. No matter how well-intentioned and meticulous volunteers may be, information professionals and their staff will probably want to look over their work and correct errors.[44]

Documentation

Managing electronic files to ensure access over any period of time requires careful and thoughtful planning and documentation of the decisions made. The importance of documenting decisions has become clear over time, and professional practice in general has arguably evolved around shared documentation. If processes and contexts are documented, best practices can be established and shared. David Seaman, associate librarian for Information Management at Dartmouth, has been known to say when making technical decisions about digital libraries that "it is better to be consistent than right."[45] This rationale makes sense given the ability to perform global updates if information is mislabeled or to use *crosswalks* to arrive at a preferable metadata standard for use at a later point in time (see sidebar 7.2 for more information about crosswalks in metadata creation and sharing). It is possible, retroactively, to make global changes only if the action, content, or procedure has been consistently applied and there is documentation. Likewise, decisions are updateable only if the context in which the decision was made is clearly documented. If certain kinds of metadata are being recorded solely for a specific stakeholder, and if that stakeholder withdraws from the project, it should be possible to revisit the decisions that were made in light of the new set of circumstances. When there is clear documentation explaining electronic file management choices, whether the choices were right or wrong at the time, the path forward is made easier for everyone.

Documentation, therefore, is essential in the decision to create and use metadata. The general term *documentation* can take on a very specific meaning in digital preservation. The Digital Preservation Coalition (DPC) defines *documentation* as "information provided by a creator and the repository [that] provides enough information to establish provenance, history, and context and to enable its use by others."[46] This kind of documentation and other documentation about digital objects that need to be stored and made accessible is managed through the creation and use of metadata.

METADATA NECESSARY FOR DIGITAL PRESERVATION

Why think of digital preservation and its metadata as being different from standard approaches to digital library metadata? The answer to this question hinges on the specialized nature of digital preservation and the digital objects being preserved. The Open Archival Information System (OAIS) Reference Model identifies *Content Information* as "a set of information that is the original target of preservation or that includes part or all of that information. It is an Information Object composed of its Content Data Object and its Representation Information."[47] In other words, it is

SIDEBAR 7.2. CROSSWALKS

NISO, in its 2004 *Understanding Metadata* report, defines and describes metadata crosswalks in the following way: "A crosswalk is a mapping of the elements, semantics, and syntax from one metadata scheme to those of another. A crosswalk allows metadata created by one community to be used by another group that employs a different metadata standard."[1] Because a variety of standards are used in different institutions, in different collections, and even in a single metadata record, documenting how standards map to each other is an essential part of enabling searchabilty and sharability of metadata records.

Metadata librarian at Tufts University, Alex May, describes crosswalking from one standard to another to be "one of the most difficult aspects of the job," requiring the information professional to take into consideration not only the semantics of the field in each standard but also the granularity of the standards in relation to each other. May explains that it is easier to go from a more-robust standard to a less-robust one but almost impossible to go the other way. Not unlike changing a .tiff (a "lossless" format) to a .jpeg (a "lossy" format), digital preservationists can create crosswalks to render more specific contents using a less-specific standard. Going from a generic standard to a more-specific one, however, will not provide high-quality results.[2]

In terms of technology, creating crosswalks frequently requires an XSLT (eXtensible Stylesheet Language Transformations). To create the new XML record for the target standard, the XSLT script must be run on the XML record that needs to be converted.

---

1. (Bethesda, Md.: NISO Press, 2004), 11, http://www.niso.org/publications/press/UnderstandingMetadata.pdf.
2. Alex May, Personal communication, October 10, 2012.

the electronic item and its metadata in tandem that must be preserved. First, digital objects in a digital preservation environment are not necessarily stored for the same uses as traditional objects maintained by cultural heritage institutions. Preservation copies may be digital copies of analog or digital resources that provide access while the original document is being kept secure. Surrogates and embedded metadata apply to an electronic document, but that document itself may be a copy of an analog document preserved using standard preservation techniques. Scans of medieval manuscripts are examples of electronic copies kept and maintained for preservation while the physical item is being preserved elsewhere. These scans have the benefit of providing access to users around the world if the institution has the rights and willingness to put them online.

Digital preservation metadata can be used within a digital preservation system to identify file formats automatically that are at risk due to obsolescence (see chapter 8 on file formats for more information about the selection of file formats for preservation). Once these file formats are identified, institutions can continue to provide long-term access to born-digital files through file format migration.

Another aspect to the specialized nature of digital preservation is the emphasis on management over time. Digital objects being preserved are designed to be moved into the future, keeping in mind all of their past and the changes that have been made to the documents so that they will remain viable and useful into the future. Metadata provides documentation of that chain of custody.

Lastly, digital preservation focuses on managing resources over time in a way that supports their authenticity and promotes their trustworthiness for users. "Confidence in the authenticity of digital materials over time is particularly crucial owing to the ease with which alterations can be made."[48] Metadata permit preservation repositories to track the chain of custody, to confirm fixity, and to ensure the integrity of the digital document.

Preservation Description Information (PDI)

Given the importance of authenticity to the management of items undergoing digital preservation, it is not surprising that the OAIS Reference Model emphasizes information necessary for asserting authenticity as part of the digital preservation metadata. Documentation and other necessary information, provided as metadata, can make strides in ensuring the authenticity and correct use of a resource. The OAIS defines *Preservation Description Information (PDI)* as "the information [that] is necessary for adequate preservation of the Content Information and [that] can be categorized as Provenance, Reference, Fixity, Context, and Access Rights Information."[49] These five kinds of information must be incorporated in digital preservation metadata, although they are not necessarily mutually exclusive. "The same bits of metadata may be used in different contexts depending on the need of the user/system/etc. It's not always cut and dry that one piece is only and always descriptive."[50] As we already saw, standard metadata in use in digital libraries can record four broad types of metadata, and those are also interpreted and used differently by different communities. For the sake of this discussion, the metadata required for PDI fits neatly into those already established categories as administrative metadata, with Authenticity as the cornerstone. *Authenticity* is defined in the OAIS as "the degree to which a person (or system) regards an object as what it is purported to be. Authenticity is judged on the basis of evidence."[51] All five kinds of information necessary for PDI can also be seen, in their own way, to contribute to the evidence needed to ensure a digital item's authenticity. Table 7.2 provides some definitions and examples of the categories of information necessary for PDI.

Table 7.2. OAIS Reference Model Information Necessary for Preservation Description Information (PDI) and Examples

Category	Definition	Examples
Provenance Information	The information that documents the history of the Content Information. This information tells the origin or source of the Content Information, any changes that may have taken place since it was originated, and who has had custody of it since it was originated. The Archive is responsible for creating and preserving Provenance Information from the point of Ingest; however, earlier Provenance Information should be provided by the Producer. Provenance Information adds to the evidence to support Authenticity.[1]	digiprovMD (for use with METS)
Reference Information	The information that is used as an identifier for the Content Information. It also includes identifiers that allow outside systems to refer unambiguously to particular Content Information. An example of Reference Information is an ISBN.[2]	EZID (long-term identifiers for texts, data, etc., created as a service of the University of California Curation Center of the California Digital Library)[3]
Fixity Information	The information that documents the mechanisms ensuring the Content Information object has not been altered in an undocumented manner. An example is a checksum for a file.[4]	Cyclical Redundancy Check (CRC) code for a file[5]
Context Information	The information that documents the relationships of the Content Information to its environment. This includes why the Content Information was created and how it relates to other Content Information objects.[6]	sourceMD: The METS source metadata element "provides a wrapper around a generic metadata section [that] should contain information regarding the original source."[7]
Access Rights Information	The information that identifies the access restrictions pertaining to the Content Information, including the legal framework, licensing terms, and access control. It contains the access and distribution conditions stated within the Submission Agreement, related to both preservation (by the OAIS–compliant system) and final usage (by the Consumer). It also includes the specifications for the application of rights enforcement measures.[8]	rightsMD Schema[9] for use with METS

---

[1] Consultative Committee for Space Data Systems (CCSDS), Reference Model for an Open Archival Information System (OAIS): Recommended Practice CCSDS 650.0-M-2; Recommendation for Space Data System Practices, Magenta Book, Recommended Practice, issue 2 (Washington, D.C.: CCSDS Secretariat, June 2012), 1–14.

[2] Ibid.

[3] Consultative Committee for Space Data Systems, Reference Model for an Open Archival Information System (OAIS), 1-11.

[4] OAIS, 2012, 1–11.

[5] Ibid.

[6] Ibid, 1–10.

[7] XML METS Schema, http://www.loc.gov/standards/mets/mets_xsdv12/mets.html.

[8] Consultative Committee for Space Data Systems, Reference Model for an Open Archival Information System (OAIS), 1-8.

[9] Rights Data Dictionary, http://www.loc.gov/rr/mopic/avprot/DD_RMD.html.

Provenance Information

Based on the history of the word and its uses in rare book librarianship, archaeology, art curation/museum studies, and archival studies, *provenance* can be said to refer "to the origins of an information-bearing entity or artifact."[52] Provenance captures information that provides proof of the chain of custody of an item, which in turn ensures its authenticity.[53] Three perspectives have been identified when considering provenance: agent-centered provenance, object-centered provenance, and process-centered provenance. Agent-centered provenance might focus on the creation of the digital file, and object-centered provenance might focus on linkages between two electronic files, especially if there is a whole/part relationship. Process-centered provenance might capture the steps that went into the creation of the digital item.[54]

The concept of provenance has been developed most extensively in archival studies as a means of organizing collections based on the *fonds* (the entirety of a collection of items by a creator) and the *original order* (the order in which the items were originally maintained). In museum studies, provenance focuses on the art object itself as a way of documenting, among other things, its authenticity. In archeology, information about provenance provides the context necessary for a better understanding of an item; consider, for example, a fragment of pottery, whose burial depth might indicate whether it had been used in cooking or, instead, if deeper in the earth, as a chamber pot.[55] In libraries, authority records created using Resource Description and Access (RDA) for publishers, creators, and works may contain information that could help identify the fonds, the original order, or the chain of custody for unique tomes.

Provenance information in the digital environment is necessary for researchers, no matter their discipline. Knowing the origin, the fonds, the chain of custody, and the original order of an item helps understand its context and can ensure its authenticity (i.e., that it has not been modified, either through negligence or for nefarious reasons). Scientists need to understand the authenticity of data and results, including provenance information concerning the lab in which the data was produced and the methodology used. Humanities researchers need to know the sources of archival materials and manuscripts to have the proper context to use them effectively. If researchers are not able to understand provenance and the chain of custody, they are unable to accept documents as authentic or effectively replicate studies.[56]

Reference Information

Depending on the item being digitally preserved, Reference Information may already be stored as administrative metadata in the form of system-generated accession numbers or as descriptive metadata recording the International Standard Book Number (ISBN), the ten- or thirteen-digit unique identifier for books. Digital Object Identifier (DOI) System can be used to register a unique identifier for a dataset, electronic article, or other electronic item.[57] Reference Information allows for Content Information to be unambiguously identified and inventoried and makes that content retrievable both within and outside of the system.

Fixity Information

Fixity is "used to verify whether an object has been altered in an undocumented or unauthorized way."[58] The concept of fixity is particularly challenging in the digital world, as this quote from Abby Smith exemplifies: "As intellectual content migrates from print, film, and tape to electronic formats, it moves from a world characterized by the fixity and relative permanence of the medium into one in which the stability of the text is easily compromised, the permanence of the intellectual content hard to ensure, and the means of accessing the information controlled by the user, not the creator, publisher, or librarian."[59] Fixity information ensures that files have not been altered since they were deposited into the digital preservation system and is associated with the Quality Assurance function. Cyclic redundancy checks (CRCs) or *checksums* can be generated for digital files that will identify errors in files that have been generated during transmission or files that have been corrupted during storage.[60] In addition to checksums, there are other methods and algorithms that can be used to test for fixity for digital preservation purposes. Some of these include message digests and digital signature. Although these "terms are frequently used interchangeably, checksums, message digests, and digital signatures are, in fact, very different tools."[61] A software program typically generates fixity metadata using a checksum (or hash) algorithm such as CRC32, SHA-1, or MD5.[62] The new checksum is compared to previous checksums—identical checksums for a file over time demonstrate that the bits and bytes of the file are unchanged and the file is uncorrupted. See table 7.3 for descriptions of the three algorithms mentioned.

Context Information

Understanding of an item's environment is necessary to understanding, ultimately, its authenticity. Context Information that can be recorded as metadata includes information about an item's provenance and other materials from the same creator. Annotations, as well, can be considered important information about items that can ensure authenticity and facilitate the use of an object.[63] Annotations contribute to the understanding of the Context Information surrounding the digital object and should therefore be preserved if at all possible.

Access Rights Information

Digital preservation is respectful of copyright and rights in general, and maintaining information about access rights is an important aspect of being "responsible stewards of the works in our collections and the digital surrogates of those works that we create."[64] Basing her suggestions on the California Digital Library (CDL)'s copyrightMD schema, Maureen Whalen goes on to recommend that institutions record five core kinds of rights information: (1) name of the creator (including nationality and date of birth and date of death if applicable), (2) year the work was created, (3) copyright status of work (including whether the copyright, assumed to be valid, is

Table 7.3. Common Algorithms Used to Generate Checksums

Fixity (or Hash) Algorithm	Description
CRC32 Algorithm	A Cycle Redundancy Check (CRC) is an error-detection code typically used on digital networks. A CRC is a form of checksum that utilizes a hash function. CRC32, which utilizes a 32-bit polynomial, is the most common type of CRC used. There are 6 different versions of CRC32. The earliest known one was published in 1975. CRC32 is also used in Gzip and Bzip2 file compression and archiving programs.[1]
SHA-1 Algorithm	The Secure Hash Algorithm (SHA) was developed by NIST (National Institute of Standards and Technology) and is specified in the Secure Hash Standard (SHS, FIPS 180). SHA-1 is a revision to this version and was published in 1994. It is also described in the ANSI (American National Standards Institute) X9.30 (part 2) standard. SHA-1 produces a 160-bit (20 byte) message digest. Although slower than MD5, this larger digest size makes it stronger against brute-force attacks.[2]
MD5 Algorithm	MD5 was developed by Professor Ronald L. Rivest in 1994. Its 128 bit (16 byte) message digest makes it a faster implementation than SHA-1.[3]

[1] Wikipedia, s.v. "Cyclic redundancy check," accessed September 29, 2013, http://en.wikipedia.org/wiki/Cyclic_redundancy_check.

[2] Hash Algorithm Directory, *The Secure Hash Algorithm Directory: MD5, SHA-1 and HMAC Resources* (N.p.: Hash Algorithm Directory, 1993–2001), http://faculty.kfupm.edu.sa/ics/darwish/swe421s26/lecturematerial/encryption/The%20Secure%20Hash%20Algorithm%20Directory%20-%20MD5,%20SHA-1,%20HMAC%20and%20other%20Cryptography%20Resources.htm.

[3] Ibid.

owned by the institution that holds the work or by a third party, whether the work is in the public domain, is an orphan work, or the copyright has not been researched), (4) publication status (published, unpublished, unknown, or not researched), and (5) date that rights research was conducted.[65] The OAIS Reference Model recommends that all digital repositories understand all questions of rights and other legal restrictions applicable to a document before that document is acquired.[66] If an item is already part of the collection and is being digitized for preservation, rights metadata will need to be researched, recorded, and continually maintained in an ongoing effort to keep rights information up to date.[67]

Digital Preservation Metadata

Metadata supporting digital preservation is, first and foremost, metadata. It includes three broad categories: (1) the metadata (data and information) described above necessary for storage and retrieval in a digital library environment, (2) the

Events for Intellectual Entity ID: IE1038

Event ID	Type	Description	Date
40956	192	A search indexes has been created for an object	Apr 20, 2011 12:47 AM
626508	186	An IE has been published	Apr 20, 2011 3:04 PM
808228	186	An IE has been published	Apr 21, 2011 10:51 AM
1016292	192	A search indexes has been created for an object	Jan 4, 2012 11:23 AM
1051661	186	An IE has been published	Jan 20, 2012 5:57 PM
1076650	192	A search indexes has been created for an object	Jan 20, 2012 6:38 PM
1101341	192	A search indexes has been created for an object	Jan 20, 2012 6:43 PM
1103996	160	The object IE1038 has been loaded by the Delivery for viewing.	Jan 25, 2012 3:39 PM
1103993	163	The Pre-Processor is processing the object IE1038 and preparing it for viewing	Jan 25, 2012 3:39 PM
1406105	186	An IE has been published	Oct 14, 2012 7:30 PM
1521243	213	User has committed changes for an object	Nov 12, 2012 2:38 PM
1522332	186	An IE has been published	Nov 12, 2012 7:45 PM
1753563	163	The Pre-Processor is processing the object IE1038 and preparing it for viewing	Feb 26, 2013 1:06 PM
1753566	160	The object IE1038 has been loaded by the Delivery for viewing.	Feb 26, 2013 1:06 PM
1759043	163	The Pre-Processor is processing the object IE1038 and preparing it for viewing	Mar 5, 2013 10:17 AM
1759046	160	The object IE1038 has been loaded by the Delivery for viewing.	Mar 5, 2013 10:17 AM
1759241	160	The object IE1038 has been loaded by the Delivery for viewing.	Mar 5, 2013 10:59 AM
1759238	163	The Pre-Processor is processing the object IE1038 and preparing it for viewing	Mar 5, 2013 10:59 AM

Figure 7.4.   Events for an Information Package in a Digital Preservation System
Used with permission.

Preservation Description Information (PDI) described above that was identified for OAIS–compliant systems to helps ensure authenticity, and (3) metadata (usually PREMIS and METS) about digital objects and their current digital environment that permits their preservation and access through the digital preservation system over the long term. PREMIS and METS will be discussed in the final section of this chapter, after additional information about metadata standards and schema are discussed. All of these kinds of metadata are housed in the digital preservation system along with the digital object. See figure 7.4 for system-related events for a digital object in a preservation repository, the Rosetta software from Ex Libris.

METADATA SPECIFIC TO DIGITAL PRESERVATION

All metadata created for access and management outside of the purview of digital preservation is and should be considered necessary for preservation. PDI requires the kinds of information that demonstrate authenticity be recorded as metadata, but what good is authenticity if a file cannot be retrieved because it is lacking any kind of descriptive metadata? As previously noted, descriptive and administrative metadata permit discovery and retrieval in a system and can allow for subsequent use,[68] but it is still necessary to consider them part of the information essential to managing Content Information to ensure access over the long term. Yale University Library is one entity that has taken this stance, affirming in their digital preservation policy that "preservation metadata are required to *describe*, manage, and preserve digital resources over time."[69] They have chosen to add the word *describe* to the definition of *preservation metadata* provided by the Digital Preservation Coalition (DPC), upon which their glossary definition was based.

Metadata used for description and access as outlined above can be useful to the digital preservation process even if it was not created with digital preservation in mind. Additional metadata is needed, however, to ensure long-term management of and access to electronic files. The PREMIS Data Model takes into account the content that is recorded in standard metadata and provides for the creation of additional metadata specific to the needs of digital preservation. The METS model also allows for metadata specific to digital preservation to be created and recorded. First we will look at PREMIS; METS will be discussed afterward.

PREMIS Model

PREMIS (PREservation Metadata: Implementation Strategies) was an international working group sponsored by OCLC and RLG starting in 2003.[70] The PREMIS working group released the first *PREMIS Data Dictionary* in 2005, and the group was retired and the ongoing maintenance of the PREMIS Data Dictionary transferred to the Library of Congress–sponsored PREMIS Metadata Maintenance Activity.[71] The current version of the *PREMIS Data Dictionary*, including the PREMIS Data Model (version 2.2 from 2012), is available online as a PDF from the Library of Congress.[72] A metadata dictionary like the *PREMIS Data Dictionary* describes

1. common metadata meanings (semantics)
2. common grammar and rules for expressing data (syntax)
3. commonly defined metadata dictionary element properties (attributes).[73]

An excellent explanation of PREMIS preservation metadata by Priscilla Caplan is available as a PDF on the Library of Congress website for those who would like a primer before delving into the full document.[74] The *PREMIS Data Dictionary*, although not a formal standard controlled by a recognized standards agency, has become "a de facto international standard for preservation metadata, . . . which has been implemented in digital preservation repositories worldwide and incorporated into a variety of digital preservation systems and tools."[75]

In the PREMIS data model, entities are defined as they appear in table 7.4. The entities and the semantic units described in the *PREMIS Data Dictionary* are not one and the same.[76] "Each semantic unit defined in the data dictionary is mapped to one of the entities in the data model. In this sense, a semantic unit may be viewed as a property of an entity. For example, the semantic unit *size* is a property of an Object entity. Semantic units have values: for a particular Object the value of *size* might be '843200004.'"[77] When possible, these semantic units can be automatically assigned, without requiring human intervention or analysis.

The PREMIS data model also takes into account that many preservation repositories may maintain multiple versions, or representations, of the same Intellectual Entity. For example, a preservation repository could have multiple representations

Table 7.4. PREMIS Data Model Entities (from *PREMIS Data Dictionary*, 2008, p. 6)

Entities	Definitions	Example
Intellectual Entity	A set of content that can logically be described as a single unit. It may have one or more digital representations.	Examples include a particular book, journal article, photograph, or dataset. It can include other Intellectual Entities; for example, a journal can include an article, and an article can include an image or a chart.
Object (or Digital Object) Entity	A discrete unit of information in digital form that consists of one or more sequences of bits stored in the repository. Object types can be a file, representation, file stream, or a bit stream.[1] It is important to "Note that the PREMIS definition of an Object entity differs from the definition of digital object often used in the digital library community, which holds a digital object to be a combination of identifier, metadata, and data. This is not intended to be a conflict."[2] The Object entity in the PREMIS model "is an abstraction defined only to cluster attributes (semantic units) and clarify relationships."[3]	Examples include a TIFF image and a PDF file or an Ogg Vorbis audio bit stream.
Event Entity	Aggregates information about actions that affect at least one object or agent in the repository.	"Documentation of actions that modify (that is, create a new version of) a digital object is critical to maintaining digital provenance, a key element of authenticity. Actions that create new relationships or alter existing relationships are important in explaining those relationships. Even actions that alter nothing, such as validity and integrity checks on objects, can be important to record for management purposes. For billing or reporting purposes some repositories may track actions such as requests for dissemination or reports."[4]

Entities	Definitions	Example
Agent Entity	Someone or something that performs a task in a digital preservation system. An Agent may be a person, organization, or software associated with Events in the life of an Object or with Rights attached to an Object.	"Agents influence Objects only indirectly through Events."[5] An example of software as an Agent Entity is a program that calculates Checksum values.
Rights Entity	An assertion of one or more rights or permissions pertaining to an Object and/ or Agent.	This includes "metadata related to intellectual property rights and permissions."[6] Examples can be copyright statement and licensing information.

Table based on information contained in: PREMIS Editorial Committee. *PREMIS Data Dictionary for Preservation Metadata*, Version 2.2. Washington, D.C.: Library of Congress, 2012. http://www.loc.gov/standards/premis/v2/premis-2-2.pdf.

[1] Priscilla Caplan and Rebecca Gunther, "Practical Preservation: The PREMIS Experience," *Library Trends* 54, no. 1 (2005): 117.

[2] PREMIS Editorial Committee. *PREMIS Data Dictionary for Preservation Metadata*, Version 2.2. Washington, D.C.: Library of Congress, 2012, 264, http://www.loc.gov/standards/premis/v2/premis-2-2.pdf.

[3] Ibid, 264.

[4] Ibid, 10.

[5] Ibid, 11.

[6] Ibid, 11.

of a photograph in different formats. One might be a high resolution TIFF file, a more Web-friendly JPEG file that will load more quickly in a Web browser and may also include a watermark, and a third, a thumbnail JPEG of the image that is used in a discovery system. PREMIS deliberately chose the word *representation* for these different versions to avoid confusion with terminology used in *The Functional Requirements for Bibliographic Records* (FRBR).[78]

Preservation metadata can span various categories of metadata including administrative, technical, and structural. This includes metadata that, (1) in the context of preservation, supports the viability, understandability, authenticity, and identity of digital object, (2) depicts information that most repositories will need to know in order to preserve digital objects in the long-term, and (3) places an emphasis on "'implementable metadata': rigorously defined, supported by guidelines for creation, management, and use, and oriented toward automated workflows."[79] PREMIS does this in a technology neutral manner, without making assumptions about specific preservation technologies or strategies. Another way of saying this is that the *PREMIS Data Dictionary* is meant to be implementation independent,[80] focusing on the

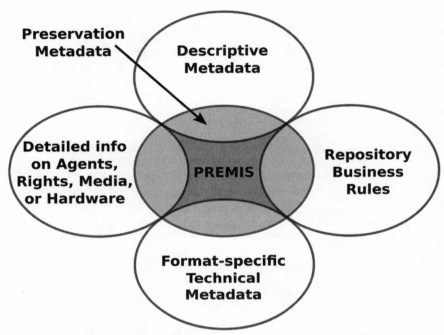

Figure 7.5. Caplan's Figure of PREMIS as a Subset of Preservation Metadata (Caplan, 2009, *Understanding PREMIS*)

metadata that is needed for preservation but that is not included in other schema. In figure 7.5 Caplan demonstrates how PREMIS is only the subsection of preservation metadata not covered by other schema. Although the *PREMIS Data Dictionary* is implementation neutral, Metadata Encoding and Transmission Standard (METS) is the most widely used framework for packaging PREMIS metadata.[81]

Metadata Encoding and Transmission Standard (METS)

Metadata Encoding and Transmission Standard (METS) is a metadata schema for complex digital objects stored in a digital library; it "is an XML schema designed for the purpose of creating XML documents that express the hierarchical structure of digital library objects, the names and locations of the files that comprise those objects, and the associated metadata."[82] The METS schema can be considered structural metadata because it keeps together and orders the different parts of an intellectual entity. Because it lends structure, we tend to hear about the METS wrapper, metadata that envelops, keeps together, and makes sense of the various files that belong with a given digital object. Seven components comprise the METS wrapper: "the METS header, descriptive metadata, administrative metadata, the file section, the structural map, structural links, and behavior metadata."[83] In providing a way to encapsulate these seven components, which in digital preservation will include PREMIS, METS allows all of the essential information to remain with the content. It also allows digital objects to be harvested and shared without losing that essential metadata. In 2007, Thomas Habing saw METS as the solution to the problem of too many kinds of repositories in use, being harvested in different ways, with integration solutions both "local and ad-hoc," and centralized preservation policy being difficult to implement.[84]

Because METS is structural metadata, it is compatible with and designed to be used with other descriptive, technical, and preservation metadata standards. Judith Pearce, et al. compare METS to LEGO™ blocks for building—much can be added together in terms of schemas, but standardization is difficult.[85] For example, it is common to use PREMIS with METS in providing digital preservation metadata in a preservation repository. Technical metadata used in METS makes use of PREMIS object entities, and digital provenance metadata in METS uses PREMIS events and agents.[86] For text-based documents, combining PREMIS, METS, and Metadata Object Description Schema (MODS) can be a good and standard solution adopted by information professionals. For visual resources, MIX (Metadata for Images in XML Schema) might be used for technical metadata, DC for description, with METS as the structural metadata wrapper.[87] The Visual Resources Association (VRA)'s VRA Core 4.0 schema has been endorsed for use with METS and "will work well as an extension schema for any METS objects that contain images of cultural heritage resources."[88]

METS Profiles

Application profiles created by an institution can center on their use of METS as structural metadata. The METS profile has the primary focus of digital preservation, repository interoperability, and Web captures. With the METS profile, the "focus [is] on preservation, not access."[89] Morgan Cundiff from the Library of Congress specifies that an application profile "describes the set of metadata elements, policies, guidelines, and vocabularies defined for a particular domain, implementation, or object type."[90] The METS website hosts an index of featured users with links to their profiles.[91] Many of these profiles hyperlink to a form describing, in human-readable language, the choices about schema, guidelines, and vocabularies. All of the featured profiles include documentation in the form of XML files that, while less easily digestible at a glance, are still human-readable.

CONCLUSION

Metadata for digital preservation supports the discovery and management of files in a digital library system as an aspect of the Technology portion of the Digital Preservation Triad. Access and usability of content are promoted through the careful creation and management of preservation metadata. When systems can ensure the authenticity of the content of their preservation repositories, users win. Usable and trustworthy content that has been carefully managed and for which the chain of custody has been documented is content that can make a difference in the future. Not unlike other kinds of metadata, preservation metadata promotes interoperability between systems through the use of standards. By standardizing the use and uses of metadata, institutions are able to streamline their operations, ensure that best practices are known and being used, and share their contents with others, if that is indeed part of their institutional mission.

Preservation systems still need to use metadata structures that will permit users to find, identify, select, and obtain documents, but for preservation to be effective these systems need to go beyond that. By using schema designed for preservation like PREMIS and METS, by building repositories that are interoperable and harvestable, and by streamlining workflows for users, successful management of the metadata question is an essential part of managing a digital preservation project in any kind of information agency that can and should be answered.

This chapter described what metadata is, demonstrated why it is important, and gave examples of how it is used in digital libraries in general and in digital preservation in particular. Without metadata in our digital preservation systems, there is no context and no authenticity. Without metadata, there is also limited retrieval and little way to group related items. Digital preservation requires metadata, pure and simple. In the next chapter, we will look at the requirements for work with another Technology: files.

NOTES

1. Consultative Committee for Space Data Systems (CCSDS), *Reference Model for an Open Archival Information System (OAIS): Recommended Practice CCSDS 650.0-M-2; Recommendation for Space Data System Practices*, Magenta Book, Recommended Practice, issue 2 (Washington, D.C.: CCSDS Secretariat, June 2012), 1-13, http://public.ccsds.org/publications/archive/650x0m2.pdf.

2. Society of American Archivists, *A Glossary of Archival and Records Terminology*, s.v. "Data," accessed September 29, 2013, http://www2.archivists.org/glossary/terms/d/data.

3. D. Grant Campbell, "Metadata, Metaphor, and Metonymy," in *Metadata: A Cataloger's Primer*, edited by Richard P. Smiraglia, 59 (New York: Routledge, 2005).

4. Marcia Lei Zeng and Jian Qin, *Metadata* (New York: Neal-Schuman, 2008), 322.

5. Laurent Romary, "Data Management in the Humanities," *ERCIM News* 89 (April 2012): 14, http://ercim-news.ercim.eu/images/stories/EN89/EN89-web.pdf.

6. Charles A. Cutter, *Rules for a Dictionary Catalog*, 4th ed., rewritten (Washington, D.C.: Government Printing Office, 1904), http://digital.library.unt.edu/ark:/67531/metadc1048/.

7. International Federation of Library Associations and Institutions' (IFLA) Study Group on the Functional Requirements for Bibliographic Records, "Functional Requirements for Bibliographic Records: Final Report," 8, September 1997, last modified February 2009, http://www.ifla.org/files/cataloguing/frbr/frbr_2008.pdf.

8. Zeng and Qin, *Metadata*, 319.

9. Ibid.

10. National Information Standards Organization (NISO), *Understanding Metadata* (Bethesda, Md.: NISO Press, 2004), http://www.niso.org/publications/press/Understanding Metadata.pdf.

11. Ibid, 1.

12. W3Schools.com, "XML Validation," accessed September 29, 2013, http://www .w3schools.com/xml/xml_dtd.asp.

13. The argument as to whether, for example, DTD, XSD, or RELAX NG is best is a long-standing argument among technologists that may never be solved, and an in-depth discussion is beyond the scope of this chapter and this endnote. However, if you are interested in a brief overview of the pros and cons of each, you may want to read the XML schema language comparison entry on Wikipedia at http://en.wikipedia.org/wiki/XML_schema_lan guage_comparison.

14. W3C, "Extensible Markup Language (XML)," last modified June 4, 2013, http://www .w3.org/XML/.

15. Chris Dietrich, "Forbearing the Digital Dark Ages: Capturing Metadata for Digital Objects" (Webinar PowerPoint presentation for the Association of Southeastern Research Libraries, April 9, 2013), http://www.aserl.org/wp-content/uploads/2013/04/Intro_ DP_2013-2_DigitalObjectMetadata.pdf.

16. Dietrich, "Forbearing the Digital Dark Ages."

17. NISO, *Understanding Metadata*.

18. Ibid, 2.

19. http://metadataregistry.org/.

20. For information on additional metadata schemas, extensions, tools, and use cases for general research data metadata, visit the General Research Data webpage of the Digital Curation Centre (DCC) at http://www.dcc.ac.uk/resources/subject-areas/general-research-data.

21. Dublin Core Metadata Initiative, "Dublin Core Metadata Element Set, Version 1.1," accessed September 29, 2013, http://dublincore.org/documents/dces/.

22. NISO, Understanding Metadata, 3.

23. Diane Hillmann, "Using Dublin Core: The Elements," Dublin Core Metadata Initiative, August 26, 2003, http://dublincore.org/documents/2003/08/26/usageguide/elements .shtml.

24. Dublin Core Metadata Initiative, "Dublin Core Metadata Element Set."

25. Dublin Core Metadata Initiative, "Dublin Core Qualifiers (SUPERSEDED, SEE DCMI Metadata Terms)," July 11, 2000, http://dublincore.org/documents/2000/07/11/ dcmes-qualifiers/.

26. Library of Congress (LOC), "Explanation: DigiProv (Digital Provenance) Extension Schema," AV Prototype Project Working Documents, February 2003, last modified August 31, 2010, http://www.loc.gov/rr/mopic/avprot/digiprov_expl.html.

27. Library of Congress (LOC), "DIGIPROVMD: Digital Production and Provenance Metadata Extension Schema," last modified August 23, 2002, http://lcweb2.loc.gov/mets/ Schemas/PMD.xsd.

28. Library of Congress (LOC), "DigiProv Data Dictionary: Audio-Visual Prototyping Project," last modified August 31, 2010, http://www.loc.gov/rr/mopic/avprot/DD_PMD.html.

29. Open Provenance Model, "The OPM Provenance Model (OPM)," "Background," accessed June 7, 2013, http://openprovenance.org/.

30. Open-biomed, "Open Provenance Model Vocabulary Specification," "Abstract," October 6, 2010, last modified June 4, 2012, http://open-biomed.sourceforge.net/opmv/ns.html.

31. W3C, "PROV-Overview," "Abstract," April 30, 2013, accessed June 7, 2013, http://www.w3.org/TR/2013/NOTE-prov-overview-20130430/.

32. W3Schools.com, "PROV-XML: The PROV XML Schema," "Section 2.3: Elements vs. Attributes," April 30, 2013, accessed June 7, 2013, http://www.w3.org/TR/prov-xml/.

33. Library of Congress (LOC), "Rights Data Dictionary," last modified August 31, 2010, http://www.loc.gov/rr/mopic/avprot/DD_RMD.html.

34. Ibid.

35. California Digital Library (CDL), *CopyrightMD User Guidelines, Version 0.91* (Oakland, Calif.: CDL, 2009), http://www.cdlib.org/groups/rmg/docs/copyrightMD_user_guidelines.pdf.

36. Library of Congress (LOC), "TextMD: Technical Metadata for Text," "News," accessed May 13, 2013, http://www.loc.gov/standards/textMD/.

37. Ibid, "About textMD."

38. http://id.loc.gov/.

39. NISO, *Understanding Metadata*, 9.

40. W3Schools.com, "XSLT Introduction," accessed September 29, 2013, http://www.w3schools.com/xsl/xsl_intro.asp.

41. Karen Coyle, "Understanding the Semantic Web: Bibliographic Data and Metadata," *Library Technology Reports* 46, no. 1 (2010): 8.

42. Susan Lazinger, *Digital Preservation and Metadata: History, Theory, Practice* (Englewood, Colo.: Libraries Unlimited, 2001).

43. http://www.citeulike.org/.

44. Rachel Jaffe, personal communication, September 4, 2012.

45. David Seaman, "XML in Action: TEI" (course presented at Rare Book School, Charlottesville, Va., June 2012).

46. Digital Preservation Coalition, "Introduction: Definitions and Concepts," accessed August 2, 2013, http://www.dpconline.org/advice/preservationhandbook/introduction/definitions-and-concepts.

47. Consultative Committee for Space Data Systems, *Reference Model for an Open Archival Information System (OAIS)*, 1–10.

48. Digital Preservation Coalition, *Preservation Management of Digital Materials: The Handbook*, in collaboration with the National Library of Australia and the PADI (Preserving Access to Digital Information) Gateway (York, Eng.: Digital Preservation Coalition, 2008), 24, http://www.dpconline.org/component/docman/doc_download/299-digital preservation-handbook.

49. Consultative Committee for Space Data Systems, *Reference Model for an Open Archival Information System (OAIS)*, 1–14.

50. Alex May, personal communication, October 2012.

51. Consultative Committee for Space Data Systems, *Reference Model for an Open Archival Information System (OAIS)*, 1–9.

52. Shelley Sweeney, "The Ambiguous Origins of the Archival Principle of 'Provenance,'" *Libraries & the Cultural Record* 43, no. 2 (2008): 193, doi:10.1353/lac.0.0017.

53. Ibid.

54. W3C, "PROV Model Primer," last modified April 30, 2013, http://www.w3.org/TR/2013/NOTE-prov-primer-20130430/.

55. Laura Millar, "The Death of the Fonds and the Resurrection of Provenance: Archival Context in Space and Time," *Archivaria* 53, no. 6 (2002): 1–15.

56. Patsy Baudoin, "The Principle of Digital Preservation," *The Serials Librarian* 55, no. 4. (2008): 556–59, doi 10.1080/03615260802291212.

57. http://www.doi.org. See the International DOI Foundation (IDF) Web site at http://www.doi.org for additional information about the Digital Object Identifier system.

58. PREMIS Editorial Committee, *PREMIS Data Dictionary for Preservation Metadata, Version 2.2* (Washington, D.C.: Library of Congress, 2012), 47, http://www.loc.gov/standards/premis/v2/premis-2-2.pdf.

59. Abby Smith, "Preface," in Enduring Paradigm, *New Opportunities: The Value of the Archival Perspective in the Digital Environment*, Anne J. Gilliland-Swetland, iv (Washington, D.C.: Council on Library and Information Resources, 2000), http://www.clir.org/pubs/reports/pub89/pub89.pdf.

60. Consultative Committee for Space Data Systems, *Reference Model for an Open Archival Information System (OAIS)*, 4–6.

61. Audrey Novak, "Fixity Checks: Checksums, Message Digests, and Digital Signatures" (committee report, Yale University Digital Preservation Committee, November 2006).

62. Novak's "Fixity Checks" goes into further details about the differences between checksums, message digests, and digital signatures. The report also provides some practical examples of how fixity checks have been used in digital preservation and discusses some issues to consider regarding fixity checks.

63. Anne J. Gilliland-Swetland, *Enduring Paradigm, New Opportunities: The Value of the Archival Perspective in the Digital Environment* (Washington, D.C.: Council on Library and Information Resources, February 2000), http://www.clir.org/pubs/reports/pub89/pub89.pdf.

64. Maureen Whalen, "Rights Metadata Made Simple," in *Introduction to Metadata*, version 3.0, edited by Murtha Baca, (Los Angeles: J. Paul Getty Trust/Gregory M. Britton, 2008), http://www.getty.edu/research/publications/electronic_publications/intrometadata/rights.pdf.

65. Ibid., 2-3 of 8.

66. Consultative Committee for Space Data Systems, *Reference Model for an Open Archival Information System (OAIS)*, 3-3.

67. Whalen, "Rights Metadata Made Simple," 8 of 8.

68. Digital Preservation Coalition, *The Preservation Management*, 26.

69. Yale University Library, "Digital Preservation Policy," November 2005, last modified February 2007, http://www.library.yale.edu/iac/DPC/final1.html. Emphasis added.

70. PREMIS Editorial Committee, *PREMIS Data Dictionary*, 1.

71. Ibid, 1.

72. *The PREMIS Data Dictionary for Preservation Metadata*, related documentation, and other materials can be downloaded at http://www.loc.gov/standards/premis/.

73. PBCore.org, "What Is a Metadata Dictionary?" accessed September 29, 2013. http://pbcore.org/PBCore/PBCorePrimer.html#02.

74. Priscilla Caplan, *Understanding PREMIS* (Washington, D.C.: Library of Congress, 2009), http://www.loc.gov/standards/premis/understanding-premis.pdf.

75. Brian Lavoie and Richard Gartner, *Preservation Metadata: Digital Preservation Coalition Technology Watch Report 13-03*, 2nd ed. (Great Britain: Digital Preservation Coalition in association with Charles Beagrie, Ltd., 2013), http://dx.doi.org/10.7207/twr13-03.

76. Caplan, *Understanding PREMIS*.

77. PREMIS Editorial Committee, *PREMIS Data Dictionary*, 6.

78. Ibid, 8.

79. Ibid, 1.

80. Ibid, 4.

81. Lavoie and Gartner, *Preservation Metadata*, 17.

82. Rebecca Guenther and Jackie Radebaugh, "What Is METS? (Schema)" (PowerPoint presented at the Standards Showcase: MODS, METS, MARCXML, the annual conference of the American Library Association, New Orleans, June 23–27, 2006), http://www.loc.gov/standards/mods/mods-mets-ala/pages/Slide21-th_gif.html; NISO, Understanding Metadata.

83. Arlene G. Taylor and Daniel N. Joudrey, *The Organization of Information* (Westport, Conn.: Libraries Unlimited, 2009), 101–2.

84. Thomas Habing, "METS, MODS and PREMIS, Oh My!" slide 5 (PowerPoint presented at the annual conference of the American Library Association, Washington, D.C., June 21–27, 2007), http://www.loc.gov/standards/mods/presentations/habing-ala07/pages/Slide05_JPG.htm.

85. Judith Pearce, David Pearson, Megan Williams, and Scott Yeadon, "The Australian METS Profile: A Journey about Metadata," *D-Lib Magazine* 14, no. 3–4 (March/April 2008), http://www.dlib.org/dlib/march08/pearce/03pearce.html.

86. Habing, "METS," slide 18, http://www.loc.gov/standards/mods/presentations/habing ala07/images/Slide18_JPG.jpg.

87. See Mingyu Chen and Michele Reilly, "Implementing METS, MIX, and DC for Sustaining Digital Preservation at the University of Houston Libraries," *Journal of Library Metadata* 11 (2011): 83–99.

88. "METS Editorial Board Endorses VRA Core 4.0 Schema: November 7, 2007." *VRA Core News*, November 8, 2012, accessed September 29, 2013, http://vracorenews.blogspot.com/2012/11/mets-editorial-board-endorses-vra-core.html.

89. Habing, "METS," slide 10, http://www.loc.gov/standards/mods/presentations/habing ala07/pages/Slide10_JPG.htm.

90. Morgan Cundiff, "METS Application Profiles" (PowerPoint presented at the METS Opening Day Program, Washington, D.C.: Library of Congress, October 27–28, 2003), www.loc.gov/standards/mets/presentations/cundiff.ppt.

91. http://www.loc.gov/standards/mets/mets-registered-profiles.html.

8

File Formats and Software for Digital Preservation

As noted, Technology can be one of the most daunting aspects of digital preservation. Technology changes at an amazingly fast rate, and it is essential to make good, informed, and well-documented decisions about the technology utilized for digital preservation. This includes file format related decisions, which are, in fact, one of the most basic, yet important aspects of digital preservation.

In order to make the best choices possible for long-term digital preservation, it is important to know exactly what type of file is being preserved. It is also important to check that the file is properly formatted and is actually in the format that it is believed to be in. This latter point may seem superfluous, but in the past it was not that uncommon for a file to have a Microsoft Word .doc extension when, in reality, the document was in Rich Text Format (.rtf extension). Microsoft Word was forgiving enough; the end user would not have noticed the difference. However, such an extension mix-up could possibly cause problems down the road for long-term preservation. Once a file's format has been identified, it is still important to decide whether the format is acceptable for digital preservation. Fortunately for digital preservationists, there are many tools including file format registries and software programs available for identifying file formats and determining the appropriate preservation strategies to preserve the digital objects in their collection.

We begin this chapter by describing file formats and evaluating their preservation qualities for a variety of different types of digital objects. Next, we focus on issues related to file formats in use. Finally, we describe software to be used by the information professional to help identify file formats.

FILE FORMATS

It is difficult to describe exactly what a file format is. It is possible to think of it as "a standard way that information is encoded for storage in a computer file. A file format specifies how bits are used to encode information in a digital storage medium."[1] When the bits are disturbed, the content is no longer intact (figure 8.1 shows an image file that has been corrupted and is no longer eye-readable). Although the above definition is accurate, it fails to tell the entire story. A file format can include bit stream encodings, wrappers and bundling formats, and classes of related formats. A very broad definition that is useful for digital preservationists, therefore, is that file formats are "packages of information that can be stored as data files or sent via network as data streams (a.k.a. bit streams, byte streams)."[2] The Global Digital Format Registry (GDFR) identifies two separate classes of formats: content stream formats and physical media formats. A *content stream format* is "independent of the

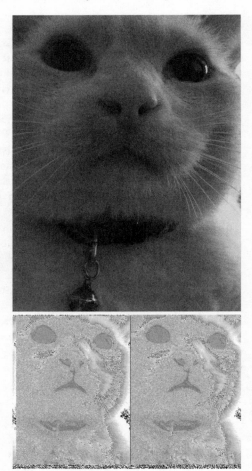

Figure 8.1. This figure contains two versions of the same photo of a cat. The top photo is the original. The bottom photo is one that has been corrupted. The corrupt photo is half the height of the original, is repeated twice, and does not have the same level of detail and clarity.

physical medium underlying its manifestation" and "is not required to have homo-geneous composition but can be defined as an aggregation of other content streams. A *physical media format* is a fixed encoding of a content stream in a tangible form on a physical storage structure."[3] Examples of content stream formats are JPEG (Joint Photographic Experts Group) and TIFF (Tagged Image File Format). One physi-cal media format is ISO 966:1988, also known as the Compact Disc File System (CDFS) that is used on CD-ROMs. In most situations, those involved with digital preservation will focus on content stream formats, since physical media formats tend to be transformed to content stream formats for digital preservation.

It is important to understand that files usually have multiple parts. For example, a PDF (Portable Document Format) consists of a file format, a wrapper, and a bun-dling format. There are also versions and subtypes (such as PDF/A, PDF/X), and a PDF may have other formats embedded, such as TIFF or JPEG images.[4] When evaluating file formats for preservation, it is important to consider these factors. If a PDF has a digital object embedded in a format that becomes obsolete, that portion of the PDF may no longer be fully preserved. This is one reason why some people prefer PDF/A, a specialized version of PDF designed for long-term digital preserva-tion. We discuss PDF, PDF/A, and other file formats for text-based and other media types in the sections that follow.

File Formats for Digital Preservation

Different organizations will have different digital preservation needs, and thus not all Archives will rely on the same file formats. However, there are some common for-mats used more often than others for digital preservation. The reason some formats are preferred is that digital preservationists are more likely to trust file formats that have a high degree of openness and ubiquity. *Openness* means that the file format's technical details are freely available to anyone and that the format does not have any patent, copyright, or other legal issues that may restrict its use. *Ubiquity* refers to how widely the format is used, both in general and by others involved with digital preservation. Often the number of software tools that can utilize the file format is included in the evaluation of ubiquity as well. These and other factors that are often taken into account when determining if a format is suitable for long-term preserva-tion will be discussed later in greater detail.

Textual and Other Document Files

The preferred text document format for most digital preservation repositories is either PDF or PDF/A. PDF, or the Adobe Portable Document Format, is a widely utilized, open international standard maintained by the International Organization for Standardization (ISO). It is designed for electronic document exchange. Reasons why PDF is extremely popular include its high readability and that it is an open standard, is trusted, works on multiple platforms, has rich file integrity, is searchable, is accessible, and has been broadly adopted.[5] Many of these reasons also make it useful in digital preservation. Although the standard PDF format is a good format for digital preservation, especially when fonts are embedded, many digital preservationists prefer the PDF/A format, which is based on PDF. PDF/A is specifically designed for digital archiving, as it removes some of the features of PDF that are less desirable for digital preservation, including the ability to link to fonts instead of embedding them within the document.

Other text formats that are commonly accepted for long-term preservation include Rich Text Format (RTF), eXtensible Markup Language (XML), and Hypertext Markup Language (HTML). For Spreadsheets, many archives prefer files that are in Comma-Separated Values (CSV) or OpenDocument Spreadsheets (ODS) formats rather than Excel (.xls, .xlsx extensions) or other proprietary and vendor-specific formats.

Still Images

Many Archives consider uncompressed TIFF the best format for digital preservation. Some Archives also use JPEG 2000. JPEG 2000 is somewhat controversial among digital preservationists, because some of them consider it a risk due to possible "submarine" patent issues.[6] Other digital preservationists believe that JPEG 2000 is not ubiquitous enough and are concerned that there are not a sufficient number of open source software products that can utilize the format. Additionally, Johan van der Knijff of the National Library of the Netherlands has written that there are a number of possible risks with the format related to the handling of ICC profiles and grid resolution, two technical issues that go beyond the scope of this book but that will be of interest to readers considering JPEG 2000.[7] Despite these concerns, JPEG 2000 is used by a number of organizations because the sizes of files are significantly smaller than equivalent TIFF files. Therefore some Archives, including the National Archives in Britain, the Library of Congress in the United States, and the National Library of Norway, have decided that JPEG 2000 is an acceptable file format. Each institution will have to decide for itself whether the risks associated with JPEG 2000 are acceptable for its digital preservation repository.

Digital Negative (DNG) is a file format for digital photographs written by Adobe. It is an open, lossless, raw image file format based on the Tagged Image File Format/ Electronic Photograph (TIFF/EP) format. One significant aspect of DNG for digital preservation is that the format mandates the significant use of metadata. Because the format is a "publicly available archival format for the raw files generated by digital cameras"[1] and includes a significant amount of metadata, some digital preservationists (and digital photographers) use DNG for preservation purposes to better ensure that digital photographs will be useable in the future. Other common image file formats used for long-term digital preservation include Portable Network Graphics (PNG) and Scalable Vector Graphic (SVG) files.

Audio and Video Files

Audio and video files can pose some unique challenges to digital preservationists because they are made up of multiple components, each with its own impact on long-term preservation. This can be true of other types of file formats as well—for example, a PDF document file may have an embedded image, but in the case of audio or video it can be more pronounced. Audio and video computer files consist "of a container holding source data [that] has been processed through a codec."[8] A *codec* is used to compress and decompress audio or video files and typically has two components: an encoder and decoder. Since some audio and video file formats such as Audio Video Interleaved (AVI) can contain source data that may be compressed using many different codecs, it is important for digital preservation purposes to know not only which format the file is in but also which codec is needed to decompress the file. Video files also have the additional complexity of having separate audio and video components that could rely on different codecs. Video may also have textual components as well that support such features as closed captioning.

Because of the complexity, "the rapidly evolving nature of digital audio and video formats, and the lack of any open, national, or international consensus standards for the creation and preservation of digital audio and video" formats, the National Archives and Records Administration (NARA) in the United States has decided not to issue "formal digital audio and digital video file format transfer guidance."[9] In all cases, digital preservationists will have to evaluate file formats carefully based on their own needs, the needs of their Consumers, and the constraints of their digital preservation systems, staffing, and content.

As an aid, NARA has identified some digital audio files that they do not consider of sufficient quality for long-term retention or preservation. These include files that are created for Internet streaming, such as RealAudio and Windows Media files. These types of files typically are designed with a small file size at the expense of quality. Likewise, NARA does not recommend most MPEG audio files such as MPEG-2 Audio Layer III files (more commonly known as MP3 files), because they use lossy compression to make smaller files, which also sacrifices quality.[10] *Lossy compression* is a data compression method that only allows for an approximation of the original data to be reconstructed; it is often used for images, audio, and video files as it can result in smaller file sizes than lossless compression.

Broadcast Wave Format (BWF) and Waveform Audio Format (WAV) are the two most common formats used for digital preservation. Some Archives will also use FLAC (Free Lossless Audio Codec) for digital preservation. A data compression method that allows for the original data to be reconstructed in full, lossless compression such as the compression used in BWF or WAV is generally desirable for digital preservation. As mentioned above, MP3 files, while ubiquitous, are often not recommended for digital preservation because MP3 utilizes lossy compression that can compromise sound quality for the sake of file size. However, depending on the content and the purpose of preserving the audio file, a digital preservationist may decide this is an acceptable tradeoff, as MP3 does offer significant storage savings.

Some digital file formats that are accepted by different digital preservation repositories include AVI, full frame (uncompressed) (.avi); WAVE PCM audio (uncompressed) (.avi); AVI, containing H.264/MPEG-v4 AVC (lossy compression)(.avi); MPEG-4, containing H.264/MPEG-4 AVC (lossy compression) (.mp4); MPEG-2

SIDEBAR 8.1 A NOTE ABOUT COMPRESSION

Many file formats have built-in compression options. Compressing files makes them smaller and reduces the amount of storage necessary. The storage savings in a large digital repository can be significant. However, compression does not come without drawbacks. When files are compressed, information can be lost. For example, when an image is compressed, some pixels may be removed. Likewise, when an audio file is compressed, sounds outside the normal range of the human ear are removed. With high-quality, modern compression algorithms, this loss may not be noticeable right away. However, if the file needs to be closely inspected in the future (for example, an extreme enlargement of a photograph), the loss of this information can make a significant difference. There are two types of compression—*lossy* and *lossless.* The types of compression described above, that are irreversible, are considered lossy, because some amount of data is lost forever in the process. Lossless compression, on the other hand, is reversible and thus preferred whenever possible for digital preservation purposes (if compression is used at all). An additional factor to keep in mind about compression is that some compression methods are proprietary or patented or come with other legal restrictions. This increases the likelihood that files compressed with these methods will be unable to be decompressed (and thus read) in the future. Like file formats, compression methods need to be considered carefully.

Video Encoding (H.262), containing H.262/MPEG- (lossy compression) (.mp2); MXF, containing Motion JPEG 2000 (lossless compression) (.mxf); and Ogg, containing Theora (lossy compression) (.ogg).

Evaluating File Formats for Digital Preservation

The University of Minnesota Digital Conservancy, as an Archive, has decided to provide three different levels of support for file formats. Level 1 is full support, which means the conservancy will take all action reasonable to maintaining usability, including migration, normalization, or emulation. It will also ensure bit-level data fixity. Level 2 provides limited support to maintain usability. This can include file migration and data fixity checks done by Archives staff. Level 3, or minimal support, means digital preservationists will only provide access to the file in its original submission format and provide for data fixity. The University of Minnesota Digital Conservancy lists the level of support and best practices on its website.[11] Following the University of Minnesota Digital Conservancy's example, Binghamton University Libraries have also committed to providing different levels of support for the digital files they preserve. Binghamton University Libraries' levels of support and evaluation of different file types, however, are not entirely the same as the University of Minnesota Digital Conservancy's. Every Archive has its own local needs and staffing and support issues and will want to consider the levels of support it is prepared to offer on its own. When considering levels of support, Binghamton University Libraries decided to offer three: basic, limited, and full. In the libraries' model, basic support means that library staff will ensure data fixity, and will provide access to the digital object in the format in which it was submitted. When providing limited support, in addition to ensuring access and data fixity, the libraries will monitor file formats and may transform files into different formats to prevent loss due to format obsolescence. When providing full support, in addition to the services provided with limited support, the libraries "will take all reasonable actions to maintain usability, including migration, emulation, or normalization."[12] To document this commitment, the Binghamton University Libraries have also published a table that lists the level of preservation support they provide in their digital preservation system based on file format. The Binghamton University Libraries' table is shown in table 8.1.[13]

Although the Binghamton University Libraries, the University of Minnesota Digital Conservancy, and other establishments provide good examples of acceptable levels of commitment for digital preservationists and their institutions, each Archive will need to make its own decisions. Digital preservationists can look at the criteria used in other digital preservation repositories as a guide when deciding what file formats to accept and maintain for long-term preservation. The Library and Archives Canada (LAC) has identified five criteria to use when evaluating file formats:

1. Openness/transparency: how easy is it to learn about the file format and its technical information?
2. Adoption as a preservation standard: to what extent have the digital preservation community, national libraries, and archives formally adopted the file format as a format suitable for digital preservation?
3. Stability/compatibility: There are three components to stability and compatibility. First, to what degree is the format backward and forward compatible? Second, to what degree is the format protected against file corruption? And third, what is the relative frequency of release of newer or replacement versions of the format?
4. Dependencies/interoperability: to what degree is the file format reliant on particular hardware or software?
5. Standardization: to what degree has the file format gone through a formal (and rigorous) standardization process?[14]

These questions may help guide digital preservationists as they begin to make decisions about levels of support they and their institutions will be able to offer over the long term.

Park and Oh's Common Criteria Used to Evaluate File Formats

Research into file formats can also guide institutional decisions about levels of support for different file formats. In a study that examined articles, institutional

Table 8.1.   Binghamton University's Digital preservation Support Based on File Type

Format	File Extension	BUL's Commitment to Support	Notes
Text and Other Document Formats			
Comma-Separated Values (CSV)	.csv	Full support	CSV files are text files structured in a spreadsheet format with rows, columns, and possibly headers. Columns are often separated by commas, but they may be separated by tabs, periods, or other delimiters. Rows are separated by new lines. Headers are optional. CSV files may be encoded as ASCII text files but today are more commonly encoded in UTF-8/16.
Microsoft .doc	.doc	Basic support	Microsoft Word switched to .docx format with the introduction of MS Word 2007. Therefore, .doc is on track to become obsolete (some earlier versions of .doc are already no longer readable by current versions of MS Word) and MS Word .doc formats should be converted to a more preservation-friendly format, such as PDF/A, before submission.
Microsoft .docx	.docx	Limited support	Microsoft Word switched to .docx format with the introduction of MS Word 2007. Though the XML-based .docx should be extensible, it is still recommended to convert files to PDF/A when possible.
PDF/A	.pdf	Full support	PDF/A is the preferred version of PDF for archival preservation. PDF/A-1 (ISO 19005-1:2005) and PDF/A/2 (ISO 19005-2:2011) are both supported. Full support is only provided for PDF/A files and PDF files with embedded fonts. Limited support is offered for other valid PDF files.

Format	File Extension	BUL's Commitment to Support	Notes
PDF (with embedded fonts)	.pdf	Full support	PDF/A is the preferred version of PDF for archival preservation. Full support is only provided for PDF/A files and PDF files with embedded fonts. Limited support is offered for other valid PDF files.
PDF (other)	.pdf	Limited support	PDF/A is the preferred version of PDF for archival preservation. Full support is only provided for PDF/A files and PDF files with embedded fonts. Limited support is offered for other valid PDF files.
Plain text	.txt	Full support	Plain text using charset encoding UTF-8, USASCII, or UTF-16 with Byte Order Mark.
WordPerfect	.wpd	Basic support	Convert files to PDF/A or PDF with embedded fonts when possible.
Image Formats			
JPEG 2000	.jp2	Full support	The use of lossless (or reversible) compression is recommended, although "visually lossless" compression (e.g., actually a lossy—irreversible—compression) is also acceptable for most images. For more details, read Robert Buckley's report "JPEG 2000 as a Preservation and Access Format for the Welcome Trust Digital Library."
TIFF	.tif, .tiff	Full support	TIFF 6.0 is considered the best format for storing master images. Best practice is to save these files with no compression.
Audio Formats			
MP3	.mp3	Full support	General preference for preservation-oriented recorded sound is uncompressed Wave. MP3 utilizes lossy (irreversible) compression, and there are

(continued)

Table 8.1. *(continued)*

Format	File Extension	BUL's Commitment to Support	Notes
			possible patent issues (all U.S. patents appear to expire on or before December 30, 2017). However, MP3 is an open ISO standard in wide use. Thus, for compressed sound MP3 is acceptable, especially at data rates of 128 Kb/s (mono) or 256 Kb/s (stereo) or higher. The patent-free, open FLAC standard that utilizes lossless (reversible) compression may be a good alternative to MP3 and Wave for some.
FLAC	.flac	Full support	FLAC is a patent-free, open standard that utilizes lossless (reversible) compression. It may be a good alternative for some who are concerned about file size.
Wave	.wav	Full support	This file format can store all the data in an uncompressed format, and its wide use suggests long-term community support.

Video Formats

Note: Video files usually contain multiple formats within a wrapper. These formats may include audio formats, text formats (for closed caption), graphical formats, and others. Typically they also have some form of compression as well. Therefore, these examples below should only be considered general guidelines, and digital video objects will need to be evaluated on a case-by-case basis.

Format	File Extension	BUL's Commitment to Support	Notes
Motion JPEG 2000	.mj2, .mjp2	Limited support	Files should be JPEG 2000 losslessly compressed video wrapped up in Material Exchange Format (MXF). Motion JPEG 2000 is under consideration as a digital-archival format by the Library of Congress. It is an open ISO standard and an advanced update to MJPEG (or MJ). Details about the Material Exchange Format (MXF) are available from the Library of Congress Sustainability of Digital Formats website.

Format	File Extension	BUL's Commitment to Support	Notes
MPEG-2	.mp2	Limited support	Details about the MPEG-2 and digital preservation are available from the Library of Congress Sustainability of Digital Formats website. Note that according to the Library of Congress's digital preservation guidelines for audio streams in MPEG-2 formats, AAC is preferred to other audio encodings.
MPEG-4 (file format version #2)	.mp4	Limited support	Details about the MPEG-4 and digital preservation are available from the Library of Congress Sustainability of Digital Formats website. Note that according to the Library of Congress's digital preservation guidelines for audio streams in MPEG-4 formats, AAC is preferred to other audio encodings.

This table and more details about the levels of support offered for digital preservation at Binghamton University Libraries are available at http://www.binghamton.edu/libraries/technology/digital preservation/levels-based-on-format.html (last accessed September 30, 2013).

reports, and other documents, Eun Park and Sam Oh identified five groups of common criteria used to evaluate file formats for digital preservation that are similar to the criteria used by LAC. The categories of criteria are "functionality, metadata, opened, interoperability, and independence."[15] Each will be discussed briefly below.

1. Functionality: The functionality of a file format is its ability to do what it is designed to do. This functionality can be thought of in two broad aspects: the "preservation of the document structure and formatting and preservation of useable content."[16] A few of the attributes of functional criteria identified include robustness (defense against a single point of failure (e.g., will one damaged bit make the whole object unreadable?), quality, compactness (how much storage is necessary), color maintenance (for high-resolution images), and compression algorithms.

2. Metadata: Metadata related-criteria refer to a file format's ability to be embedded with technical and descriptive metadata. When this type of information is embedded into the document, as long as the file itself is preserved it

will be possible to determine what the file is at a later point should external metadata be lost. Metadata-related criteria identified in the study include criteria "expressed as metadata support, self-documentation (self-documenting), documentation, content-level (as opposed to presentation-level) description, self-describing, self-describing files, formal description of format, etc."[17]

3. Opened: The opened (or *openness*) criteria refers to whether the file format's specifications are openly available. *Openly available* means that the specifications are available to and accessible by the public at large. Some people may use phrases such as *open standard*, *open availability*, or *nonproprietary* or might indicate that the specification is independent of any single vendor when describing openness-related criteria.

4. Interoperability: Interoperability of a file format refers primarily to "the ability of a file format to be compatible with other formats and to exchange documents without loss of information."[18] A file format has high interoperability if it is supported by multiple software applications on multiple operating systems. Usually, if the file format is an open standard, it will have high interoperability.

5. Independence: Independence means that digital objects on the file format are free from specific, proprietary software applications or hardware. As with interoperability, this set of criteria is closely related to openness. Other factors leading to high interoperability include the lack of password restrictions and the absence of Digital-Rights Management (DRM) features. Patent and copyright issues can also affect the level of independence a file format has.

Along with the five groups of criteria listed above, Park and Oh also identify a number of other attributes that are often used by digital preservationists when making decisions about file formats. These attributes are adoption, authenticity, presentation, preservation, protection, reference, and transparency. Of these, they identify authenticity as "one of the most important attributes in archives and records management."[19]

File Migration Considerations

Many digital preservationists decide to migrate or normalize digital objects before depositing them into the repository. The specific reasons for doing this can vary, but in general it is easier to migrate a format upfront; not only is there a better chance that the appropriate tools will be available, but it is also more likely that someone familiar with the content will be available. It is nonetheless recommended that digital preservationists hedge their bets by storing both the digital object in the format as it was received and a migrated or normalized copy in the digital preservation system. This way, if someone in the future needs to see the original file for a purpose not considered when the file was formatted or if an error in migration is discovered down the road, another file format migration or the use of an emulation strategy would still be a possibility. Preserving the original files may also aid in matters of authenticity and provenance as well. This second method is ideal if resources allow. The main downside to this approach is that additional storage is necessary to keep copies of the digital object in both its original and migrated format.

DETERMINING FILE FORMATS

In some instances, digital preservationists will receive content for the digital preservation repository that is already in electronic form. This is especially true of content that was born digital and that must be preserved into the future without any kind of analog corollary. In these cases, it will be up to the digital preservationist to figure out what kind of file is being presented. After that, she will be able to make further decisions about that file's suitability for long-term preservation.

File Extensions

Perhaps the easiest way to identify an unfamiliar format is to use a search engine such as Google or Bing to search for the filename extension (a *file extension* is the suffix separated by a dot in a filename—e.g., .doc, .jpg, or .csv). Most of the time useful information will appear on the first page of results. If someone winds up looking for information about filename extensions often, it is a good idea to bookmark a few websites dedicated to providing information about file formats. A few of the most popular are dotWhat?, the Central File Extensions Registry, File Extensions Database, and FILExt.com.[20] Besides identifying the filename extension, these websites often provide information about which programs can read or write files that have this format and which programs can convert the file into a different format. Wikipedia also has a good deal of information about filename extensions.[21]

While filename extensions are a good place to begin when trying to identify a file format, the extensions may not always be accurate. Even when the filename extension is accurate, it may not be specific enough. In some cases there may be multiple competing file formats with the same extension or multiple revisions of a file format. For example, a file with a .doc extension can be described as a "Word processing document created by Microsoft Word, a word processor included with all versions of Microsoft Office; may contain formatted text, images, tables, graphs, charts, page formatting, and print settings."[22] However, there are at least four different versions of .doc files created with Microsoft Word—"(1) Word for DOS; (2) Word for Windows 1 and 2; Word 4 and 5 for Mac; (3) Word 6 and Word 95 for Windows; Word 6 for Mac; (4) Word 97 and later for Windows; Word 98 and later for Mac."[23] While software manufacturers typically aim to keep new versions of software backward compatible and able to open older files, there are limits to this, and eventually the older formats become unsupported by newer versions of the software. According to Microsoft, the newest version of .DOC supported by Word 2013 is the one that first appeared with Word 97. If an Archive has a document made with a version of

Word that is older than the Word 97 version of the program, it may not be able to open it in Word 2013. This example shows that we need to know more than the file extension to determine what type of file it is.[24]

MIME Internet Media Types

MIME, or Multipurpose Internet Mail Extensions, is a standard developed to allow nontext file attachments and multiple content items to be sent via e-mail. MIME types are now used for a number of Internet protocols, including Hypertext Transfer Protocol (HTTP). HTTP identifies the MIME type of content in the Content-Type header.[25] While the use of the term *MIME type* is common, the newer naming convention is to use the term *Internet Media Type*, since the standard is now used for many Internet protocols and not just for e-mail. Some common examples are *image/jpeg* (used for JPEG images), *audio/mpeg* (used for MP3 audio files), and *application/vnd.openxmlformats-officedocument.wordprocessingml.document* (used for .docx Microsoft Word documents).[26]

MIME Media types may be useful for identifying file format types, especially when content from websites is harvested automatically using a tool like Heretix. There are some issues with using MIME Media types for digital preservation as pointed out in the Digital Curation Centre (DCC)'s *Digital Curation Manual* by Stephen Abrams, Harvard University Library's Digital Library program manager from 1999 to 2008.[27] Some of these issues include that the MIME registry was designed to be read by humans and not machines, the information in the registry is rather minimal and is not always complete, and, "perhaps most significantly, . . . MIME types are defined at a fairly coarse granularity. For example, in many important curation contexts the variant 'profiles' of TIFF, such as TIFF/EP (ISO 12234-2), TIFF/IT (ISO 12639), GeoTIFF, and DNG, can be considered to have quite different sets of significant properties, necessitating independent workflows, yet all are defined by the same MIME type, 'image/tiff.'"[28] Despite these limitations, "MIME type is [the] most widely used authority list" in the PREMIS formatDesignation field.[29]

File Format Registries

There are literally thousands of different file formats that have been created and identified. The dotWhat? website, for example, has indexed almost eleven thousand different file extensions alone,[30] and many of these have multiple file format versions. Many of these file formats will need either specific software or hardware to be usable. Luckily there are a number of different tools and strategies available to help identify many of the common file types in use today. Common file format names, filename extensions, and MIME Media Types are "too generic to distinguish between significantly different subtypes and versions."[31] Therefore, digital preservationists need a more sophisticated method of determining exactly what type of file they have. This is where file format registries come in. A file format registry is a database that contains file "format–related representation information [that] can be expressed by a single reference to the database."[32] These registries aim to provide detailed information that is "intended to support preservation of digital content."[33] An advantage of this approach is that when file format information needs to be added or updated, it only has to be done in one place. A file format registry can be a local registry created by an individual repository or can be a registry used by multiple repositories. A discussion of various global efforts to create file format registries follows.

PRONOM

PRONOM was the first major effort to create a public file format registry.[34] PRONOM was initially developed in March 2002 by the National Archives in the U.K.'s Digital Preservation Department. PRONOM became Web-enabled with the release of PRONOM 3 in February 2004, which "represented the starting point for the development of PRONOM as a major online resource for the international digital preservation community."[35] The content contained in PRONOM has continued to grow. As of January 2014, PRONOM contained over eight hundred individual file format entries, and work is continuing "to improve the information and coverage of file formats in the registry."[36] In 2012 alone the National Archives added one hundred file formats and 177 file format signatures to PRONOM.[37] The National Archives announced in early 2013 that they are working on a linked data version of PRONOM. This work is being done in conjunction with Tessella Scientific Software Solutions.[38] Various software programs utilize the PRONOM registry's knowledge base to automatically identify file formats and properties. The most widely recognized of these programs is DROID (Digital Record Object Identification), which, like PRONOM, was developed by the National Archives. DROID and other tools will be discussed later in this chapter.

Global Digital Format Registry (GDFR)

The Global Digital Format Registry (GDFR) was an effort that came out of a $600,000 grant from the Andrew W. Mellon Foundation awarded to Harvard University Libraries in late 2005. The purpose of the grant was the "development of a registry of authoritative information about digital formats."[39] Although the grant was awarded in 2005, the project can be traced back to meetings sponsored by the Digital Library Federation (DLF) in 2003, "which established an ad hoc group to work on a plan."[40] Harvard University Libraries collaborated with Online Computer Library Center (OCLC) on the project, which concluded in 2008. GDFR was a very complex undertaking and has been criticized for ending "in 2008 or so without producing either usable software or a practical repository."[41]

Unified Digital Format Registry (UDFR)

The Unified Digital Format Registry (UDFR) seeks to combine the holdings and function of both GDFR and PRONOM. Developed by the University of California Curation Center, UDFR was released for production use in July 2012 at http://udfr .org. According to the project's final report, the UDFR meets all "major functional requirements [identified at the beginning of the project], except for the ability to export a PRONOM signature file."[42] Although the project managed to produce a functioning product, it is unclear what will happen to UDFR. While community involvement was high at the beginning, it "wasn't sustained after the final deployment of the software. There was a general sense of exhaustion at the end, leaving no one to rally the community to continue updating it."[43] There is still the possibility that an organization or some other group of people will continue UDFR's work. Its future is nonetheless uncertain.

DBpedia

DBpedia could possibly be used as a file format registry or as a source of information to be included in such a registry. "DBpedia is a crowd-sourced community effort to extract structured information from Wikipedia and make this information available on the Web" as linked data.[44] A digital preservationist could use DBpedia to, among other things, gather file format information that has been included in Wikipedia. Although the information is available for machine queries, "the data there, extracted from infoboxes on Wikipedia pages, is too inconsistent for structured queries to be of much use."[45] Another problem with DBpedia is that, even if the information were more consistent, "Wikipedia is directed at the general reader and mostly lacks the detailed technical information that's needed for preservation efforts. It often has links to that kind of information, though, including specifications."[46]

Just Solve the Problem

Just Solve the Problem is a wiki created to address "the issue that there is a lot of spread-out information about file formats in the world and almost universal acknowledgement that there are too many to keep track of and too much information in too-spread-out an area for it ever to be assembled."[47] The people behind the Just Solve the Problem wiki believe that by crowdsourcing the file format registries problem the information can be compiled in one place, making it easier for everyone who needs to find out about specific file formats. This is similar to the goals of PRONOM (and other file format registries), but while PRONOM accepts recommendations from the public, there sometimes can be delays in making the most up-to-date information available. The project initially began as a month-long endeavor in November 2012, but it is still ongoing at the time of writing. In the first month of its operation, Just Solve the Problem already contained "a huge amount of information [. . . although] the quality, completeness, and reliability vary[;] but in sheer breadth of information it could be a valuable resource."[48]

Why Are Registries So Difficult?

As described above, despite a number of efforts, the file format registry problem remains. A significant amount of information is required to create a file format registry. Not only does the information need to be gathered initially, but the information must also be revised and updated continuously as new file formats and updated versions of existing formats appear.

In some cases, information about older file formats may already be lost. According to Jim Thatcher, principal program manager lead for Office standards at Microsoft, Microsoft does "not currently have specifications for these older [Microsoft Office] file formats, [and it] is likely that those employees who had significant knowledge of these formats are no longer with Microsoft."[49] This is not a lone example, nor is it a new problem. The *Encyclopedia of Graphics File Formats*, published in 1994, discusses a once highly used file format, a Harvard Graphics file, that is no longer commonly used. The authors of the encyclopedia reportedly "just admit[ted] defeat in getting information" about this file format to include in the publication and subsequently left out important details about the file format because that information was no longer accessible.[50]

The good news is that many people realize the problem of losing information about file formats exists and there are ongoing efforts including PRONOM and Just Solve the Problem to help provide documentation into the future. Because of its longevity and continued development, in many ways PRONOM is not only the first but also possibly the best file format registry.

SOFTWARE TO HELP IDENTIFY FILE FORMATS

There are many different tools that a digital preservationist can use to identify and analyze files to determine the format and whether they were properly formatted. Below are some tools that someone working on digital preservation should be aware of. Due to the rapidly evolving nature of these and similar resources, this list is meant to give an idea of the kinds of tools one might find, not be comprehensive.

Generic Tools

DROID (Digital Record Object Identification) is a tool that can be used to identify file formats automatically. It can be used to identify files in batch. DROID, which is developed by the National Archives, "is designed to meet the fundamental requirement of any digital repository to be able to identify the precise format of all stored digital objects and to link that identification to a central registry of technical information about that format and its dependencies."[51] DROID identifies files using signatures from the PRONOM technical registry. Figure 8.2 shows the output DROID produced when it was run on a folder containing various types of digital objects.

FIDO (Format Identification for Digital Objects) is a free, easily installable tool written in the Python programming language with similar functionality to DROID. It differs from DROID in that it does not have a graphical user interface. Like DROID, it uses signatures from the PRONOM registry. One of FIDO's strengths is that it is very fast.[52]

JHOVE (JSTOR/Harvard Object Validation Environment) "provides functions to perform format-specific identification, validation, and characterization of digital objects."[53] *Format identification* is the process of determining what format a file has. *Validation* is confirming that the file is in compliance with the file format it is supposed to be in. *Format characterization* can be described as the "process of determining the format-specific significant properties of an object of a given format."[54] In the process of format identification, validation, and characterization, JHOVE can provide a large amount of information about the technical properties of a file. JHOVE should not be confused with JHOVE2. While JHOVE and JHOVE2 have similar purposes, JHOVE2 has a completely different code base. JHOVE is under continual development, with version 1.11 released in September of 2013.

JHOVE2 tries to address some of the perceived shortcomings of JHOVE by providing answers to four questions about a file: (1) What format is the file (identification)? (2) What about it (Feature extraction)? (3) What is the file, really (validation)? (4) So what does this mean (assessment)?. JHOVE2 is open source software being developed in a collaborative effort between California Digital Library, Stanford, and Portico.[55]

The UNIX/Linux file command was one of the first tools designed to determine file types. It originally appeared in 1973. BSD and Linux systems use a version that can be traced back to Ian Darwin's rewrite of the code in the mid-1980s.[56] The file

DROID Example · Resource	Extension	Size	Last modified	Format	Version	Mime type	PUID	Method
/home/ecorr...	zip	189.8 MB	4/22/13 3:22 PM	ZIP Format		application/zip	x-fmt/263	Signature
Link-Aviatio...	tif	91.6 MB	8/3/12 11:57 AM	Tagged Image File Format		image/tiff	fmt/353	Signature
Link-Aviatio...	tif	90.4 MB	8/3/12 11:55 AM	Tagged Image File Format		image/tiff	fmt/353	Signature
Link-Aviatio...	tif	88.3 MB	8/3/12 11:53 AM	Tagged Image File Format		image/tiff	fmt/353	Signature
/home/ecorr...	csv	868.2 KB	4/22/13 2:42 PM	Comma Separated Values		text/csv	x-fmt/18	Extension
/home/ecorr...	jpg	107.3 KB	5/26/13 1:05 PM	JPEG File Interchange Format	1.02	image/jpeg	fmt/44	Signature
/home/ecorr...	jpg	1.2 MB	6/6/12 3:37 PM	Raw JPEG Stream		image/jpeg	fmt/41	Signature
/home/ecorr...	jpg	1.1 MB	2/8/13 11:25 AM	JPEG File Interchange Format	1.01	image/jpeg	fmt/43	Signature
/home/ecorr...	jpg	1.3 MB	6/7/13 3:58 PM	JPEG File Interchange Format	1.02	image/jpeg	fmt/44	Signature
/home/ecorr...	ogg	7.7 MB	6/8/13 7:06 PM	Ogg Vorbis Codec Compress...		audio/ogg	fmt/203	Signature
/home/ecorr...	pdf	590.8 KB	5/30/13 3:10 PM	Acrobat PDF 1.4 - Portable D...	1.4	application/pdf	fmt/18	Signature
/home/ecorr...	pdf	306.3 KB	4/19/13 11:52 AM	Acrobat PDF 1.4 - Portable D...	1.4	application/pdf	fmt/18	Signature
/home/ecorr...	png	91.8 KB	5/30/13 6:46 PM	Portable Network Graphics	1.0	image/png	fmt/11	Signature
/home/ecorr...	tif	92.8 MB	8/3/12 12:03 PM	Tagged Image File Format		image/tiff	fmt/353	Signature
/home/ecorr...	xlsx	654.6 KB	4/22/13 12:37 PM	Microsoft Excel for Windows	2007 onwards		fmt/214	Container

Figure 8.2.   File format Information about Various Files Detected by the DROID Software

command relies on a "Magic File" database that contains information about what a file looks like. While it is a useful tool, it is limited in both digital preservation and security purposes because it only describes what a file appears to be, not necessarily what the file actually is.

ExifTool is an open source Perl Library and command line tool developed by Phil Harvey. It can be used "for reading, writing, and editing meta information in a wide variety of files."[57] While ExifTool supports a wide variety of formats, its strength is with graphic files and, to a lesser extent, audio and video file formats. It also supports a wide variety of metadata formats. ExifTool is not a file format validator, but "it often reports useful information in case of defective files."[58]

Apache Tika is an open source program designed to extract information from digital objects. "Tika allows search engines, content management systems, and other applications that work with various kinds of digital documents to easily detect and extract metadata and content from all major file formats."[59] Though Tika supports more file formats than DROID, it does not identify different versions of file formats. Therefore, the two tools might be best used in combination with each other.

XENA (Xml Electronic Normalising for Archives) is a tool designed to assist in long-term digital preservation by performing two tasks: the first is to detect the file format of a digital object, the second to convert "digital objects into open formats for preservation."[60] XENA is an open source software package developed by the National Archives of Australia as part of its Digital Preservation Software Platform. Figure 8.3 shows the results screen of a successful normalization process run on five files of different types.

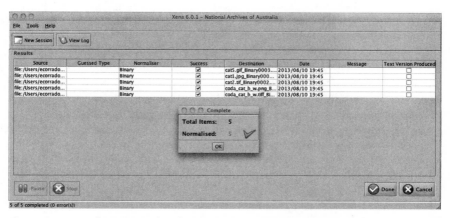

Figure 8.3. Results Screen of a File Format Demonstrating the Normalization Process within the Xena Digital Preservation (Open Source) Software. Created by the National Library of Australia. Image retrieved June 8, 2013 from http://xena.sourceforge.net/ help.php?page=normfile.html.

File Type Specific Tools

Along with the above tools that can be used to identify file formats and other file characteristics, there are many tools that have been designed to work with specific file formats or types of file formats that can be useful for digital preservation. A brief description follows of a few of the more popular tools utilized by digital preservationists.

PDF Tools

There are many software tools designed to work with Portable Document Format (PDF) files. One obvious tool that can be used is Adobe's Acrobat program. Adobe originated the PDF format, and many PDF files are created using its software, so it makes sense for digital preservationists to have Acrobat in their toolkit.

PDFTron's PDF/A Manager is a validation and conversation tool that can convert PDF documents to PDF/A–compliant documents. During this process, PDF features that are not suitable for long-term preservation are replaced with PDF/A equivalents. Some PDF features that are not suitable for digital preservation include "encryption, obsolete compression schemes, missing fonts, or device-dependent color."[61] According to PDFTron, the modifications are only those that are absolutely necessary; therefore, any information loss in the process is minimal and there is a full report of any changes. Besides converting files, PDFTron can also be used to validate a file against the PDF/A specification. Unlike PDF Toolkit (see below), PDF/A Manager is a commercial tool. However, there is a free developer license available. It can run on Linux, Mac OS/X, or Windows.

The PDF Toolkit (PDFtk) is a command line tool used for PDF files licensed under GNU General Public License (GPL) Version 2. PDFtk can perform a number of different tasks on PDF files. Some of the tasks that might be interesting to a digital preservationist include merging or splitting documents, rotating documents or pages, or applying watermarks or stamps. It can also sometimes repair corrupted or ill-formatted PDF files. PDFtk can run on Linux, MacOS/X, and Windows.

Xpdf is an open source PDF viewer. While one of its major features is viewing PDF files on computers running the X Windows system, Xpdf "also includes command-line information extractor and font analyzer utilities."[62] The *pdfinfo* and *pdffonts* utilities are particularly useful for digital preservation. *Pdfinfo* prints the contents of the "Info" dictionary contained in a PDF file. Some of the information printed includes page counts, encryption information, PDF version, and embedded metadata. *Pdffonts* lists which fonts are contained in a PDF file. It also lists some information for the fonts, including its name and type and whether the font is embedded in the document.

Microsoft Office Format Tool

The Dependency Discovery Tool was designed to search through binary Microsoft Office files (in the .doc, .ppt, or .xls formats) in an attempt "to find any documents or files that are linked to the document."[63] The tool has a command-line interface, and there is also an API available. Output can be in text, .XML, or .CSV formats.

Image Format Tools

There are many different tools designed to work with images that are of interest to digital preservationists. Two particularly useful tools are ImageMagick and ImageVerifier.

ImageMagick is a software suite designed to create, edit, compose, or convert bitmap images. ImageMagick can read and write more than 100 different image file formats. Digital preservationists may want to take advantage of ImageMagick's ability to identify the format and technological attributes of an image or use it to convert an image to a different format that may be deemed to be more preservation-worthy or more user-friendly for access purposes. It can also be used to watermark display copies of images.

ImageVerifier (IV) is commercial software that crawls a hierarchy of file folders to look for image files to verify. It is useful when dealing with a large number of files and should easily be able to handle more than 100,000 images. Among the image formats that IV can verify are TIFF and JPEG. IV checks the structure of files "by reading the actual image data, decompressing as necessary. This can find many errors but not all, as some errors are indistinguishable for image data."[64]

Audio/Video File Format Tools

As with image tools, there are many audio and video tools useful for digital preservation. Two tools specifically worth mentioning are FFmpeg and MediaInfo. FFmpeg is a complete, crossplatform solution to record, convert, and stream audio and video. One reason FFmpeg is useful for digital preservation is that it supports a wide range of formats from "the most obscure ancient formats up to the cutting edge."[65] FFmpeg includes various other tools. One of them that would be useful for digital preservationists is FFprobe, which gathers various bits of information about a multimedia stream and displays or prints it in machine- and human-readable formats. Figure 8.4 shows the human-readable output from FFprobe on a live audio recording from a Grateful Dead concert.

MediaInfo is a tool that can be used to view technical and tag information about audio and video files. MediaInfo supports a wide range of audio and video file formats. MediaInfo can be used to display container information including "format, profile, commercial name of the format, duration, overall bit rate, writing application and library, title, author, director, album, track number, date," and more.[66] It can display various details about audio and video information including format, codec, and bit rate. MediaInfo also can display information about text tracks (such as those used for subtitles) and chapter information. There is a graphical user interface for most operating systems and a command-line interface for all supported platforms.

```
ecorrado@ecorrado:~$ ffprobe gd_song.ogg
avprobe version 0.8.6-4:0.8.6-0ubuntu0.12.04.1, Copyright (c) 2007-2013 the
Libav developers
  built on Apr  2 2013 17:02:36 with gcc 4.6.3
Input #0, ogg, from 'gd_song.ogg':
  Duration: 00:08:00.25, start: 0.000000, bitrate: 133 kb/s
    Stream #0.0: Audio: vorbis, 44100 Hz, stereo, s16, 128 kb/s
    Metadata:
      TITLE           : The Music Never Stopped
      ARTIST          : Grateful Dead
      ALBUM           : 1977-11-06 - Broome County Arena
      track           : 12
ecorrado@ecorrado:~$ ▮
```

Figure 8.4. Output Produced by Executing the FFprobe Command Line Program on an Audio File

For more information about the tools discussed above and to learn about additional software useful for digital preservation, visit the Open Planets Foundation Digital Preservation Tool Registry.[67]

While these and other file format and analysis tools are extremely useful for digital preservationists, they are not completely foolproof. When working with "older files in particular, PRONOM/Droid and Linux file[s] fail pretty badly. This is particular[ly] important for the older files, as there can often be less information or metadata on those files than for more recent ones. The detection tools do not come up with reasonable results for older WordStar, WordPerfect, MS-Word,. . . and files [...] from old databases."[68] Because of this, digital preservationists may need to use other tools and their best judgment at times to determine the types and the validity of files they are entrusted to preserve.

CONCLUSION

As Park and Oh describe, many Archives use similar types of criteria when evaluating file formats.[69] It makes sense since, while the goals may differ, the staff operating these digital preservation repositories are all interested in long-term preservation. The importance of each of these criteria, however, will likely vary between organizations based on the unique circumstances of each digital preservation project. This is one thing that makes determining what file formats to use for digital preservation so hard. While one Archive may believe that PDF/A is a highly desirable file format for digital preservation, another may decide not to accept it at all, in part because "PDF/A does not offer the same editing functionality available in datasets."[70] Each Archive has its own mission and goals and has Consumers with different needs. Therefore, it is not realistic to say that any one particular file format is or is not the best. It is probably not even realistic to say that a file format is or is not proper for digital preservation. Each Archive needs to make its own Technology decisions, but this chapter should serve as a good resource for information about the issues at hand. Next, in part IV, we consider the Content housed by and made available through the Technologies reviewed in art III.

NOTES

1. Wikipedia, s.v. "File Format," last modified April 4, 2013, http://en.wikipedia.org/w/index.php?title=File_format&oldid=548699192.
2. Library of Congress (LOC), "Formats, Evaluation Factors, and Relationships," last modified March 20, 2013, http://www.digitalpreservation.gov/formats/intro/format_eval_rel.shtml.
3. Global Digital Format Registry, "Format Registry Ontology," last modified March 10, 2003, http://www.gdfr.info/docs/Ontology-v1-2003-03-10.pdf.
4. LOC, "Formats, Evaluation Factors, and Relationships."
5. Adobe, "About Adobe PDF," accessed September 29, 2013, http://www.adobe.com/products/acrobat/adobepdf.html.
6. For a brief introduction to possible legal issues with JPEG 2000, see Wikipedia, s.v. "JPEG 2000: Legal Issues," accessed September 29, 2013, http://en.wikipedia.org/wiki/JPEG_2000#Legal_issues.
7. Johan van der Knijff, "JPEG 2000 for Long-Term Preservation: JP2 as a Preservation Format," *D-Lib Magazine* 17, no. 5–6 (2011), http://www.dlib.org/dlib/may11/vanderknijff/05vanderknijff.html.
8. National Archives (U.S.), "Frequently Asked Questions (FAQ) about Digital Audio and Video Records," accessed April 23, 2012, http://www.archives.gov/records-mgmt/initiatives/dav-faq.html.
9. Ibid.
10. Ibid, question 11.
11. University of Minnesota Digital Conservancy, "University Digital Conservancy Preservation Policy," accessed April 23, 2013, http://conservancy.umn.edu/pol-preservation.jsp.
12. Binghamton University Library, "Digital Preservation Levels Based on Format," accessed November 11, 2013, http://www.binghamton.edu/libraries/technology/digital-preservation/levels-based-on-format.html.
13. The chart here was slightly modified for purposes of this book. The current version of this chart as used by Binghamton University Libraries can be found at http://www.binghamton.edu/libraries/technology/digital-preservation/levels-based-on-format.html.
14. Library and Archives Canada, "Library and Archives Canada, Local Digital Format Registry (LDFR) File Format Guidelines for Preservation and Long-term Access Version 1.0," accessed April 23, 2013, http://www.collectionscanada.gc.ca/obj/012018/f2/012018-2200-e.pdf.
15. Eun G. Park and Sam Oh, "Examining Attributes of Open Standard File Formats for Long-Term Preservation and Open Access," *Information Technology and Libraries* 31, no. 4 (Dec. 2012): 44–65, doi:10.6017/ital.v31i4.1946. The article also includes a useful appendix that defines the various attributes identified in the study.
16. Ibid.
17. Ibid.

18. Ibid. In coming up with this definition, Park and Oh reference Judith Rog and Caroline van Wijk, *Evaluating File Formats for Long-Term Preservation* (The Hague: National Library of the Netherlands, 2008; and ECMA International, "Standard ECMA-376: Office Open XML File Formats," accessed September 29, 2013, http://www.ecma-international.org/publications/standards/Ecma-376.htm.

19. Ibid.

20. Found at dotwhat.net, FileInfo.com, filedesc.com, and FILExt.com, respectively.

21. The alphabetical list of filename extensions on Wikipedia can be found at "List of File Formats (Alphabetical)," last modified November 6, 2013, http://en.wikipedia.org/wiki/List_of_file_formats_%28alphabetical%29.

22. FileInfo.com, ".DOC File Extension," accessed April 23, 2013, http://www.fileinfo.com/extension/doc. FileInfo.com "contains a searchable database of thousands of file extensions with detailed information about the associated file types" ("Welcome to FileInfo.com," accessed April 23, 2013, http://fileinfo.com).

23. Wikipedia, s.v. "Microsoft Word: File Formats," accessed April 23, 2013, http://en.wikipedia.org/wiki/Microsoft_Word#File_formats.

24. TechNet, "File Format Reference for Office 2013," accessed April 23, 2013, http://technet.microsoft.com/en-us/library/dd797428.aspx.

25. Adam Barth, Juan Caballero, and Dawn Song, "Secure Content Sniffing for Web Browsers, or How to Stop Papers from Reviewing Themselves" (paper presented at the thirtieth IEEE Symposium on Security and Privacy, Oakland, Calif., May 2009) (Washington, D.C.: IEEE Computer Society, 2009), 360–71, doi:10.1109/SP.2009.3.

26. A list of MIME Media types is available at Internet Assigned Numbers Authority, "MIME Media Types," last modified January 30, 2013, http://www.iana.org/assignments/media-types.

27. LinkedIn, "Stephen Abrams," accessed April 13, 2013, http://www.linkedin.com/pub/stephen-abrams/11/370/591.

28. Stephen Abrams, "DCC | Digital Curation Manual: Instalment on 'File Formats,'" Edinburgh Research Archive, last modified October 2007, https://www.era.lib.ed.ac.uk/bitstream/1842/3351/1/Abrams%20file formats.pdf.

29. Angela Dappert, "The *PREMIS Data Dictionary*: Information You Need to Know for Preserving Digital Documents," slide 43 (paper presented in Prague, October 14, 2008).

30. The DotWhat? website (http://dotwhat.net/) claims to have "one of the world's largest and most detailed databases of file extension information." However, it is by no means comprehensive. For example, in 2004, a now defunct "File Extensions Collection" website claimed to have indexed over fifteen thousand different file formats according to Lars R. Clausen, *Handling File Formats* (Copenhagen: n.p., 2004), accessed April 23, 2013, http://citeseerx.ist.psu.edu/viewdoc/download?doi=10.1.1.2.1801&rep=rep1&type=pdf.

31. Caroline Arms and Carl Fleischhauer, "Digital Formats: Factors for Sustainability, Functionality, and Quality" (paper presented at the IS & T Archiving 2005 Conference, Washington, D.C., April 26–29, 2005), http://memory.loc.gov/ammem/techdocs/digform/Formats_IST05_paper.pdf.

32. Alex Ball, "Briefing Paper: File Format and XML Scheme Registries," May 31, 2006, http://www.ukoln.ac.uk/projects/grand-challenge/papers/registryBriefing.pdf.

33. Arms and Fleischhauer, "Digital Formats."

34. Chris Rusbridge, "Excuse Me . . . Some Digital Preservation Fallacies?" *Adriane* 46 (Feb. 2006), accessed April 23, 2013, http://www.ariadne.ac.uk/issue46/rusbridge. Although,

as pointed out on Wikipedia (s.v. "PRONOM," accessed April 23, 2013, http://en.wikipedia
.org/w/index.php?title=PRONOM&oldid=534676523), it should be noted that the "Magic
File" repository used by the UNIX/Linux file command has served this role in a less formal
capacity for two decades.

35. National Archives (U.K.), "PRONOM," accessed February 5, 2014, http://www.nation
alarchives.gov.uk/aboutapps/PRONOM/default.htm.

36. Ibid.

37. David Clipsham, "Bring Out Your Dead (Files)," *National Archives Blog*, February 8,
2013, http://blog.nationalarchives.gov.uk/blog/bring-out-your-dead-files/.

38. Actually, they have been working on one in beta for a while, but with the help of Tessella it is expected that a production-quality implementation will be made available. This update was presented in David Clipsham, "Recent Developments in DROID and PRONOM:
What Happened in 2012?" (presentation for the National Archives, January 28, 2013), http://
www.dpconline.org/component/docman/doc_download/813-2013fileformatsclipsham.

39. "University Library Receives Grant," *Harvard Gazette*, February 2, 2006, accessed September 29, 2013, http://news.harvard.edu/gazette/story/2006/02/university-library-receives
-grant/.

40. Gary McGath, "The Format Registry Problem" *Code4Lib Journal* 19, accessed April
23, 2013, http://journal.code4lib.org/articles/8029.

41. Ibid.

42. U.C. Curation Center, *Unified Digital Format Registry (UDFR) Final Report* (Oakland,
Calif.: California Digital Library, 2012), http://udfr.org/project/UDFR-final-report.pdf.

43. McGath, "Format Registry Problem."

44. DBpedia, "About," accessed April 23, 2013, http://dbpedia.org/About.

45. Gary McGath, "Format Registries Don't SPARQL," *File Formats Blog*, September 6,
2012, http://fileformats.wordpress.com/2012/09/06/sparql/.

46. McGath "Format Registry Problem."

47. Fileformats.archiveteam.org, "Statement of Project," last modified October 28, 2012,
http://fileformats.archiveteam.org/wiki/Statement_of_Project.

48. McGath, "Format Registry Problem."

49. Chris Rusbridge, "Response to the Open Letter on Obsolete Microsoft File Formats," *Unsustainable Ideas Blog*, November 26, 2012, http://unsustainableideas.wordpress
.com/2012/11/26/response-open-letter-obsolete-ms-formats/.

50. Gary McGath, "Defining the File Format Registry Problem," *File Formats Blog*, September 3, 2013, http://fileformats.wordpress.com/2012/09/03/registry-problem/. According
to McGath's blog post, the *Encyclopedia of Graphics File Formats* "covers about a hundred different formats, generally in enough detail to give you a good start at implementing a reader.
There are names [that] are still familiar: TIFF, GIF, JPEG. Many others aren't even memories
except to a few people. DKB? FaceSaver?" The second edition of *Encyclopedia of Graphics
File Formats* is available as an Open Access book at http://www.fileformat.info/resource/
book/1565921615/index.htm (first ed.: James D. Murray and William Van Ryper, *Encyclopedia of Graphics File Formats* [Sebastopol, Calif.: O'Reilly & Associates, 1994]).

51. National Archives (U.K.), "Download DROID: File Format Identification Tool,"
accessed April 23, 2013, http://www.nationalarchives.gov.uk/information-management/
projects-and-work/droid.htm.

52. Adam Farquhar describes FIDO's impressive performance in his blog post "Fido: A
High Performance Format Identifier for Digital Objects" (*Adam Farquhar's Blog*, November

3, 2010, http://www.openplanetsfoundation.org/blogs/2010-11-03-fido-%E2%80%93-high
-performance-format-identifier-digital objects). According to the post, FIDO can identify
over seventeen million files in a single day using standard computing equipment.

53. SourceForge, "JHOVE: JSTOR/Harvard Object Validation Environment," last modified February 25, 2009, http://jhove.sourceforge.net/.

54. Ibid.

55. More information about JHOVE2 can be found at Bitbucket, "JHOVE2 Frequently
Asked Questions (FAQ)," last modified March 18, 2013, https://bitbucket.org/jhove2/main/
wiki/JHOVE2_Frequently_Asked_Questions_%28FAQ%29.

56. Ian F. Darwin, "Fine Free File Command," accessed August 1, 2013, http://darwinsys
.com/file/.

57. ExifTool by Phil Harvey, "ExifTool by Phil Harvey: Read, Write, and Edit Meta Information!" accessed April 23, 2013, http://www.sno.phy.queensu.ca/~phil/exiftool/.

58. Open Planets Knowledge Base, s.v. "ExifTool," last modified December 18, 2012,
http://wiki.opf-labs.org/display/TR/ExifTool.

59. Apache Software Foundation, "Apache Tika," accessed April 23, 2013, http://tika
.apache.org/.

60. "National Archives of Australia, "Xena Digital Preservation Software," accessed September 29, 2013, http://xena.sourceforge.net/.

61. PDFTron, "PDFTron: PDF/A Manager," accessed September 29, 2013, http://www
.pdftron.com/pdfamanager/.

62. Open Planets Knowledge Base, s.v. "Xpdf," last modified August 20, 2013, http://wiki
.opf-labs.org/display/TR/Xpdf.

63. SourceForge, "Dependency Discovery Tool," accessed April 23, 2013, http://source-
forge.net/projects/officeddt/.

64. Marc Rochkind's Apps and Books, "ImageVerifier," accessed April 23, 2013, http://
basepath.com/site/detail-ImageVerifier.php.

65. FFmpeg, "About FFmpeg," accessed April 23, 2013, http://www.ffmpeg.org/about
.html.

66. MediaArea.net, "MediaInfo," accessed April 23, 2013, http://mediainfo.sourceforge
.net/en.

67. At http://wiki.opf-labs.org/display/TR/Home.

68. Dirk von Suchodoletz, "Practical Issues with Currently Available File Format Software," (comment on *Bill Robert's Blog*, "File Format Registry Report Released," February 16,
2011), http://www.openplanetsfoundation.org/comment/92#comment-92.

69. Park and Oh, "Examining Attributes of Open Standard File Formats."

70. Rog and van Wijk, "Evaluating File Formats."

IV

CONTENT-RELATED ASPECTS

9

Collection Development

According to the Digital Preservation Triad, Content is the third and final area necessary to a successful digital preservation initiative. Collections are valuable, and the content they contain is the reason for any digital preservation initiative in the first place. All of the work done in Management and in working with Technology serves to preserve and make available digital content that is ultimately of value to the Designated Community.

The Blue Ribbon Task Force on Sustainable Digital Preservation and Access (BRTF-SDPA) reminds us that "without preservation, there is no access."[1] That said, digital preservation is not an inexpensive proposition and in order for it to be sustainable there needs to be demand for digital preservation and for digital preservation–related services. One potential factor influencing demand is the ability to access digital content (typically over some length of time, when discussing access in terms of digital preservation). In order to help create and cultivate this demand, there needs to be content in the digital preservation system that people will want, or need, to access. This access does not always have to be immediate, and access may only be available to a limited number of people for legal or other reasons; however, a well-articulated demand will go a long way toward helping a digital preservation initiative become financially sustainable.[2] One of the main ways a digital preservation initiative can increase demand for its services is by collecting digital objects that people desire to access now and in the future, and by actively securing the interest of stakeholders at the same time, if possible.

Collection development has been described in this book as the selection and deselection of objects for a collection. Collection development may be called by various terms in different domains. For instance, museums may use the term *curation*, and in archival science sometimes the word *appraisal* is used to describe activities similar to collection development. One of the mandatory responsibilities in the OAIS

Reference Model for an organization operating a digital preservation system is to "have established some criteria that aid in determining the types of information that it is willing to, or it is required to, accept."[3] Regardless of the terms used, if an organization desires to become fully compliant with the OAIS Reference Model, it is prudent to have a well-thought-out policy in place for the types of objects digital preservationists will accept.

Mike Kastellec described three general models of digital object selection for which the amount of human intervention required can be placed on a sliding scale.[4] On one end of the scale is the *selective* model. In this model, which is the closest to the traditional collection development process in the analog world, the subject specialist selects individual digital objects (or small sets of digital objects) that are to be preserved. On the other end of the scale is the *whole domain* model, where everything that can be harvested is preserved. The *whole domain* digital object selection model is often used when collecting a large number of websites. For instance, the National Library of New Zealand periodically crawls all of the .nz top level domains and preserves the content. The downside of this method is that it is "wasteful" and can be expensive, since "everything found is kept, irrespective of potential value."[5] The method can also create quality control issues, since, because of the scale, not everything can be verified to have been harvested completely and saved in a manner that is useful or useable by the Designated Community. In between the *selective* and *whole domain* models on the scale are the *thematic* and *collaborative* models of digital collection development. The *thematic* model can apply either selective or whole domain approaches to relatively narrow domains, such as specific events, topics, or communities. The *collaborative* model is one "in which archival institutions negotiate agreements with publishers to deposit content."[6] Figure 9.1 offers one way of looking at this model.

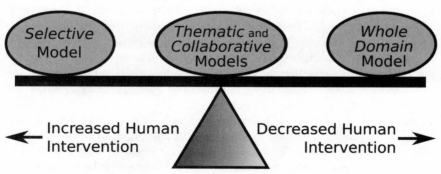

Figure 9.1.   Collection Development Models for Digital Preservation

CRITERIA

According to the IBM website on big data, "90 percent of the data in the world today has been created in the last two years alone."[7] It may not be surprising, then, that the amount of digital content created every year is more than all of the data storage capacity in the world.[8] Because of this, the libraries, archives, and museums (LAM) community is clearly unable to collect everything. Therefore, LAM professionals should want to establish criteria to aid in the selection process. In a recent European-wide survey of research libraries, the "main criteria identified for selecting digital material for long-term preservation are historical value, user demand, and usefulness."[9] These three factors are a good place to start, but there are other factors an organization may wish to consider as well. The OAIS Reference Model suggests that selection "criteria may include, among others, subject matter, information source, degree of uniqueness or originality, and the nature of the techniques used to represent the information (e.g., physical media, digital media, format)."[10] Some of the other factors that may be considered are copyright and other intellectual property issues, existing descriptive metadata, staffing issues, and the availability of external funding. Table 9.1 offers information related to these factors that may be important when developing collections.

Existing Collections

Most organizations that embark on a digital preservation program will already have existing collections. These collections may contain digital objects as well as analog objects that may be suitable for digitization. An organization that is undertaking digital preservation may choose to identify and inventory the digital content already in the collections. As part of this process, tangible items such as floppy disks, external hard drives, and CD-ROMs and their associated contents should be inventoried. Physical items that may be suitable for digitization could also be identified. The process of identifying items for digital preservation that are already in the organization's possession will usually include many of the same evaluation criteria against which new additions to the standard collections are evaluated. In particular, the review should include an overview of any legal issues such as copyright and other intellectual property issues that may restrict the ability of the organization to be able to legally make digital copies for preservation and/or access purposes. Often the agreements made in the past do not cover such activities, and the digital preservationist or subject specialist may need to reach out to the copyright holder to secure the rights necessary to take the appropriate actions to preserve this content digitally.

New Collections

Outreach to faculty and other producers of content, in some ways a Management task, may be a key component in obtaining new digital content in support of the

Table 9.1. Factors that May Influence Collection Development Policies

Factor	Selected Questions to Consider
Subject matter	• Is the subject matter appropriate for the mission of the organization? • To what degree is there demand for this content? • Will the content be useful immediately and/or in the future?
Source of content	• Is the source of the content a prominent member of the community? For example, is the source of the content affiliated with the parent institution? • Does the repository have a legal, procedural, or other obligation to preserve the content due to the position or role of the person or entity providing it?
Degree of uniqueness or originality	• Is the content at risk because it is one of a kind or one of a few? • Is someone else already responsible for preserving the content? For example, is the content in the form of a journal article that is already being preserved by Portico?
Nature of the techniques used to represent the information	• What type of physical media or digital media is the content on? • If digital, what file formats are used, and are they acceptable to the organization? • Are these physical media, digital media, or file formats in danger of obsolescence? If so, how quickly do they need to be preserved? • Do the materials need to be digitized or migrated to different file formats? If so, by whom?
Copyright and other intellectual property issues	• Are there any copyright or other intellectual property issues that will need to be addressed in order to make the content available to the Designated Community? • Can the content be made openly accessible? • Can or will the content provider transfer or grant the necessary intellectual property rights to the Archive so that it will have sufficient control of the content in order to perform digital preservation actions such as file format migration?
Existing metadata	• Is there a need to create substantial amounts of descriptive metadata for the objects or collection? If so, who will do it? • If descriptive metadata already exists, can it easily be reused in the digital preservation system?
Staffing issues	• Is there adequate staff in place to process the collection? If not, does the content provider have staff that is able to perform some of the processing?
Funding issues	• Is there external funding available from the content provider or other sources that can be used to offset costs of processing, maintaining, and preserving the materials?

Digital Preservation Triad's Content area. Who, when, and how this outreach is performed will vary greatly by organization. In some cases archivists, museum curators, subject librarians, or other content specialists should be enlisted to help in this effort by reaching out to stakeholders who are producing digital content, since these information professionals generally will have a better understanding as to what content is out there that should be preserved. Another way of obtaining content for new collections is to partner with other organizations. A small- or medium-sized cultural heritage organization, such as a regional opera house or local historical society, may very well have content that is worth preserving but may not have the expertise or funding to undertake digital preservation initiatives on its own. It may, however, be able to do so in partnership with a large university that already has a digital preservation system in place. For example, the University of Oregon's Digital Library Services has been working with the Oregon Arts Commission to create digital collections based on their content.[11]

Digital preservation systems may also act as an institutional or subject-specific repository that allows self- and unmediated submission of digital objects. When this is the case, there should be a clear policy as to what type of content is appropriate as well as a generic agreement for the person submitting the content that includes statements providing the organization sufficient control to undertake the steps necessary to enabling long-term preservation. See chapter 3's discussion of the OAIS Reference Model for more information.

The issue of descriptive metadata, while not necessarily, or specifically, a collection development issue, should be considered at the time of obtaining a new collection. In some cases the collection may already have descriptive metadata that will come with the collection. In these cases, the metadata will have to be evaluated to see if, how, and by whom it will be transformed for the purposes of being deposited it into the digital preservation system. If there is no descriptive metadata available at the time the content's transfer and ingest is being negotiated, it must be asked who will create this metadata and in what format will it be created.

Similarly, digitizing or reformatting already digital content should be undertaken at the time the rights to a collection are obtained. Just because an object is already digital does not mean that it is in a file format suitable for digital preservation. If a file needs to be migrated or normalized into a different format before being preserved, it must be determined who is responsible for doing that and to what file formats the content will be migrated. The same applies to content that needs to be digitized—determining who will be responsible for digitizing the content and what file format and specifications will be used for the preservation and, optionally, the display copies is crucial.

CONCLUSION

As the Digital Preservation Triad makes clear, digital preservation is very much a Content issue, intertwined with both Management and Technology. Management policies and institutional missions will shape the content being collected and will guide work with stakeholders. Technology will be necessary to supporting the various kinds of digital or digitized content, from text-based to 3-D and everything in between.

Because technological as well as human and financial resources are not unlimited, not every digital object can be preserved. The suitability of a digital object (or digitized object) for preservation needs to be judged on technical, social, and administrative criteria. If the digital object is not useful for the Designated Community, the expense of preserving the object is not a wise choice. By having a clearly articulated and potentially creative collection development policy, an organization not only can satisfy one of the mandatory responsibilities of the OAIS Reference Model but will also be seen as more transparent, potentially yielding a more-sustainable digital preservation system. This collection development policy should address both existing and new acquisitions of digital content. By formalizing partnerships with individual stakeholders as part of that policy, creative digital preservationists can envision going beyond the scope of institutional MOUs, discussed in chapter 5, to garner support and collect useful content directly from among the stakeholders.

Each type of digital object and each subject domain will raise slightly different issues and concerns and may require slightly different approaches, as alluded to in chapter 4. The next couple of chapters will look at preservation issues involved in two domains that have been receiving a lot of attention recently. Chapter 10 will look at the preservation of scientific research data, and chapter 11 will explore the preservation of digital humanities content.

NOTES

1. Blue Ribbon Task Force on Sustainable Digital Preservation and Access (BRTF-SDPA), *Sustainable Economics for a Digital Planet: Ensuring Long Term Access to Digital Information* (San Diego: San Diego Supercomputer Center, 2010), 9, http://brtf.sdsc.edu/biblio/BRTF_Final_Report.pdf.

2. Ibid.

3. Consultative Committee for Space Data Systems (CCSDS), *Reference Model for an Open Archival Information System (OAIS): Recommended Practice CCSDS 650.0-M-2; Recommendation for Space Data System Practices*, Magenta Book, Recommended Practice, issue 2 (Washington, D.C.: CCSDS Secretariat, June 2012), 3-2, http://public.ccsds.org/publications/archive/650x0m2.pdf.

4. Mike Kastellec, "Practical Limits to the Scope of Digital Preservation," *Information Technology and Libraries* 31 (June 2012).

5. Ibid, 67.

6. Ibid.

7. IBM, "Big Data at the Speed of Business," para. 1, accessed August 13, 2013, http://www-01.ibm.com/software/data/bigdata/.

8. Francine Berman, "Got Data?" *Communications of the ACM* 51 (Dec. 2008): 50, http://portal.acm.org/citation.cfm?id=1409360.1409376.

9. Alliance Permanent Access to the Records of Science in Europe Network (APARSEN), *Trust Is Fundamental to the Working of Society* (Dorset, Eng., and The Hague: APARSEN, 2012), 40, http://www.alliancepermanentaccess.org/wp-content/uploads/downloads/2012/09/APARSEN-Trust-Brochure-Low-Res-Web-Version.pdf.

10. CCSDS, *Reference Model*, 3-2.

11. University of Oregon Libraries, "Instruction and Outreach," accessed June 8, 2013, http://library.uoregon.edu/diglib/instruction.html.

10

Preserving Research Data

Content to support research is increasingly important to preserve digitally. To the layman, *research* might mean looking into a topic for the first time; teenagers working with prebuilt electrical circuits using a battery-powered circuit board might be *researching* electricity. At more advanced levels, though, formal approaches to the topic of research exist. Universities and other institutions responsible for encouraging knowledge creation generally consider research to be "a systematic investigation including research development, testing, and evaluation, designed to develop or contribute to generalizable knowledge."[1]

Research as a systematic investigation to develop or contribute to generalizable and new knowledge is a major component of the sciences and the social sciences, and it is research that allows these fields to advance. Formal research, including research projects, is an essential part of grant and other funding opportunities in a number of fields. Funding agencies that sponsor this kind of research are increasingly requiring research outputs, including the data created as part of the research, to be managed, preserved, and made available to other researchers.

When data is managed and stored properly, it can easily be shared with any number of researchers over time and beyond the walls of the institution where it was originally created. But why are funding agencies so concerned with sharing? It turns out that there are numerous benefits to sharing, for both individual researchers and for the research community at large. As the U.S. National Institute of Health (NIH) explains, "sharing data reinforces open scientific inquiry, encourages diversity of analysis and opinion, promotes new research, makes possible the testing of new or alternative hypotheses and methods of analysis, supports studies on data collection methods and measurement, facilitates the education of new researchers, enables the exploration of topics not envisioned by the initial investigators, and permits the creation of new datasets when data from multiple sources are combined."[2] The movement to require researchers to preserve and share data is growing. This move to share is, by default, increasingly putting the institutions that support research in the business of preserving data so that it can be shared.

Keeping in mind this shared data environment, this chapter on Content will describe some of the challenges of preserving research data, will look more closely at some of the trends in the requirements to preserving data and making it open, will examine the growth of big data in the repository setting, and will explore some issues surrounding the preservation of data relating to human subjects.

RESEARCH DATA

Research data supports and promotes research and inquiry. The volume of scientific data has been increasing at an extraordinary rate throughout the twentieth and twenty-first centuries. In 1945, Vannavar Bush first suggested a new, futuristic machine called a Memex, which, if created, was to have helped researchers find and annotate their way through the information glut.[3] Bush's proposed Memex was a response to the intensive research that was carried out during World War II and was being generated at a rate far too rapid for any single researcher to internalize and make sense of. Information and computer scientists tend to agree that the Memex, as envisioned, was a kind of precursor to the World Wide Web and Web 2.0, perhaps giving some insight into the rationale behind the push for preservation and sharing.

Research data can be difficult to curate for a number of reasons. One reason is that the sheer scale of research data is a "daunting curatorial task."[4] Another factor is that, although some research data is not any more complicated than a photograph or a book, in many cases it is heterogeneous, unstructured, or in a variety of different formats. Likewise, "there are many different information standards used (and not used) as well as many different approaches to information structure (e.g., XML–structured documents versus fixed image and textual file formats)."[5] There can also be distinct discipline-specific differences to the approach to researching data. A biochemist may very well not wish to organize, store, and share data in the same way that an astronomer does.

Research Data Life Cycle

Logically, research data is not a static thing. All research data goes through a life cycle from the point at which it was conceptualized through its phases of use. There are various research data life cycle models that demonstrate this. Two of the more prominent examples are from DataOne and the UK Data Archive. Both of these models (and many other models) show the life cycle of research data to be a circular pattern where data moves through stages starting with creation and going through analysis and preservation to reuse. At that point, when the data is reused, the process can potentially start again when new or complementary data is created. Not all data will go through every stage in every case. Figure 10.1 shows the UK Data Archive Research Data Lifecycle and highlights the tasks involved with the preserving data stage of the life cycle.

The UK Data Archive's Research Data model has six stages. The first stage is *creating data*, in which the researcher designs her research, creates data management plans, locates existing data, collects data, and captures and creates metadata.

During the second stage, *processing data*, data is digitized, transcribed, or translated as necessary; validated and cleaned; anonymized; described; and managed and stored.

The third stage is the *analyzing data* stage, at which point data is interpreted and research outputs are produced (including author publications). During this stage data is also prepared for the next stage, preservation.

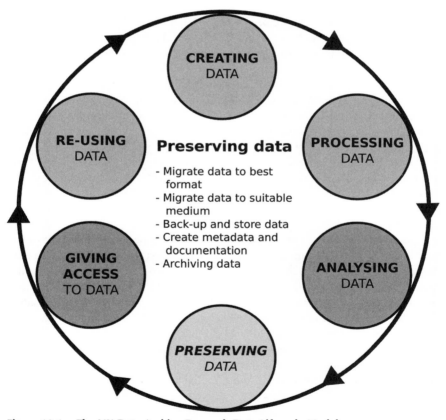

Figure 10.1.   The UK Data Archive Research Data Lifecycle Model
© 2013 Veerle Van Den Eynden, Data Life Cycle & Data Management Planning. http://ukdataservice.ac.uk/media/187718/dmplanningdm24apr2013.pdf

During the *preserving data* stage, data is migrated to the best format and to a suitable medium. Data is also backed up and stored. The metadata and documentation necessary for long-term preservation is created, and, finally, data is archived. If preservation were considered earlier in the data life cycle process, it would make preserving the data an easier undertaking at the preservation stage.

The fifth stage of the UK Data Archive Research Data Lifecycle model is *giving access to data*. During this stage, data is distributed, shared, and promoted. It is also necessary at this stage to implement any appropriate access controls and establish copyright.

The sixth stage is *reusing data*. The reuse of data may be by the original researcher or a different researcher. Reusing data may include follow-up research, new research, reviewing research, and scrutinizing findings and for educational purposes such as teaching and learning.

Provenance of Research Data

Organized access to authentic prior work is important in both the hard sciences and the social sciences. In the next chapter, chapter 11, we will discuss the situation involving preservation and access in the humanities. In the hard sciences, researchers must be able to verify and test the experiments by replicating them in their own labs.

Within scientific discourse the methodology employed in the process of generating scientific information has been traditionally called the inquiry's "provenance." This provenance is carefully recorded in lab notebooks or similar records during the inquiry and then becomes an integral element of the published results. This provenance explains where the information came from and permits replication experiments, central to scientific practice, to confirm the information's quality. Such provenance may include descriptions of equipment employed, mathematical and logical operations applied, controls, oversight operations, and any other process elements necessary to making both the inquiry and its results clear and transparent to scientific colleagues and the interested public.[6]

Access to the product of the research, the scholarly paper with its analysis of the experiment, is important but, increasingly, so is access to the raw, uninterrupted data itself as well as, potentially, the notes and information on provenance. In the social sciences, much of the same holds true. Social scientists need access to the research papers that are the end result of the research, the ultimate creation of new knowledge. They also need access to the data sets, however, not only to replicate the studies but also to be able to analyze the data in new and different ways.

Another complication of research data is that there are different types of research data that may require digital preservation and a project may have one or more of these data types. Daniel Lemire and Andre Vellino have identified three types of data that may need to be preserved: raw data, derived data, and resultant data. *Raw data* might come directly from a simulation or experiment, or it could come from legacy sources. *Derived data* is the result of processing raw data. This includes correcting errors and combining different data sets into a new data set. *Resultant data* is the final product that "might be published by the authors along with their research article."[7] While in some situations it may be tempting to preserve only the resultant data, there are at least two problems that Lemire and Vellino have identified with that approach. First, other researchers may not trust the resultant data, since they will not be able to verify it, and, secondly, "it is difficult to predict how and in what format the data might be useful to others, even with the best of intentions."[8]

All of this means that research data, whether empirical or qualitative, wherever it is being used, needs to be carefully preserved so that it can be consulted and verified into the future. To ensure future use, not only does the data need to be accurately and carefully managed and preserved so that the original data is not changed, but the origins of that data also need to be clear and the authenticity of that data demonstrated.

Big Data

What big data is and why it is important to research may depend on an individual's point of view. Big data is the rapidly growing collection of datasets that are too big to be stored, analyzed, and used in traditional ways. What separates "big data" from other data sets is its volume, velocity, and variety (the three Vs), making it particularly appealing to researchers.[9] Scientists are using big data to study a variety of topics in novel ways. Take the field of medical science, for example. The World Economic Forum reports that mobile phone data has been used to map the spread of malaria in Kenya.[10] Google search logs have enabled researchers to link drug interactions and symptoms,[11] and Kaiser Permanente, an integrated managed care consortium, foresees a day when big data from personal devices like cell phones will help monitor patients with depression, signaling the need for intervention before issues arise.[12]

All of this voluminous and varied data that has been created quickly has implications for the rest of us, too. Journalists describe the social effects of big data, saying it is "shorthand for advancing trends in technology that open the door to a new approach to understanding the world and making decisions."[13] Researchers studying sociotechnical aspects of communication may view big data as "a cultural, technological, and scholarly phenomenon that rests on the interplay of (1) Technology . . . (2) Analysis . . . [and] (3) Mythology."[14] Regardless, one thing seems to be certain: big data is a trend that is new and promising for research, and the preservation of big datasets presents new challenges for digital preservationists wishing to support these research initiatives.

In terms of curated data that was produced with the intention of being used, "the digital collections of scientific and memory institutions—many of which are already in the petabyte range—are growing larger every day."[15] Preserving big data is a big challenge, one that traditional preservation repositories are ill equipped to handle. "Diversity of data, formats, metadata, semantics, access rights, and associated computing and software tools for simulation and visualization add to the complexity and scale of the challenge" of preservation and sustainable access.[16]

One project coordinated by the Austrian Institute of Technology (AIT) is the Scalable Preservation Environments (SCAPE) project. It is designed to provide scalable preservation services.[17] As SCAPE points out, current tools break down when dealing with digital objects that are very large or complex; they also break down when faced with very large numbers of objects or heterogeneous collections. The SCAPE project seeks to remedy this and is currently working with three large-scale test beds, one of which is digital repositories of interest to the information professional community.[18]

Internet Archiving

Digital preservationists working with large research datasets and other big data projects can learn from other large-scale digital projects, such as Google Books or the Internet Archive, that also deal with similar challenges related to preserving and providing access to large volumes of digital information. Web contents, including Web pages, videos, blogs, and other somewhat ephemeral content, can contribute to the big data that is studied, especially by social sciences researchers. The Internet Archive is one institution attempting to rise to the challenge of preserving the contents of the World Wide Web for future research and study. "The Internet Archive is a 501(c)(3) nonprofit that was founded to build an Internet library. Its purposes include offering permanent access for researchers, historians, scholars, people with disabilities, and the general public to historical collections that exist in digital format."[19] Carefully chosen mirror sites, sites with all of the same content that serve as backups but also as sources, are part of the plan to make Web content accessible indefinitely.[20] Smaller-scale projects aimed at making Web content available into the future tend to be called *Web archiving* projects. In addition to Web archiving, the Internet Archive also maintains other types of content. For example, they provide storage and access to over a million videos ranging from cartoons, to out-of-copyright movies, to news broadcasts.[21] They also have a large-scale digital book and text project and provide access to live concert recordings by bands such as the Grateful Dead.[22] If a library, archive, or museum has collections that meet the guidelines for inclusion into these Internet Archive services, they may wish to include the Internet Archive as part of their digital preservation strategy.

Digital preservationists generally are not responsible for Web archiving projects as far-reaching and as ambitious as preserving the entire Web. Digital preservationists may be required, however, to provide long-term access to Web based data and information that will benefit future research. Developments in the sciences and the social sciences are contingent on researchers being able to create new knowledge and share that knowledge with other researchers; increasingly, information repositories are being recognized as an enticing way to ensure long-term access to scholarly content—including research data.

Small Data as Big Data's Counterpart

Big data receives a great deal of attention; however, most scientific research is performed on a smaller scale, and "relatively little attention is given to the data that is being generated by the majority of scientists."[23] A survey at one public research university of faculty who had, or submitted proposals for, external funding showed that almost three-quarters had research datasets of fewer than 100 MB.[24] While funding for large amounts of storage hardware is less of a challenge for small data, small data does have its own share of digital preservation challenges.

One of these challenges is that small amounts of data are less likely to be preserved to begin with. Many researchers working with small data store it on their local computer, or a departmental server at best.[25] Small data is less likely than its big brother to be in a standardized format and is more likely to be heterogeneous in nature.[26] Both of these factors make reuse and preservation more difficult. Additionally, metadata creation tools are not always common in the small data realm, so metadata cannot always be automatically created. Researchers may lack the expertise, resources, or desire to create metadata themselves. Because of the lack of metadata and the spread-out nature of small data (even when it is available online, it is often on an individual researcher's website), discovery of these datasets can prove difficult. Also, without a long-term storage plan, the datasets may change URLs or be removed from the Web completely. Academic libraries and other organizations with metadata knowledge and information repositories may be well positioned to make a lasting impact in this area, even with limited resources.

METADATA SCHEMA FOR SCIENCE DATA

As discussed in chapter 7, recording information about digital content is essential to ensuring its proper use and reuse. Technical, administrative, and descriptive metadata along with the necessary preservation data must be included in order for the digital object to be viable into the future. The following section describes a sampling of schema used in the sciences to record data and make it searchable. Although these or other schema are necessary for the description and ultimately access, they must be used in conjunction with preservation metadata to ensure long-term access.

Directory Interchange Format (DIF)[27]

The National Aeronautics and Space Administration (NASA) maintains the Global Change Master Directory (GCMD), "an extensive directory of descriptive and locational information about datasets and services relevant to global change research. . . . The GCMD includes metadata from disciplines including atmospheric science, biology, oceanography, ecology, geology, hydrology, and human dimensions of climate change."[28] The metadata schema used to encode these datasets, the Directory Interchange Format (DIF), has been in existence since 1987.[29] DIF is composed of eight required elements, eighteen highly recommended elements, and ten recommended elements (the elements being called *attributes*).[30]

The Content Standard for Digital Geospatial Metadata (CSDGM)

Related to the DIF is the Content Standard for Digital Geospatial Metadata (CSDGM). "In the United States, the Office of Management and Budget's (OMB) Circular A-16 for the improved coordination of spatial data among federal agencies led to the establishment of the Federal Geographic Data Committee (FGDC) and the FGDC Clearinghouse. The GCMD serves as NASA's FGDC Clearinghouse node for geospatial metadata. Elements of the Content Standard for Digital Geospatial Metadata (CSDGM) were incorporated in the DIF in 1994."[31] As a stand-alone schema, the CSDGM "is the current U.S. Federal Metadata standard. The FGDC originally adopted the CSDGM in 1994 and revised it in 1998."[32] As expected, this schema, along with ISO 19115, is strongly associated with geospatial metadata.

Darwin Core Schema[33]

Government is not the only group interested in scientific data and exchange. Darwin Core is maintained by a nongovernmental and not-for-profit association promoting science and education, known as the Biodiversity Information Standards (TDWG), or the Taxonomic Databases Working Group.[34] The Darwin Core standard supports two XML schemas and is intended "to provide a stable standard reference for sharing information on biological diversity."[35] "The primary purpose of Darwin Core is to create a common language for sharing biodiversity data that is complementary to and reuses metadata standards from other domains wherever possible."[36] The standard is designed to be an extension of the Dublin Core Metadata Initiative, specifically encoding information relevant to biodiversity.[37] Dublin Core (DC) Terms used in Darwin Core "may include a description and comments adapted for the biodiversity community."[38] Figure 10.2 demonstrates the diverse roots and subsequently the fields of application for the Darwin Core standard.

Core Scientific Metadata Model

The Core Scientific Metadata Model (CSMD) is a "model for the representation of scientific study metadata developed within the Science and Technology Facilities Council (STFC) to represent the data generated from scientific facilities."[39] This model is hierarchical in structure and can incorporate both studies and investigations. One of the strengths of CSMD is that it is "generic enough to apply to a variety of disciplines but also detailed enough to enable reuse and repurposing of data within and across scientific disciplines."[40]

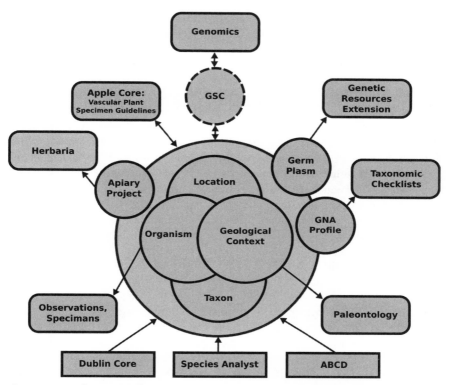

Figure 10.2.   The Scope of Darwin Core and Its Relation to Other Schema and to Relevant Domains
Image © John Wieczorek, David Bloom, Robert Guralnick, Stan Blum, Markus Döring, Renato Giovanni, Tim Robertson, and David Vieglais; used under a Creative Commons Attribution License.

Harvestable Scientific Metadata

Scientific data and datasets are resources that additionally can have metadata created for them to help ensure their authenticity and to make them discoverable and shareable. Stand-alone organizations like DataCite provide services that allow members to mint DOIs and register metadata for datasets.[41] Because they now adhere to Open Archives Initiative Protocol for Metadata Harvesting (OAI-PMH) standards, data and datasets in the DataCite Metadata Store (MDS) can be harvested and ultimately shared.[42]

OPEN DATA INITIATIVES

Sharing data, big and small, well into the future is important to furthering science. As Clifford Lynch puts it, "to enable reuse, data must be well preserved. In some cases the effects of data loss are economic, because experiments have to be rerun. In other cases, data loss represents an opportunity lost forever. Funders now rightly view data as assets that they are underwriting and so seek the greatest pay-off for their investments."[43] A series of statements and position papers supports the move to make research data open.[44] The Paris-based international Organisation for Economic Co-operation and Development's (OECD) *Principles and Guidelines for Access to Research Data from Public Funding* was published in 2007. The open principles it includes are ones of interest to us in preservation—*openness, transparency, interoperability, quality,* and *sustainability*.[45] More recently, the Toronto Statement, which was issued in 2009 in *Nature* and was a continuation of work in Bermuda in 1996, 1997, and 1998 and in Fort Lauderdale in 2003, promotes the rapid prepublication of "large reference datasets in biology and medicine that have broad utility."[46]

In some instances, the journals themselves can be the ones to require (or highly suggest) data archiving. An example is Dryad, "a nonprofit organization and an international repository of data underlying scientific and medical publications."[47] The Joint Data Archiving Policy (JDAP) is supported by a number of journals, including *Nature* and *PLOS*, although data archiving policies are not necessarily strictly adhered to at the present time.[48] The reality that researchers are not uniformly making their research data available when mandated is disappointing. Yet, unless they are experts in information management, researchers will need to seek assistance in identifying the standards and policies relating to storage and long-term access.

Also in line with this movement promoting open access, major funding agencies in the United States and around the world are starting to require researchers to document how they will store and preserve data as part of the application process. Information professionals in academic and research settings will need to be prepared to assist researchers and may find they are needed from the preliminary phases of a project through its completion.

Next, we will look at some of the requirements for preservation and access by funding agencies in the United States and move to a brief overview of additional English-speaking countries—the United Kingdom, Canada, and Australia.

The U.S. National Science Foundation

The U.S. National Science Foundation (NSF) is a federal funding organization that requires data management plans that consider topics related to digital preservation and sharing. In the NSF *Grant Proposal Guide*, a data management plan is described in order to assist researchers seeking funding to understand what is required of the process.[49] These researchers must include data management plans in their applications in order to receive funding. The data management plan should support a policy of sharing and preservation, and the guide indicates that it can include

1. the types of data, samples, physical collections, software, curriculum materials, and other materials to be produced in the course of the project

2. the standards to be used for data and metadata format and content (where existing standards are absent or deemed inadequate, this should be documented along with any proposed solutions or remedies)
3. policies for access and sharing, including provisions for appropriate protection of privacy, confidentiality, security, intellectual property, or other rights or requirements
4. policies and provisions for reuse, redistribution, and the production of derivatives, and
5. plans for archiving data, samples, and other research products and for preservation of access to them.[50]

Researchers are experts in the types of materials produced, yet the question of standards, metadata, policies, and plans for archiving and preservation may elude even the most experienced researcher.

The U.S. National Institute of Health

The U.S. National Institute of Health (NIH) also requires preservation and sharing of data created through funded research. Final research data must be shared in either a *data archive* or a *data enclave*, two common means of preserving and sharing data that might be listed in a data management plan. Data archives permit the further analysis of machine-readable data by the scientific community. Data enclaves house restricted data resources in a protected environment. Content in data enclaves is only accessed and used by authorized researchers, and precautions to keep the data safe may include not publishing it to the Internet or requiring keyed entry to the room where it is held.[51] This restricted data may be derived from research involving human subjects, especially data that includes what is known as PHI, or protected health information, as identified through the U.S. Health Insurance Portability and Accountability Act (HIPAA).[52]

Other U.S. Initiatives

The NSF and the NIH are only two among many governmental funding agencies that are requiring data sharing and preservation plans. Other U.S. funding agencies with specific data sharing policies include the U.S. Department of Education's Institute of Education Sciences (IES) and the Howard Hughes Medical Institute (HHMI). The IES requires that final research data be released in a timely fashion and in a way that is respectful of human subjects participants after the research is complete. The IES clarifies in a generic way the meaning of final research data, the kind of data that is the focus of NSF and NIH policy as well. "Final research data," it says, "does not mean summary statistics or tables but rather the factual information on which summary statistics and tables are based. For the purposes of this policy, final research data do not include laboratory notebooks, partial datasets, preliminary analyses, drafts of scientific papers, plans for future research, peer-review reports, or communications with colleagues."[53]

Final research data for the IES may be maintained by the researcher, in data archives, or in data enclaves. The HHMI funds research in the health sciences, and, for the reasons mentioned in this section, it also requires the sharing of data when a project is completed.[54]

Along with funding agencies, organizations that support scholars and research are interested in providing access to data. One example is the Interuniversity Consortium for Political and Social Research (ICPSR). The ICPSR is a consortium of institutions affiliated with the University of Michigan's Institute for Social Research. It has a mission to provide "leadership and training in data access, curation, and methods of analysis for a diverse and expanding social science research community."[55] This data, curated and made available through the ICPSR website, can be used by social sciences researchers. Researchers can also upload their data directly to the website.

ICSPR is not the only organization that works to provide access to data. There are, in general, two different types of data warehouses. *Domain specific* warehouses might include ISCPR and GenBank (a database of genetic sequences). *Integrated data* warehouses, on the other hand, "provide a uniform layer of abstraction from the data domain"[56]—like the Australian National Data Service (ANDS), the UK Data Archive, and other national initiatives around the world, for example. Digital preservationists working with scientists may wish to investigate whether any of these national or subject-specific data repositories can be effectively integrated into their workflows.

It is not only funding agencies and scholarly organizations that require access to the products of scholarly research. As mentioned above, scholarly journals may require access to raw data supporting journal articles. Other initiatives also focus on the data that is analyzed in order for these papers to be written. In early 2013 the U.S. Senate and House of Representatives began consideration of the Fair Access to Science and Technology Research Act (FASTR),[57] which, if passed, would require "the collection and depositing of research papers."[58]

English-Speaking Countries: Approaches to Open Data

In the United Kingdom, many governmental and private funding bodies are requiring that researchers make their data available. The U.K.'s Medical Research Council (MRC), for example, requires a data management plan to be submitted with applications for funding.[59] The preservation of this data, including metadata and ensured long-term access, will maximize access that will enable research opportunities.[60] The U.K.'s Biotechnology and Biological Sciences Research Council (BBSRC) also "expects research data generated as a result of BBSRC support to be made available with as few restrictions as possible in a timely and responsible manner to the scientific community for subsequent research."[61] Finally, as an example of a private-funding organization requiring that data be shared, the U.K.'s Wellcome

Trust "expects all of its funded researchers to maximise the availability of research data with as few restrictions as possible."[62] Additionally, the Research Councils UK (RCUK) requires open access to manuscripts that have been created as part of publicly funded research.[63] This is in line with the Finch Group's report promoting open access to scholarly journal articles.[64]

Elsewhere in the English-speaking world, efforts are also underway to promote open access to data. Research Data Australia is a portal providing access to research data created by Australian researchers.[65] Collections include "datasets from observations, investigations, instruments, surveys, etc., recordings, images, video, software, [and] text."[66] Research is carried out by researchers and is maintained by them, but access to their content is provided through the portal.[67] In Canada, currently, of the three major governmental funding bodies, only the Social Sciences and Humanities Research Council (SHHRC) requires that data be shared, but this is expected to change in the future.[68]

HUMAN SUBJECTS AND DATA PRESERVATION

Depending on the discipline and the approach, research can involve human participants, also known as human subjects. Human subjects are often used in medical research (including research testing new drugs, new therapies, new approaches, etc.) and the social sciences (including research that studies behaviors, attitudes, actions, etc.) to delve more deeply into a problem. The Code of Federal Regulations, Title 45, Part 46, governs the protection of human subjects in research carried out by researchers affiliated with institutions in the United States.[69]

Challenges with Preserving Human Subjects Data

The CITI (Collaborative Institutional Training Initiative) course on the use of human subjects in the social sciences recommends that data be safeguarded so as to minimize the risk of a confidentiality breach.[70] This is important because, depending on the kind of research and the funding body, the research data may need to be retained and made available. When research involves human subjects, depending on the research protocol, the data collected and preserved may need to be maintained for a certain period of time and then destroyed. Although the destruction of data is not generally a topic addressed in works on preservation, the life cycle of the material, including its required destruction, needs to be kept in mind by those managing the data.

Another aspect of maintaining data, especially when human subjects are involved, is the need for data to be kept *confidential*. According to the *IRB Guidebook*, published by the Office for Human Research Protections (OHRP), *confidentiality* "pertains to the treatment of information that an individual has disclosed in a relationship of trust and with the expectation that it will not be divulged to others without permission in ways that are inconsistent with the understanding of the original disclosure."[71] Confidentiality, therefore, must be insured when working with content that will be preserved. Strategies for safeguarding data involve a combination of common sense and tech savvy. Any one strategy might suffice, and using more than one insures a maximum of confidentiality for the data provided by subjects involved in the research. When the confidentiality of data is protected, the privacy of subjects is respected.

CONCLUSION

This chapter described some of the requirements for preservation of Content that are starting to become commonplace in the scientific and social science research disciplines. These and future developments are important for both researchers and information professionals to follow. If the current trends relating to open access, open data, and open research continue, it will become much more difficult in the future to receive funding without a well-thought-out data management plan, and digital preservationists will need to be actively involved in that planning process.

The responses to these challenges will be unique, depending on the field of study, the requirements of the funding organization, the researcher, and the resources available. As with other aspects of preservation, a one-size-fits-all solution is not possible at this time. This is particularly true with small data. In understanding some of the important elements of preserving and providing access to data and content in the hard sciences and the social sciences, information professionals can provide additional guidance to researchers throughout the process of creating and sharing new knowledge. In the next chapter, we will look at preserving digital Content in a field that has not traditionally had digital Content: the humanities.

NOTES

1. U.S. Department of Health and Human Services (HHS), "Code of Federal Regulations: §46.102 Definitions," accessed September 29, 2013, http://www.hhs.gov/ohrp/humansubjects/guidance/45cfr46.html#46.102.

2. National Institutes of Health, "NIH Data Sharing Policy and Implementation Guidance: Goals of Data Sharing," last modified March 5, 2003, http://grants.nih.gov/grants/policy/data_sharing/data_sharing_guidance.htm#goals.

3. Vannavar Bush, "As We May Think," *Atlantic Monthly* 176, no. 1 (July 1945): 101–8, http://www.theatlantic.com/magazine/archive/1945/07/as-we-may-think/303881/.

4. National Digital Stewardship Alliance. *National Agenda for Digital Stewardship 2014.* Washington, D.C.: Library of Congress, 2014,11, accessed September 29, 2013, http://www.digitalpreservation.gov/ndsa/documents/2014NationalAgenda.pdf.

5. Ibid, 12.

6. Mark Mudge, Michael Ashley, and Carla Schroer, and Cultural Heritage Imaging, "A Digital Future for Cultural Heritage," edited by A. Georgopoulos and N. Agriantonis (paper presented at Cipa 2007: Anticipating the Future of the Cultural Past, Athens, October 1–7, 2007), http://culturalheritageimaging.org/What_We_Do/Publications/cipa2007/CIPA_2007.pdf.

7. Daniel Lemire and Andre Vellino, "Extracting, Transforming and Archiving Scientific Data" (paper presented at the fourth Workshop on Very Large Digital Libraries, Berlin, September 29, 2011), http://arxiv.org/abs/1108.4041.

8. Ibid.

9. Doug Laney, "3D Data Management: Controlling Data Volume, Velocity, and Variety," META Group Application Delivery Services, file 949, February 6, 2001, (Stamford, Conn.: Meta Group, Inc., 2001), http://blogs.gartner.com/doug-laney/files/2012/01/ad949-3D-Data management-Controlling-Data-Volume-Velocity-and-Variety.pdf.

10. World Economic Forum, in collaboration with The Boston Consulting Group, "Unlocking The Values of Personal Data: From Collection to Usage," February 2013, http://www3.weforum.org/docs/WEF_IT_UnlockingValuePersonalData_CollectionUsage_Report_2013.pdf.

11. John Markoff, "Unreported Side Effects of Drugs Are Found Using Internet Search Data, Study Finds," *New York Times Online*, March 6, 2013, accessed September 29, 2013, http://www.nytimes.com/2013/03/07/science/unreported-side-effects-of-drugs-found-using-internet-data-study-finds.html.

12. Steve Lohr, "Big Data Is Opening Doors, but Maybe Too Many," *New York Times*, March 23, 2013, accessed September 29, 2013, http://www.nytimes.com/2013/03/24/technology/big-data-and-a-renewed-debate-over-privacy.html.

13. Steve Lohr, "The Age of Big Data," *New York Times*, February 13, 2012. Accessed September 29, 2013, http://www.nytimes.com/2012/02/12/sunday-review/big-datas-impact-in-the-world.html.

14. danah boyd and Kate Crawford, "Critical Questions for Big Data," *Information, Communication & Society* 15, no. 5 (2012): 663.

15. Ross King, Rainer Schmidt, Christoph Becker, and Sven Schlarb, "SCAPE: Big Data Meets Digital Preservation," *ERCIM News* 89 (April 2012): 30–31, http://ercim-news.ercim.eu/images/stories/EN89/EN89-web.pdf.

16. Kostas Glinos, "Keynote: E-infrastructures for Big Data: Opportunities and Challenges," *ERICM News* 89 (2012): 2–3, http://ercim-news.ercim.eu/images/stories/EN89/EN89-web.pdf.

17. SCAlable Preservation Environments (SCAPE), "SCAlable Preservation Environments," accessed September 29, 2013, http://www.scape-project.eu/.

18. SCAlable Preservation Environments (SCAPE), "Preservation," accessed September 29, 2013, http://www.scape-project.eu/about/preservation. For a discussion of the SCAPE project, see King et al., "SCAPE."

19. Internet Archive, "About the Internet Archive," accessed September 29, 2013, http://archive.org/about/.

20. For a discussion of the XS4ALL European mirror of the Internet Archive, see Cory Doctorow, "Welcome to the Petacentre," *Nature* 455, no. 4 (September 2008): 16–21, http://www.nature.com/news/2008/080903/full/455016a.html.

21. Internet Archive, "Movie Archive," accessed September 29, 2013, http://archive.org/details/movies/.

22. Internet Archive, "Ebook and Texts Archive," accessed September 29, 2013, http://archive.org/details/texts/; Internet Archive, "Audio Archive," accessed September 29, 2013, http://archive.org/details/audio/.

23. P. Bryan Heidorn, "Shedding Light on the Dark Data in the Long Tail of Science," *Library Trends* 57, no. 2 (2008): 280–81, doi:10.1353/lib.0.0036.

24. This study was performed in 2011 by Jim Wolf, director of Academic Computing, retired, as a special project for Binghamton University. It was reported in Edward M. Corrado, "Preservation and Research Data at Binghamton University Libraries" (presented at the University at Albany Libraries' Open Access Week, Albany, October 23, 2012), http://codabox.org/114/.

25. Ibid.

26. Dianne Dietrich, "Metadata Management in a Data Staging Repository." *Journal of Library Metadata* 10, no. 2–3 (2010): 79–98.

27. For information on additional metadata schemas, extensions, tools, and use cases for metadata used in the earth sciences, visit Digital Curation Centre (DCC), "Earth Science," accessed September 29, 2013, http://www.dcc.ac.uk/resources/subject-areas/earth-science.

28. Global Change Master Directory, "What Is the Global Change Master Directory (GCMD) and How Can It Help Me?" last modified June 2013, http://gcmd.nasa.gov/learn/faqs/about.html.

29. Global Change Master Directory, "Metadata Protocol and Standards," last modified June 2013, http://gcmd.nasa.gov/add/standards/index.html;
Lola Olsen, "What Is a DIF? A Short History of the Directory Interchange Format (DIF)," *Global Change Master Directory: Discover Earth Science Data and* Services, last modified June 2013, http://gcmd.gsfc.nasa.gov/add/difguide/whatisadif.html.

30. Global Change Master Directory, "Write a DIF (Version 6)," November 2010, http://gcmd.nasa.gov/add/difguide/WRITEADIF.pdf.

31. Olsen, "What Is a DIF?"

32. Federal Geographic Data Committee, "Geospatial Metadata Standards: The Content Standard for Digital Geospatial Metadata (CSDGM)," last modified September 6, 2012, http://www.fgdc.gov/metadata/geospatial-metadata-standards#csdgm.

33. For information on additional metadata schemas, extensions, tools, and use cases for metadata used in biological sciences, visit Digital Curation Centre, "Biology" accessed September 29, 2013, http://www.dcc.ac.uk/resources/subject-areas/biology.

34. Biodiversity Information Standards: TDWG, "About Us," last modified January 13, 2011, http://www.tdwg.org/about-tdwg/.

35. Biodiversity Information Standards: TDWG, "Darwin Core," last modified October 8, 2009, http://rs.tdwg.org/dwc/.

36. John Wieczorek, David Bloom, Robert Guralnick, Stan Blum, Markus Döring, Renato Giovanni, Tim Robertson, and David Vieglais, "Darwin Core: An Evolving Community-Developed Biodiversity Data Standard," *PLoS ONE* 7, no. 1 (2012): 2, doi:10.1371/journal.pone.0029715, http://www.plosone.org/article/info%3Adoi%2F10.1371%2Fjournal.pone.0029715.

37. Biodiversity Information Standards: TDWG, "Darwin Core."

38. Biodiversity Information Standards: TDWG, "Darwin Core Terms: A Quick Reference Guide." February 12, 2009, last modified October 26, 2011, http://rs.tdwg.org/dwc/terms/.

39. Brian Matthews, Shoaib Sufi, Damian Flannery, Laurent Lerusse, Tom Griffin, Michael Gleaves, and Kerstin Kleese, "Using a Core Scientific Metadata Model in Large-Scale

Facilities," *The International Journal of Digital Curation* 5, no. 1 (2010), http://www.ijdc.net/index.php/ijdc/article/view/149/211.

40. Lemire and Vellino, "Extracting, Transforming and Archiving," 5.

41. DataCite, "DataCite Services," accessed June 7, 2013, http://datacite.org/services.

42. Oai.datacite.org, "OAI-PMH Data Provider (Beta)," accessed June 7, 2013, http://oai.datacite.org/.

43. Clifford Lynch, "Big Data: How Do Your Data Grow?" *Nature* 455, no. 4 (2008): 28, http://www.nature.com/nature/journal/v455/n7209/pdf/455028a.pdf.

44. Wellcome Trust, "Policy on Data Management and Sharing," august 2010, http://www.wellcome.ac.uk/About-us/Policy/Policy-and-position-statements/WTX035043.htm.

45. Organisation for Economic Co-operation and Development (OECD), *OECD Principles and Guidelines for Access to Research Data from Public Funding* (Paris: OECD, 2007), http://www.oecd.org/sti/sci-tech/38500813.pdf.

46. Toronto International Data Release Workshop Authors, "Prepublication Data Sharing." *Nature* 461 (Sept. 2009): 168, doi:10.1038/461168a, http://www.nature.com/nature/journal/v461/n7261/full/461168a.html.

47. Dryad, home page, accessed March 24, 2013, http://datadryad.org/.

48. Dryad, "Joint Data Archiving Policy (JDAP)," last modified April 7, 2013, http://datadryad.org/pages/jdap;

Timothy H. Vines, Rose L. Andrew, Dan G. Bock, Michelle T. Franklin, Kimberly J. Gilbert, Nolan C. Kane, Jean-Sébastien Moore, Brook T. Moyers, Sébastien Renaut, Diana J. Rennison, Thor Veen, and Sam Yeaman, "Mandated Data Archiving Greatly Improves Access to Research Data," *The FASEB Journal* 27, no. 4 (April 2013): 1304–8, doi:10.1096/fj.12-218164. http://www.fasebj.org/content/early/2013/01/07/fj.12-218164.full.pdf.

49. National Science Foundation (NSF), *Proposal and Award Policies and Procedures Guide*, NSF 13-1, OMB Control Number: 3145-0058 (Washington, D.C.: NSF, 2012), http://www.nsf.gov/pubs/policydocs/pappguide/nsf13001/nsf13_1.pdf.

50. Ibid, II-20.

51. Institute of Education Sciences (IES), "Resources for Researchers: Data Sharing Implementation Guide," accessed September 29, 2013, http://ies.ed.gov/funding/datasharing_implementation.asp.

52. Health Insurance Portability and Protection Act (HIPPA), "HIPAA 'Protected Health Information': What Does PHI Include?" accessed September 29, 2013, http://www.hipaa.com/2009/09/hipaa-protected-health-information-what-does-phi-include/.

53. Institute of Education Sciences (IES) Centers, "Policy Statement on Data Sharing in IES Research Centers," footnote 1, accessed September 29, 2013, http://ies.ed.gov/funding/datasharing_policy.asp.

54. Howard Hughes Medical Institute (HHMI), "Research Policies: Sharing of Publication-Related Materials, Data and Software (SC-300)," accessed September 29, 2013, http://www.hhmi.org/about/research/sc_300.pdf.

55. Interuniversity Consortium for Political and Social Research (ICPSR), "About ICPSR," accessed September 29, 2013, http://www.icpsr.umich.edu/icpsrweb/content/membership/about.html.

56. Lemire and Vellino, "Extracting, Transforming and Archiving."

57. Library of Congress (LOC), "Bill Summary and Status: 113th Congress (2013–2014); S.350," accessed September 29, 2013, http://thomas.loc.gov/cgi-bin/bdquery/z?d113:s.350:; Library of Congress (LOC), "Bill Summary and Status: 113th Congress

(2013–2014); H.R.708," accessed September 29, 2013, http://thomas.loc.gov/cgi-bin/bdquery/z?d113:h.r.708:.

58. Library of Congress (LOC), "Bill Text: 113th Congress (2013–2014); S.350.IS," accessed September 29, 2013, http://thomas.loc.gov/cgi-bin/query/z?c113:S.350:.

59. Medical Research Council (MRC), "MRC Guidance in Data Management Plans," accessed September 29, 2013, http://www.mrc.ac.uk/Ourresearch/Ethicsresearchguidance/datasharing/DMPs/index.htm.

60. Medical Research Council (MRC), "Data Sharing," accessed September 29, 2013, http://www.mrc.ac.uk/Ourresearch/Ethicsresearchguidance/datasharing/index.htm.

61. Biotechnology and Biological Sciences Research Center (BBSRC), *BBSRC Data Sharing Policy, Version 1.1* (Swindon, Eng.: BBSRC, June 2010), 5, http://www.bbsrc.ac.uk/web/FILES/Policies/data-sharing-policy.pdf.

62. Wellcome Trust, "Policy on Data Management and Sharing."

63. Research Councils UK, "RCUK Policy on Open Access and Supporting Guidance," accessed September 29, 2013, http://www.rcuk.ac.uk/documents/documents/RCUKOpenAccessPolicy.pdf.

64. Working Group on Expanding Access to Published Research Findings, "Accessibility, Sustainability, Excellence: How to Expand Access to Research Publications" ["The Finch Report"], *Research Information Network*, June 2012, http://www.researchinfonet.org/wp-content/uploads/2012/06/Finch-Group-report-FINAL-VERSION.pdf.

65. http://researchdata.ands.org.au/.

66. Australia National Data Service, "Register My Data," accessed September 29, 2013, http://www.ands.org.au/services/register-my-data.html.

67. Australia National Data Service "Research Data Australia," accessed September 29, 2013, http://www.ands.org.au/guides/research-data-australia.html.

68. Pascal Calarco, personal communication, April 4, 2013.

69. U.S. Department of Health and Human Services, "§46.101 To What Does This Policy Apply?" in *Code of Federal Regulations: Title 45, Public Welfare; Part 46, Protection of Human Subjects* (Washington, D.C.: HHS, 2009), http://www.hhs.gov/ohrp/policy/ohrpregulations.pdf.

70. CITI Collaborative Institutional Training Initiative, "CITI Human Subjects Research Educational Program Information (CITI)," accessed September 29, 2013, https://www.citiprogram.org/citiinfo.asp.

71. U.S. Department of Health and Human Services (HHS): Office for Human Research Protections (OHRP), *Institutional Review Board Guidebook*, s.v. "Confidentiality," last modified 1993, http://www.hhs.gov/ohrp/archive/irb/irb_glossary.htm.

11

Preserving Humanities Content

The humanities are an integral part of what cultural heritage institutions seek to collect, organize, maintain, and make accessible. Humanities Content is not new. There are a few ways of looking at the humanities, but scholars generally agree that, at a minimum, the humanities include the study of languages and literatures, art, and philosophy, or "human constructs and concerns."[1] The study of history can also be seen as a *humanistic* study. As well, some of the social sciences, especially fields studying humans and their cultural artifacts instead of the written word, can likewise be considered the humanities. Not unlike computing, the humanities "primarily study human-created artifacts."[2] Humanists, therefore, study and analyze human-created artifacts, including the written word and visual resources, with an interest in the context in which they were created.

The digital humanities, a new field of interest to digital preservationists, take the humanities and applies computing power. A single unified definition of *digital humanities* has not yet been accepted across the board. Descriptions of the general approaches to digital humanities, however, can be found. "The Digital Humanities Manifesto, 2.0" describes the digital humanities as "an array of convergent practices that explore a universe in which: (a) print is no longer the exclusive or the normative medium . . . ; and (b) digital tools, techniques, and media have altered the production and dissemination of knowledge."[3] Similarly, from a library professional's viewpoint, "the digital humanities use information technologies like high-speed computing, textual analysis, digitization, data visualization, and geospatial mapping techniques in support of research and teaching in fields like literature, languages, history, art history, and philosophy."[4] The digital humanities combine the study of human artifacts with techniques that have emerged in the computer age. Part of the appeal of the digital humanities is the flexibility of applying technology to different humanities problems in novel ways. In some respects, though, unlike in the sciences,

197

use of digital humanities techniques are specialized; because of this the techniques have the potential to differ from researcher to researcher.[5]

Although the digital humanities are emerging as scholars adopt new methods to study problems relating to human artifacts, the digital humanities are rooted in another field, *humanities computing.*[6] According to Matthew Gold, "Father Roberto Busa, an Italian Jesuit priest, is generally credited with having founded humanities computing in 1949 when he began collaborating with IBM on a machine that could be used to create a concordance of all words ever published by Thomas Aquinas. After thirty years of work, Busa published the Index Thomisticus first in print and later on CD-ROM and the Web."[7] Computer-mediated work in the humanities is increasingly common, as evidenced by the success of formal venues for humanities scholars to convene, as well as *unconferences*, such as THATcamp,[8] to unite scholars, information professionals, technologists, and other interested parties in discussing ideas and practices relating to the digital humanities.

Gregory Crane, editor-in-chief of the Perseus Digital Library,[9] chair of the Department of Classics, and adjunct professor of Computer Science at Tufts University, has written on the impact of the digital humanities.[10] Crane sees the digital humanities as having three influences on humanities scholarship: (1) advancing established scholarship, (2) enabling new research, and (3) redefining who can contribute to scholarship.[11] For Crane, the digital humanities lower the barriers to access, permitting the involvement of a wider group of participants than ever before. This, in turn, advances the humanities in ways that were unimaginable before computers were recruited to assist in the study of human artifacts. Crane's interest in the digital humanities seems to be in line with the approach adopted by the manifesto, where the digital humanities "[recast] the scholar as curator and the curator as scholar."[12]

Yet the role of preservation is unclear in a field where computing power is intended to assist with understanding. In chapters 1 and 2 of this book we saw how digital preservation is a Management activity, envisioned by the information professional and carefully acted on in the computer environment. This computer-based approach to the study and analysis of the humanities is new and noteworthy since the humanities have traditionally been an area focusing on the analog resource, carried out via the close analysis of scholars. The addition of computers, since "they can help make generalizations about fairly large bodies of texts,"[13] permits humanists to explore even more within texts, performances, and the like, to create different output, and from that, to create new knowledge. "The challenge—and commitment—here centers on preservation and access. How do we ensure that books or images that we digitize this year will be viewable the next? What about documents created using obsolete or comparatively ancient software? Does your Archive have a WordStar or MP3 expert on staff? What about materials saved on 'the cloud' like Google documents or files on external servers or hard drives? How do we present these kinds of materials for our users and how do we make sure they don't go up in so much electronic smoke?"[14] The challenge of digital preservation is not mitigated with the simple digitization of materials that were traditionally studied as analog artifacts. Although the challenges facing digital preservation in the humanities are not entirely unique, they are different enough to warrant a chapter to investigate them in more detail. This chapter on digital preservation in the digital humanities begins with a look at digital humanities resources, then examines work being done to preserve texts and visual resources. Finally, we conclude with a look at how preservation will permit sharing in the digital humanities into the future.

COMPUTERIZING THE HUMANITIES

A number of groups have recently been interested in supporting humanists in their efforts to create new humanities knowledge through the use of computer-based techniques. Two recent examples are DARIAH and Project Bamboo. DARIAH (Digital Research Infrastructure for the Arts and Humanities[15]) is a project from the European Union with the goal to "create a sound and solid infrastructure to ensure the long-term stability of digital assets, as well as the development of a wide range of thus-far unanticipated services to carry out research on these assets."[16] DARIAH is designed to support the digital humanities in Europe but will surely be of interest to digital preservationists wishing to learn more about the digital humanities from an information point of view. Project Bamboo,[17] a digital humanities initiative that was active from 2008 to 2012, was "led by University of California–Berkeley and includ[ed] Australian National University, Indiana University, Northwestern University, Tufts University, University of Chicago, University of Illinois at Urbana-Champaign, University of Maryland, University of Oxford, and University of Wisconsin–Madison."[18] Like DARIAH, Project Bamboo was not intended specifically to support preservation. Instead, it was meant to be an overall "cyberinfrastructure initiative." Funded through the Andrew W. Mellon Foundation, Project Bamboo held a series of workshops, developed demonstrators to support the workshop discussions, and ultimately brought together ten partner institutions to work on big-picture digital humanities issues, "not trying to create a single tool or to solve a single problem."[19] Although the project is no longer active, the software it created has been made available at SourceForge,[20] and its Web pages have been archived and remain accessible.

Big Data in the Digital Humanities

Although big data has been getting a lot of attention in the sciences, it is also a major component of the digital humanities movement. "Big data science emerges as a new paradigm for scientific discovery that reflects the increasing value of observational, experimental, and computer-generated data in virtually all domains, from physics to the humanities and social sciences."[21] The variety of kinds of research in the digital humanities all tend to focus on work that could not be done were it not for the use of computing technology and computing power. Investigating the use of certain words, over time, in published books that have been scanned as part of the Google Books project would not have been possible before scanning and search techniques were perfected on a large scale. And before the computer age analyzing recorded sounds, images, or ephemera like Web pages would also not have been possible in the way that the digital humanities now permit.

FUNDING FOR THE DIGITAL HUMANITIES

In the United States, it is the National Endowment for the Humanities (NEH) that has led the way in providing funding for work in the digital humanities. The NEH created an Office for Digital Humanities in 2008.[22] The NEH has been active in finding funding partners to support the digital humanities as well. "The NEH has also partnered with the National Science Foundation (NSF), the Social Science and Humanities Research Council (SSHRC) in Canada, the Institute of Museum and Library Services (IMLS), Jisc (formerly known as JISC, the Joint Information Systems Committee) in the U.K., and the Netherlands Organisation for Scientific Research to organize the 'Digging into Data Challenge.'"[23] Because funds are supplied by agencies that require data be preserved, digital humanities work funded through these U.S. bodies will be subject to the requirements for data preservation described in chapter 10's section on research data.

Digital humanities projects need ongoing support and funding as much as any other project requiring the use of long-term digital repositories. One long-term humanities project, the Linguistic Atlas Project (LAP), was begun in 1929. It first became a digital humanities project when it was converted to digital in 1980. Because of its longevity, the project had to "go through several generations of programming and computer tools," eventually leaving the principle investigator in a situation where he had to "spend more and more time soliciting grant funding just to keep the operation alive."[24] LAP found an electronic home in the university library, but such luck may not be likely for all digital humanities projects that begin with a bit of funding but aren't, ultimately, able to secure long-term funding and support. Securing funding in the digital humanities is just as important for long-term preservation as in any other discipline. With digital humanities, the emphasis can sometimes be placed on the immediate deliverable, but researchers need the help of the digital preservationists from the very beginning to envision ways to make the project sustainable. For more discussion about sustainability, see chapter 5.

HUMANITIES SOURCES

Work in the digital humanities can easily include the close study of texts that have been digitized and made searchable. Some projects are done through academic institutions, such as the Roman de la Rose project. "The well-known Roman de la Rose project started in 1996 when a Johns Hopkins professor approached the university library about digitizing French medieval manuscripts to use in teaching. Fifteen years later, the project has grown in scope to include libraries in the [United States], [United Kingdom], Japan, and France and a team of librarians, programmer-analysts, and specialists in medieval art and literature."[25] Most publicly available projects featuring access to digitized texts involve only works that are out of copyright. For example, NINES (Networked Infrastructure for Nineteenth-Century Electronic Scholarship) attempts to assist scholars and students in using primary source documents from the nineteenth century in a twenty-first-century computerized environment.[26] These documents are considered to be in the public domain around the world and therefore are no longer subject to national copyright laws protecting intellectual property.

Metadata Schema for Published Texts

As with any other digital preservation project, metadata to record information about content is key in preserving digital humanities content.[27] In order to describe the published books often used in text-based digital humanities projects, two related metadata encoding standards should be mentioned: MARC and MODS. Although related, both serve a place in the digital preservation landscape by providing description and access in the electronic environment. Both also can be used in conjunction with the content schema used in libraries, Resource Description and Access (RDA), the 2013 replacement to the long-used Anglo-American Cataloguing Rules, 2nd ed. (AACR2).

MAchine-Readable Cataloging (MARC)

MAchine-Readable Cataloging (MARC) was first created by the Library of Congress in the late 1960s and has been used ever since for the encoding of metadata about published texts and other resources. MARC is currently used to encode surrogates in integrated library systems (ILSs). Because the origins of MARC go back many decades, the format of MARC records is not ideal for today's computers and programming languages. For this reason, the Library of Congress developed the MARCXML framework in 2002, which enables the use of MARC data in an XML environment. MARC has been marked for replacement by the BIBFRAME (Bibliographic Framework) standard, which is currently under development, in the future.

Metadata Object Description Schema (MODS)

In a general statement to be used in the formulation of future enhancements, the Library of Congress gives the following general description of the Metadata Object

Description Schema (MODS): "an XML schema and guidelines for encoding a resource description[, MODS] supports discovery and management of resources, and
access to them, as well as exchange and management of encoded descriptions."[28] Unlike MARC, MODS was meant to work "with other XML standards/initiatives"[29];
currently, it is in version 3.5, which was released in July 2013.[30] Because MODS
grew out of MARC,[31] it is also related to MARCXML and is perhaps best used to
provide descriptive metadata for published resources that are text-based or even
audio-visual in nature.

Metadata Schema for Digital Texts

Digital texts used in the digital humanities are generally unpublished manuscripts
from archives or special collections. Archival standards for access may include the
schema used by the library community to catalog published books (including RDA/
AACR2 and MARC). To provide access to digitized texts, the Dublin Core Metadata
Element Set (DCMES) (see chapter 7 on Metadata for digital preservation) might be
used with DACS (Describing Archives: A Content Standard) Schema. DACS, maintained by the Society of American Archivists (SAA), Describing Archives: A Content
Standard (DACS), "is an output-neutral set of rules for describing archives, personal
papers, and manuscript collections and can be applied to all material types."[32] As
well, the two schema described below may be used to mark up texts (TEI) or to
encode the finding aids used in the archives (EAD).

Text Encoding Initiative (TEI)

TEI is a "standard for the representation of texts in digital form" developed and
maintained by the TEI Consortium.[33] Like the other schema in use in digital libraries, TEI is a very powerful mark-up language used to encode electronic versions of
texts including prose and poetry, manuscripts and publications, and correspondences
and treatises "such as novels, plays, and poetry, primarily to support research in the
humanities. In addition to specifying how to encode the text of a work, the *TEI
Guidelines for Electronic Text Encoding and Interchange* also specify a header portion,
embedded in the resource, that consists of metadata about the work."[34] Indeed, for
some, the header may be the part of the TEI file that they have heard about, since
this is where additional information is stored, including descriptive metadata from
additional metadata standards. TEI Lite is a version of TEI used to communicate
with vendors and will not, in most likelihood, be the version of TEI that a digital
preservation system will adopt. TEI is increasingly where digital humanities work is
occurring. However, there is no one standard, monolithic TEI in use. Instead, there
are many individual projects working under the umbrella term. For librarians and
archivists involved in digital preservation, managing the many different implementations of TEI may become a real challenge in the future.

Encoded Archival Description (EAD)

The EAD 2002 standard's Document Type Definition (DTD) is endorsed by the Society of American Archivists (SAA) for the encoding of finding aids; the SAA is the maintenance agency for the EAD DTD along with the Library of Congress.[35] EAD is a powerful XML mark-up language for encoding finding aids. "Finding aids may vary somewhat in style, their common purpose is to provide detailed description of the content and intellectual organization of collections of archival materials. EAD allows the standardization of collection information in finding aids within and across repositories."[36] Primarily, discussions about EAD focus on the DTD, but there is an EAD Schema as well.[37] A revision to EAD began in October 2010.[38] A beta release of the revise schema was released for comment in August 2013 and the final EAD schema revision is expected to released in May 2014.[39]

Metadata Schema for Encoding Visual Resources: Museum Artifacts

Searching for information on digital preservation in the humanities can be frustrating: unfortunately, the uninitiated seem to think that digitization *is* preservation! To these people, having a digital copy equates to a step in the preservation process. Clearly, such misguided humanists and technologists need to refer to chapter 1 of this book for a discussion about why this digitization is a good start but cannot be confused with digital preservation!

Perhaps the most exciting thing to happen to digital museum content in recent years is the three-dimensional rendering of objects and artifacts. For example, in 1966 Donatello's 1455 wooden sculpture, *Maddalena*, was damaged in a Florentine flood. By 2003 researchers were able to render a three-dimensional version largely using photographs in a technique called photogrammetry. This along with the use of scanning allowed the researchers to avoid creating contact between the exploring sensor and the damaged statue. As a result, conservationists were able successively to restore the damaged sculpture.[40] Now, however, the question remains as to how such three-dimensional renderings can be preserved for the use and enjoyment of future generations. Digital preservation in the past could include printouts of digitized content as a method of preservation, but with the increasing sophistication of digital content to be preserved new methods will need to be explored.[41]

The creation of digital files to support work with 2- and 3-D artifacts is a logical progression of steps in the sharing of and access to digitized versions for instance.[42] This is especially true when access to the original is not possible for reasons of the original's fragility or geographic location relative to the humanist who would like to study it. As we saw in chapter 7, it is necessary for preservation metadata to accompany digitized content in order for that content to be findable and ultimately usable. The following schema are used to record information about two-dimensional works of art in digital repositories and preservation repositories alike.

As with text-based resources, visual resources must first be described and encoded in order to be retrieved. Below, three encoding schemas are described that are used in the encoding of visual resources, such as resources held in museums or other cultural-heritage institutions. As the Canadian Heritage Information Network (CHIN) states in its best practices documentation for digital preservation in museums, "for museums, having sound policy that maintains human accessibility to the digital objects is critical. The preservation of digital cultural objects will ultimately be found in the overall commitment to preserve our society's culture and heritage regardless of technical issues."[43] The metadata that should be included in museum digital preservation efforts should adhere to global standards unless there is a "compelling reason to create a local standard."[44] Below, we discuss three popular metadata schema with global buy-in that are used in recoding information specific to visual resources: CDWA, VRA Core, and MIX.

Categories for the Description of Works of Art (CDWA) Schema

Categories for the Description of Works of Art (CDWA) is maintained by the Getty Museum. According to them, the CDWA articulates a framework "for describing and accessing information about works of art, architecture, other material culture, groups and collections of works, and related images." [45] Much bigger than the Dublin Core Metadata Element Set, CDWA has a total of 532 categories and subcategories with some elements from some of the categories said to be "core." For example, for description of objects, core categories are the following: catalog level, object/work type, classification term, title or name, measurements description, materials and techniques description, creator description, creator identity, creator role, creation date, earliest date, latest date, subject matter, current location repository name/geographic location, and current repository numbers. Marcia Lei Zeng and Jian Qin consider CDWA more a framework than a set of elements.[46] CDWA Lite "is an XML schema to describe core records for works of art and material culture based on the Categories for the Description of Works of Art (CDWA) and Cataloging Cultural Objects: A Guide to Describing Cultural Works and Their Images (CCO)."[47] Maintained by the Visual Resources Association (VRA), "'Cataloging Cultural Objects: A Guide to Describing Cultural Works and Their Images (CCO)' is a manual for describing, documenting, and cataloging cultural works and their visual surrogates."[48] CCO is, therefore, a data content standard for the cultural heritage community that is encoded in CDWA metadata records.

VRA Core Schema

Not unlike CCO, the VRA Core is maintained by the Visual Resources Association (VRA).[49] The VRA was founded by slide librarians, and the encoding schema VRA Core was also developed by slide librarians. VRA Core is currently in version 4.0. "The VRA Core is a data standard for the description of works of visual culture as well as the images that document them. The standard is hosted by the Network Development and MARC Standards Office of the Library of Congress (LOC) in partnership with the Visual Resources Association."[50] As with other metadata schemas described here, VRA Core 4.0 is composed of elements, subelements, and attributes; not all elements must be used in a given record, and elements are repeatable.

One of the key aspects of VRA Core is that the VRA Data Standards Committee has continued to follow the 1:1 principle—that is, "only one object or resource may be described within a single metadata element record."[51] This is especially important in instances where multiple versions of a file may be housed in a repository: one file, for example, as a lossless preservation copy, one as a Web-ready but lossy file that is smaller, and one as a thumbnail. Institutions are able to define levels of description locally, giving them a good deal of flexibility in deciding which levels of description to use and how labor-intensive to make the metadata creation process. Because of this built-in flexibility, a VRA Core 4 Lite is not needed.[52]

NISO Metadata for Images in XML (MIX) Schema

The NISO standard, *Data Dictionary: Technical Metadata for Digital Still Images* (ANSI/NISO Z39.87-2006[53]) is known among information professionals as the NISO Metadata for Images in XML (MIX) schema.[54] The abstract to the data dictionary explains that this standard, an XML schema, "defines a set of metadata elements for raster digital images to enable users to develop, exchange, and interpret digital image files."[55] Currently in version 2.0, "MIX is maintained for NISO by the Network Development and MARC Standards Office of the Library of Congress with input from users."[56]

Metadata Schema for Encoding Video and Sound

Video and sound files may be used in a number of cultural heritage institutions to support digital humanities work. In libraries, videos may be published items to be consulted and studied, on par with a book or a journal article. In archives and in museums, video and sound files may be carefully curated and documented unpublished or published recordings. In libraries, metadata schema used to describe and encode video files, including streaming video, are identical to the ones used to for other library resources: MARC and RDA/AACR2. Other communities, however, have created more specialized schemas to deal with audio-visual files. One example is the PBCore schema, described below.

PBCore Schema

The Public Broadcasting Metadata Dictionary Project's schema, PBCore, is designed to describe digital and analog media and is used by public broadcasting companies, especially to provide access to digital content from their websites.

Currently in its second version, PBCore is an XML schema.[57] A user guide with links to PBCore training documentation, mappings and crosswalks, and other useful resources is available online.[58] Although more affiliated with recording descriptive metadata than with supporting preservation, PBCore provides valuable metadata for search and retrieval. Local PBS stations tend to use PBCore to encode video files of programs for organization and retrieval in their digital library systems.

CONCLUSION

Because of digital humanities' focus away from the study of analog texts and audio-visual resources and its requisite move to focus on the digital, the question of preservation of that created digital data looms large. As with other kinds of digital preservation initiatives, Management is key to a project's success. In this chapter we have explored the meaning of the digital humanities, what data is like in the digital humanities, and institutions supporting digital humanities research. Then, in the second part of the chapter we explored a number of specifics relating to metadata supporting digital humanities work, with considerations for digital preservation as part of the overarching conversation about providing long-term access and use of digital humanities resources. Although there are certainly other kinds of digital Content housed in digital preservation systems beyond scientific research and digital humanities research, this part on Content chose to focus two chapters on scientific research and digital humanities research because of the particular challenges they pose. We hope that this discussion will help in thinking about the specifics of digitally preserving Content that may not be part of the traditional collections housed in an Archive.

NOTES

1. Merriam-Webster Dictionary, s.v. "Humanity," accessed May 12, 2013, http://www.merriam-webster.com/dictionary/humanity.

2. Paul S. Rosenbloom, "Towards a Conceptual Framework for the Digital Humanities," *Digital Humanities Quarterly* 6, no. 2 (2012): para. 12, http://www.digitalhumanities.org/dhq/vol/6/2/000127/000127.html. In this same section, Rosenbloom also references and cites Herbert A. Simon as being relevant to the question of defining the humanities in relationship to computing: Herbert A. Simon, *The Sciences of the Artificial* (Cambridge: MIT Press, 1969).

3. Humanities Blast: Engaged Digital Humanities Scholarship, "The Digital Humanities Manifesto 2.0," 2, accessed May 1, 2013, http://www.humanitiesblast.com/manifesto/Manifesto_V2.pdf.

4. Geoffrey Little, "We Are All Digital Humanists Now," *The Journal of Academic Librarianship* 37, no. 4 (2011): 352, doi:10.1016/j.acalib.2011.04.023.

5. Laurent Romary, "Data Management in the Humanities," *ERCIM News* 89 (April 2012): 14, http://ercim-news.ercim.eu/images/stories/EN89/EN89-web.pdf. Specifically, Ro-

mary states that "there is little notion of data centre in the humanities, since data production and enrichment are anchored on the individuals performing research."

6. Jennifer L. Adams and Kevin B. Gunn, "Keeping Up with . . . Digital Humanities," *Keeping Up With* (April 2013), Association of College and Research Libraries, accessed May 12, 2013, http://www.ala.org/acrl/publications/keeping_up_with/digital_humanities. For example, in their introduction Adams and Gunn describe the digital humanities as an "emerging, interdisciplinary movement."

7. Matthew K. Gold, "The Digital Humanities Moment," in *Debates in the Digital Humanities*, edited by Matthew K. Gold, (Minneapolis: University of Minnesota Press, 2012), xiv, note 1. A digital edition is also available online at http://dhdebates.gc.cuny.edu/debates/text/2.

8. The Humanities and Technology Camp, http://thatcamp.org/.

9. http://www.perseus.tufts.edu/hopper/.

10. Gregory Crane's curriculum vitae is posted to the Perseus Digital Library Project website at http://www.perseus.tufts.edu/~gcrane/grc.cv.pdf.

11. Gregory Crane, "Give Us Editors! Re-inventing the Edition and Rethinking the Humanities," *Connexions*, last modified by Ben Allen on May 14, 2010, http://cnx.org/content/m34316/1.2/.

12. Humanities Blast, "The Digital Humanities Manifesto 2.0," 2.

13. Donald Ross Jr., "Computer-Aided Study of Literary Language," *Computer* 11, no. 8 (Aug. 1978): 32.

14. Little, "We Are All Digital Humanists Now," 352–53.

15. http://www.dariah.eu/.

16. Romary, "Data Management in the Humanities," 14.

17. Archived at http://www.projectbamboo.org/.

18. Emma Millon, "Project Bamboo: Building Shared Infrastructure for Humanities Research," *Blog of the Maryland Institute for Technology in the Humanities*, July 1, 2011, http://mith.umd.edu/project-bamboo-building-shared-infrastructure-for-humanities-research/.

19. University of California–Berkeley and University of Chicago, "Bamboo Planning Project: Final Report to the Andrew W. Mellon Foundation," "Challenges Met, Challenges Remaining," 6, December 21, 2010, https://googledrive.com/host/0B3zU098zQ8VMc2xfMUJZaWxXNWs/wp-content/uploads/Project-Bamboo-Planning-Project-Final-Report.pdf.

20. http://sourceforge.net/.

21. Kostas Glinos, "Keynote: E-infrastructures for Big Data: Opportunities and Challenges," *ERICM News* 89 (2012): 2–3, http://ercim-news.ercim.eu/images/stories/EN89/EN89-web.pdf.

22. Little, "We Are All Digital Humanists Now," 352.

23. Ibid.

24. William A. Kretzschmar and William Gray Potter, "Library Collaboration with Large Digital Humanities Projects," *Literary and Linguistic Computing* 25 no. 4 (Sept. 2010): 440, doi:10.1093/llc/fqq022.

25. Little, "We Are All Digital Humanists Now," 353.

26. NINES, "What Is NINES?," accessed May 12, 2013, http://www.nines.org/about/what-is-nines/.

27. For information on additional metadata schemas, extensions, tools, and use cases for metadata used in the social sciences and humanities, visit the Digital Curation Centre

(DCC)'s "Social Science and Humanities" page at http://www.dcc.ac.uk/resources/subject-areas/social-science-humanities.

28. Library of Congress (LOC), "Design Principles for Enhancements to MODS and MADS," September 2009; last modified October 18, 2010, http://www.loc.gov/standards/mods/design-principles-mods-mads.html.

29. Rebecca Guenther, "The Metadata Object Description Schema (MODS)," slide 19, (PowerPoint presented at the NISO Metadata Workshop, Washington, D.C., May 20, 2004), www.loc.gov/standards/mods/presentations/niso-mods.ppt.

30. Library of Congress (LOC), "MODS: Metadata Object Description Schema," accessed September 29, 2013, http://www.loc.gov/standards/mods/.

31. Guenther, "The Metadata Object Description Schema (MODS)," slide 19.

32. Society of American Archivists, "Describing Archives: A Content Standard (DACS)," accessed September 29, 2013, http://www.archivists.org/governance/standards/dacs.asp.

33. Text Encoding Initiative (TEI), "TEI: Text Encoding Initiative," accessed September 29, 2013. http://www.tei-c.org/index.xml.

34. National Information Standards Organization (NISO), *Understanding Metadata* (Bethesda, Md.: NISO Press, 2004), 4, http://www.niso.org/publications/press/UnderstandingMetadata.pdf.

35. Library of Congress (LOC), "Development of the Encoded Archival Description DTD," last revised December 2002, http://www.loc.gov/ead/eaddev.html; Society of American Archivists, "Encoded Archival Description (EAD) Roundtable," accessed September 29, 2013, http://www2.archivists.org/groups/encoded-archival-description-ead-roundtable; and Library of Congress (LOC), "Other Web Sites Related to EAD," accessed September 29, 2013, http://www.loc.gov/ead/eadother.html.

36. Library of Congress (LOC), "About EAD," last modified July 11, 2012, http://www.loc.gov/ead/eadabout.html.

37. Library of Congress (LOC), "EAD 2002 Schema," last modified July 17, 2012, http://www.loc.gov/ead/eadschema.html.

38. Library of Congress (LOC), "EAD Revision Under Way," last modified November 8, 2013, http://www.loc.gov/ead/eadrevision.html.

39. Society of American Archivists (SAA), "EAD Revision," accessed January 1, 2014, http://www2.archivists.org/groups/technical-subcommittee-on-encoded-archival-description-ead/ead-revision.

40. Gabriele Guidi, J.-Angelo Beraldin, and Carlo Atzeni, "High-Accuracy 3-D Modeling of Cultural Heritage: The Digitizing of Donatello's 'Maddalena,'" *IEEE Transactions on Image Processing* 13, no. 3 (March 2004): 370–80, doi:10.1109/TIP.2003.822592.

41. Julie Doyle, Herna Viktor, and Eric Paquet, "Long-Term Digital Preservation: Preserving Authenticity and Usability of 3-D Data," *International Journal on Digital Libraries* 10 (2009): 33–47.

42. Fr. Michael Suarez, director of the Rare Book School, amply made this point in a presentation at Washington University in St. Louis. Michael Suarez, "Rare Books in a Digital World," (paper presented at Washington University, St. Louis, February 16, 2012). Fr. Suarez showed different digitizations of the same painting where, in each instance, the color, shading, and dimensions were different.

43. CHIN's Professional Exchange, "Recommendations for Museums," "Conclusion," last modified February 15, 2013, http://www.pro.rcip-chin.gc.ca/contenu_numerique-digital_content/preservation_numerique-digital_preservation/recommand-recommend-eng.jsp.

44. CHIN's Professional Exchange, "Checklist for Creating a Preservation Policy," "Metadata," last modified February 2, 2013, http://www.pro.rcip-chin.gc.ca/contenu_numerique -digital_content/preservation_numerique-digital_preservation/annexeA-appendixA-eng.jsp.

45. J. Paul Getty Trust, "Categories for the Description of Works of Art: Introduction," last modified March 11, 2009, http://www.getty.edu/research/publications/electronic_publi cations/cdwa/introduction.html.

46. Marcia Lei Zeng and Jian Qin, *Metadata* (New York: Neal-Schuman, 2008), 33.

47. J. Paul Getty Trust, "Categories for the Description of Works of Art: CDWA Lite," last modified February 7, 2011, http://www.getty.edu/research/publications/electronic_publica tions/cdwa/cdwalite.html.

48. Cataloging Cultural Objects, "Brochure," accessed September 29, 2013, http://www .vraweb.org/ccoweb/cco/about.html.

49. VRA Core, "VRA Core Support Pages," accessed September 29, 2013, http://www .vraweb.org/projects/vracore4/.

50. Library of Congress (LOC), "VRA CORE Schemas and Documentation," last modi- fied April 16, 2012, http://www.loc.gov/standards/vracore/.

51. Library of Congress (LOC), "VRA Core 4.0," "Introduction," 1, March 9, 2007, http://www.loc.gov/standards/vracore/VRA_Core4_Intro.pdf.

52. VRA Core, "Frequently Asked Questions," accessed September 29, 2013, http://www .vraweb.org/projects/vracore4/vracore_faq.html.

53. National Information Standards Organization (NISO), *Data Dictionary: Technical Metadata for Digital Still Images* (Bethesda, Md.: NISO Press, 2006), http://www.niso.org/ kst/reports/standards/kfile_download?id%3Austring%3Aiso-8859-1=Z39-87-2006.pdf&pt =RkGKiXzW643YeUaYUqZ1BFwDhIG4-24RJbcZBWg8uE4vWdpZsJDs4RjLz0t90_d5_ ymGsj_IKVaGZww13HuDlSn6cvwjex0ejiIKSaTYlErPbfamndQa6zkS6rLL3oIr.

54. Library of Congress (LOC), "MIX," accessed September 29, 2013, http://www.loc .gov/standards/mix/.

55. NISO, *Data Dictionary*, i.

56. LOC, "MIX."

57. PBCore, "Schema," accessed September 29, 2013, http://www.pbcore.org/schema/.

58. PBCore, "User Guide to PBCore Public Broadcasting Metadata Dictionary," accessed September 29, 2013, http://pbcore.org/PBCore/UserGuide.html.

12

Conclusion

In many ways, digital preservation is a new frontier in access that is both exciting and daunting. Digital preservation allows information professionals and those working in cultural heritage institutions to preserve, for the long term, content that otherwise, if not cared for, would unquestionably be lost. We have all had experiences where digital content that we wanted to save for personal use has not been retrievable. This can happen for a variety of reasons: the e-mail being sought was accidently deleted, one specific digital photo from vacation was not adequately tagged and is indistinguishable from legions of nearly identical photos, the DVD got jammed in the machine and broke, the hard drive crashed, etc. It is heartbreaking when personal digital content is lost. Put in perspective, though, the loss of a personal item is not as serious as the loss of a carefully curated digital artifact that is part of a unique collection of interest to a designated group of stakeholders. Institutions simply cannot risk loss of digital content over time, and digital preservationists must systematically take steps to collect, organize, maintain, and provide appropriate access to digital objects in a way that is rational, responsible, and well documented.

As we have seen, according to the Digital Preservation Triad, digital preservation requires three simultaneous foci for an initiative to be successful: management aspects that pertain to policy, resources, and organizational structures; technological aspects that support the long-term access to the digital objects themselves; and the content of the digital preservation system itself. Not a hierarchy, this Triad requires that each area be present equally, and, as we have seen, all areas are fundamentally interrelated. We cannot preserve in a digital preservation system if there is no content. Likewise, in order to have sound digital preservation systems we need to understand and respect the technology and the practices and standards of the information and cultural heritage communities. Finally, there will be no one to collect and organize content if there is no overarching context in which to work, that of the digital preservation initiative that is rigorously thought-out, managed, and documented by information professionals with specialized knowledge and experience in the field.

We hope that in reading this book readers will be comfortable with all three areas of the Digital Preservation Triad and will understand their importance and their interrelation. As digital preservationists continue on their journey, they are welcome to examine the resources that are presented in the appendix, pursue additional educational opportunities mentioned in chapter 4, and examine more closely the resources that were consulted in writing this book by choosing relevant readings from the bibliography. Indeed, it is our hope that this book will not be a stopping point in readers' study of digital preservation but, rather, a systematic and foundational cornerstone to thinking about the many complex and interrelated aspects of digital preservation that will help anchor readers into the future.

Appendix A

Select Resources in Support of Digital Preservation

The following is an incomplete list of organizations, reports, Web resources, initiatives, and events that may be helpful to digital preservationists working in LAM institutions.

SELECTED DIGITAL PRESERVATION ORGANIZATIONS (ALPHABETICAL)

Alliance for Permanent Access. http://www.alliancepermanentaccess.org/.
> Primarily working to support access to science-related content in Europe, the alliance publishes reports and sponsors events that will be of interest to digital preservationists around the world.

Digital Curation Centre (DCC). http://www.dcc.ac.uk/.
> U.K.–based group supporting digital preservation, especially in the sciences. The DCC sponsors an international conference, hosts training, and makes available a wealth of resources through its website.

Digital Preservation Coalition. http://www.dpconline.org/.
> Supports member organizations in digital preservation with a primary focus on U.K. institutions. A series of publications of interest to digital preservationists worldwide has been posted to their Web site.

Digital Preservation Europe (DPE). http://www.digitalpreservationeurope.eu/.
> Fosters collaboration and synergies between various existing European national initiatives.

Digital Preservation Network. http://www.dpn.org/.
> Launched early in 2012 with over fifty members and an intent to enable "higher education to own, maintain, and control the scholarly record throughout time."[1]

International Council of Museums (ICOM), CIDOC Digital Preservation Working Group. http://network.icom.museum/cidoc/working-groups/digital preservation/.
> Inactive since 2006, this group may yet provide good information for museum professionals on digital preservation in the museum context.

International Internet Preservation Consortium (IIPC). http://netpreserve.org/.
> Membership-based group supporting the preservation of Web resources or, as they term it, *web archiving*. IIPC supports the tools that have become the standards for Web capture around the world.

Library of Congress's Digital Preservation. http://www.digitalpreservation.gov/.
> The online home of the National Digital Stewardship Alliance, Digital Preservation Outreach and Education, and the National Digital Information Infrastructure and Preservation Program, with a variety of online resources available.

SPRUCE Project (Sustainable PReservation Using Community Engagement). http://www.dpconline.org/advocacy/spruce/.
> A two-year Jisc–funded partnership between the University of Leeds, the British Library, the Digital Preservation Coalition, the London School of Economics, and the Open Planets Foundation that aims to foster a vibrant and self-supporting community of digital preservation practitioners and developers via a mixture of online interaction and face-to-face events.

TIMBUS Project (Timeless Business Process and Services). http://timbusproject.net/.
> The European Union–funded TIMBUS Project focuses on resilient business processes. It plans to deliver activities, process, and tools that ensure continued access and services to produce the context within which information can be accessed, properly rendered, validated, and transformed into knowledge. The TIMBUS project believes this approach extends traditional digital preservation approaches by introducing the need to analyze and sustain accessibility to business processes and supporting services.

SELECTED DIGITAL PRESERVATION CONSORTIUM/GROUP INITIATIVES

Data Preservation (alphabetical)

Australian Data Archive (ADA). http://www.ada.edu.au/.
> A national service for the collection and preservation of digital research data. ADA makes these data available to academic researchers for secondary analysis and other purposes.

Data Archiving and Networked Services (DANS). http://www.dans.knaw.nl/en.
> Based in the Netherlands, promotes sustained access to digital research data. For this purpose, DANS encourages researchers to archive and reuse data in a sustained manner. DANS was the original developer of the Data Seal of Approval.

Data Preservation Alliance for the Social Sciences (Data-PASS). http://www.data pass.org/.

A voluntary partnership of organizations created to archive, catalog, and preserve data used for social science research. Data-PASS uses the Lots of Copies Keeps Stuff Safe (LOCKSS) open source software program (see below for more information about LOCKSS).

Inter university Consortium for Political and Social Research (ICPSR). http://www .icpsr.umich.edu.

Seeks to process, preserve, and disseminate data and documents created by researchers, government entities, and research agencies in the social sciences. ICPSR has received the Data Seal of Approval.

Lots of Copies Keeps Stuff Safe (LOCKSS) Networks. http://www.lockss.org/.

An open source program designed by libraries to duplicate content automatically between participants for preservation purposes. Libraries can join various public and private LOCKSS networks or can start their own. Three prominent LOCKSS implementations are listed below (with lists of other networks and access to software available on the LOCKSS website).

- Global LOCKSS Network (GLN). http://www.lockss.org/community/ publishers-titles-gln/.

  Libraries participating in GLN are building and preserving collections of open-access titles and e-journals and e-books that they subscribe. GLN includes more than 10,000 e-journal titles from over 500 publishers.

- Controlled LOCKSS (CLOCKSS). http://www.clockss.org/.

  A not-for-profit joint venture between academic publishers and research libraries whose mission is to build a sustainable, geographically distributed dark archive with which to ensure the long-term survival of Web-based scholarly publications for the benefit of the greater global research community.

- MetaArchive Cooperative. http://www.metaarchive.org/.

  A community-owned, community-led initiative comprised of libraries, archives, and other digital memory organization that collaborate to preserve very high-value locally created digital materials. MetaArchive is the largest Private LOCKSS Network implementation.

UK Data Archive. http://data-archive.ac.uk/.

Acquires, curates, and provides access to social and economic data. It is the U.K.'s largest collection of digital data in the disciplines it covers.

Other Initiatives (alphabetical)

Chronopolis. http://chronopolis.sdsc.edu/.

This digital preservation network provides services for the long-term preservation and curation of America's digital holdings.

DuraCloud. http://duracloud.org/.

A service that makes it easy to move copies of your content into the cloud and store them with several different cloud storage providers, all with just one click. Providers include Amazon and the San Diego Super Computing Center.

216

Internet Archive. http://archive.org/.

A 501(c)(3) nonprofit building a digital library of Internet sites and other cultural artifacts in digital form. Besides preserving Web sites, the Internet Archive also preserves e-books, audio, and video. Organizations can use their Archive-It service (http://archive-it.org/) to build and preserve their own Web archives of digital content through a user-friendly Web application that doesn't require any technical expertise or hosting facilities.

OCLC Digital Archive. http://www.oclc.org/digital-archive.en.html.

Provides a secure storage environment for digital preservationists to manage and monitor the health of master files and digital originals.

REPORTS

General Reports on Digital Preservation (from most recent)

2014 National Agenda for Digital Stewardship, National Digital Stewardship Alliance, http://www.digitalpreservation.gov/ndsa/documents/2014NationalAgenda.pdf.

Reference Model for an Open Archival Information System (OAIS): Recommendation for Space Data System Practices, Consultative Committee for Space Data Systems, June 2012, http://public.ccsds.org/publications/archive/650x0m2.pdf.

Sustainable Economics for a Digital Planet: Ensuring Long-Term Access to Digital Information, Blue Ribbon Task Force on Sustainable Digital Preservation and Access, February 2010, http://brtf.sdsc.edu/biblio/BRTF_Final_Report.pdf.

Sustaining Digital Resources: An On-the-Ground View of Projects Today, Nancy L. Maron, K. Kirby Smith, and Matthew Loy, April 2009, http://www.jisc.ac.uk/publications/programmerelated/2009/scaithakaprojectstoday.aspx.

International Study on the Impact of Copyright Law on Digital Preservation, June M. Besek et al., July 2008, http://www.digitalpreservation.gov/documents/digital_preservation_final_report2008.pdf.

In its own words, "this study focuses on the copyright and related laws of Australia, the Netherlands, the United Kingdom, and the United States and the impact of those laws on digital preservation of copyrighted works. It also addresses proposals for legislative reform and efforts to develop nonlegislative solutions to the challenges that copyright law presents for digital preservation."

The Preservation Management of Digital Material Handbook, Digital Preservation Coalition, November 2008, http://www.dpconline.org/component/docman/doc_download/299-digital preservation-handbook.

Mind the Gap: Assessing Digital Preservation Needs in the UK, Martin Waller and Robert Sharpe, 2006 (available at http://www.dpconline.org/advocacy/mind-the-gap).

This report performed a needs assessment for digital preservation in the United Kingdom. Two goals of this report were to go beyond "preaching to the converted" and "build a detailed picture of the current situation in the UK."

A Continuing Access and Digital Preservation Strategy for the Joint Information Systems Committee (JISC) 2002–2005, Neil Beagrie, October 1, 2002, http://www.jisc .ac.uk/media/documents/publications/strategypreservation.pdf.
A foundational report on digital preservation strategy.

Preserving Digital Information: Report of the Task Force on Archiving of Digital Information, Task Force on Archiving of Digital Information, May 1, 1996, http:// www.oclc.org/content/dam/research/activities/digpresstudy/final-report.pdf.
One of the preliminary reports on the challenges and rewards of digital preservation from a cultural heritage perspective.

Archives

Enduring Paradigm, New Opportunities: The Value of the Archival Perspective in the Digital Environment, Anne J. Gilliland-Swetland (Washington, D.C.: Council on Library and Information Resources, February 2000), http://www.clir.org/pubs/reports/pub89/pub89.pdf.

Museums

Digital Preservation: Best Practices for Museums, Canadian Heritage, last modified February 15, 2013, http://www.pro.rcip-chin.gc.ca/contenu_numerique-digital_content/preservation_numerique-digital_preservation/index-eng.jsp.
Although not a report per se, this online guide designed for museum professionals contains elements that will be helpful to digital preservationists.

Metadata

Preservation Metadata, 2nd ed., Brian Lavoie and Richard Gartner, May 2013 (Great Britain: Digital Preservation Coalition in association with Charles Beagrie, Ltd., 2013), http://dx.doi.org/10.7207/twr13-03.
Focuses on new developments in preservation metadata that have been made possible because of PREMIS emerging as a de facto international standard.

PREMIS Data Dictionary for Preservation Metadata, Version 2.2, PREMIS Editorial Committee, July 2012, http://www.loc.gov/standards/premis/v2/premis-2-2.pdf.
Information on the PREMIS data model and data dictionary.

File Formats

File Format Guidelines for Management and Long-Term Retention of Electronic Records, State Archives of North Carolina, September 10, 2012, http://www.records .ncdcr.gov/guides/file_formats_in-house_preservation_20120910.pdf.
Helpful overview of file types, including for documents, e-mails, and Web pages.

Moving Images

The Digital Dilemma 2: Perspectives from Independent Filmmakers, Documentarians and Nonprofit Audiovisual Archives, Science and Technology Council (Beverly Hills, Calif.: Academy of Motion Picture Arts and Sciences, 2012).

Music

The Library of Congress National Recording Preservation Plan, National Recording Preservation Board (Washington, D.C.: Council on Library and Information Resources and The Library of Congress, December 2012), http://www.loc.gov/rr/record/nrpb/PLAN%20pdf.pdf.
Although not only about digital preservation, this title's sections on recorded music's preservation will be of interest to digital preservationists working with sound recordings.
The State of Recorded Sound Preservation in the United States: A National Legacy at Risk in the Digital Age, Council on Library and Information Resources and The Library of Congress (Washington, D.C.: LOC, August 2010), http://www.clir.org/pubs/reports/pub148/pub148.pdf.
Includes the chapter "Technical Issues in Digital Audio Preservation"; other chapters contain related content. Includes an annotated bibliography of audio-preservation resources.

WEBLIOGRAPHIES AND WEBINARS

Webliographies (alphabetical)

"Digital Materials," ACLTS, in *Preserving Your Memories*. Preservation Week, http://www.ala.org/alcts/confevents/preswk/tools#7.
Links to resources as varied as documentation to help with CDs and DVDs, to online tutorials through Cornell and ICPSR.
Digital Curation and Preservation Bibliography 2010, Charles W. Bailey Jr. (Houston: Digital Scholarship, 2011), http://digital-scholarship.org/dcpb/.
A freely available resource published under the Creative Commons Attribution-Noncommercial license that features over five hundred resources on the topic of digital preservation.
Digital Preservation Readiness Webliography, Liz Bishoff (LYRASIS, June 2009), http://www.lyrasis.org/LYRASIS%20Digital/Documents/Digital%20Toolbox/webliography.pdf.
A bit dated, but broad in scope with some foundational resources that will be of current interest.

"Bibliography," Canadian Heritage, in *Digital Preservation: Best Practices for Museums*, http://www.pro.rcip-chin.gc.ca/contenu_numerique-digital_content/preser vation_numerique-digital_preservation/bibliographie-bibliography-eng.jsp. Contains best practices guides, information concerning the museum context, and links to a number of online reports.

Web Archiving Bibliography, International Internet Preservation Consortium, http://netpreserve.org/web-archiving/bibliography. Although none of the resources are more current than 2009, the content is still worthy of digital preservationists' attention, especially if there is a need to review resources on the preservation of Web content.

Webinars

Webinars and Events, ALCTS, Preservation Week, http://www.ala.org/alcts/confe vents/preswk/alctsevents. Links to free webinars and webcasts from past and future Preservation Weeks.

BOOKS, GUIDES, AND TEXTBOOKS

Chowdhury, G. G., and Schubert Foo. *Digital Libraries and Information Access: Research Perspectives*. Chicago: Neal-Schuman, 2012. Contains articles about digital libraries written from a wide range of perspectives.

"DH Curation Guide: A Community Resource Guide to Data Curation in the Digital Humanities." In *Digital Humanities Data Curation*. http://guide.dhcuration .org/contents/. Guide to digital curation and preservation focused on content in the humanities; overseen by Digital Humanities Data Curation, a collaborative research project.

Harvey, Ross. *Digital Curation: A How-to-Do-It Manual*. New York: Neal-Schuman, 2010. A how-to manual for digital preservation.

McGath, Gary. *Files that Last: Digital Preservation for Everygeek*. N.P.: Smashwords, 2013. https://www.smashwords.com/books/view/307057. An e-book available in a variety of formats for just about any reader. Written for the preservation geek, it focuses on files and formats, including Web archiving.

McMillan, Gail, Matt Schultz, and Katherine Skinner. *Digital Preservation*. Washington, D.C.: Association of Research Libraries, 2011. Explores the strategies that Association of Research Libraries (ARL) members are utilizing for digital preservation.

Nelson, Naomi L. *Managing Born-Digital Special Collections and Archival Materials: August 2012*. Washington, D.C.: Association of Research Libraries, 2012.

This book looks at tools, workflow, and policies that can be utilized by staff working in special collections and archives to assist in processing and managing born-digital materials.

Skinner, Katherine, and Matt Schultz, eds. *A Guide to Distributed Digital Preservation.* Atlanta: Educopia Institute, 2010. http://digital.library.unt.edu/ark:/67531/metadc12850/.

An overview of geographically distributed digital preservation.

Online Digital Preservation Glossaries

Alliance for Permanent Access's *DPGlossary.* http://www.alliancepermanentaccess .org/index.php/knowledge-base/dpglossary/.

Archives New Zealand's Glossary Definitions Full List. http://archives.govt.nz/ad vice/continuum-resource-kit/glossary/definitions-full-list.

Digital Preservation Coalition's *Preservation Management of Digital Materials: The Handbook,* "Introduction: Definitions and Concepts," http://www.dpconline .org/advice/preservationhandbook/introduction/definitions-and-concepts.

International Research on Permanent Authentic Records in Electronic Systems's *The InterPARES 2 Project Glossary,* http://www.interpares.org/ip2/ip2_terminol ogy_db.cfm.

LIFE (Life Cycle Information for E-Literature)'s *LIFE: Glossary and Reference,* http:// www.life.ac.uk/glossary/.

PREMIS Data Dictionary's "Glossary" (pp. 257–63), http://www.loc.gov/standards/ premis/v2/premis-2-2.pdf.

Reference Model for an Open Archival Information System (OAIS): Recommendation for Space Data System Practices's "Terminology" (pp. 1–8, 1–16), http://public.ccsds .org/publications/archive/650x0m2.pdf.

Storage Networking Industry Association's *2013 SNIA Dictionary,* http://snia.org/ sites/default/files/SNIADictionary2013.pdf.

Directories for Digital Preservation Education

Program, Planning and Publications Committee, Preservation and Reformatting Section (PARS), comp. and ed. *Preservation Education Directory,* 9th ed. With the Association of Library Collections and Technical Services (ALCTS) and American Library Association. 2012. http://www.ala.org/alcts/sites/ala.org.alcts/files/ content/resources/preserv/preseddir/Preservation_Education_Dir_9thEd.pdf.

Society of American Archivists. *Directory of Archival Education.* http://www2.archi vists.org/dae.

National Council for Preservation Education. *Guide to Academic Programs.* http:// www.ncpe.us/academic-programs/#.UaTSzZyhrUQ.

CENTERS SUPPORTING RESEARCH AND TEACHING IN DIGITAL PRESERVATION (ALPHABETICAL)

Carolina Digital Curation Curriculum Project at the University of North Carolina at Chapel Hill's School of Information and Library Science. http://www.ils.unc.edu/digccurr/.

Center for Informatics Research in Science and Scholarship at the University of Illinois at Urbana-Champaign. http://www.lis.illinois.edu/research/projects.

Digital Curation Unit (DCU) at the IMIS Athena Research. http://www.dcu.gr/.

Digital Curriculum Laboratory. Simmons University Graduate School of Library and Information Science. http://calliope.simmons.edu/dcl/.

Digital Humanities Data Curation. Maryland Institute for Technology in the Humanities (MITH), University of Maryland, Women Writers Project, Brown University, and the Center for Informatics Research in Science and Scholarship, Graduate School of Library and Information Science, University of Illinois at Urbana-Champaign. http://www.dhcuration.org/.

Digital Research and Curation Center at The Johns Hopkins University's Sheridan Libraries. http://old.library.jhu.edu/departments/dkc/.

Distributed Data Curation Center at the Purdue University Library. http://d2c2.lib.purdue.edu/.

Digital Curation Institute at the University of Toronto's iSchool. http://dci.ischool.utoronto.ca/.

University of California Curation Center at the California Digital Library. http://www.cdlib.org/services/uc3/.

CONFERENCES AND IN-PERSON EVENTS

The University of Oregon maintains a list of upcoming conferences of interest to data curation at http://datacure.uoregon.edu/.

Core Conferences on Digital Preservation

International Association for Social Science Information Services & Technology (IASSIST), http://www.iassistdata.org/conferences.

International Conference on Preservation of Digital Objects (iPRES), http://ipres2013.ist.utl.pt/ (2013 website).

International Digital Curation Conference (IDCC) (through the Digital Curation Centre), http://www.dcc.ac.uk/events/international-digital-curation-conference-idcc.

Preservation and Archiving Special Interest Group (PASIG) International Meeting, http://www.preservationandarchivingsig.org.

Society for Imaging Science and Technology (IS&T) Archiving Conference, http://
www.imaging.org/ist/conferences/archiving/.

Related Conferences on Digital Preservation

Aligning National Approaches to Digital Preservation (ANADP) (through the Educopia Institute), http://rhizome.org/announce/opportunities/59553/view/.
CODATA (Committee on Data for Science and Technology) International Confer-
ence, http://www.codata.org/archives/conferences.html.
CULTURAL HERITAGE On Line: Trusted Digital Repositories and Trusted Pro-
fessionals, http://www.rinascimento-digitale.it/Conference2012.phtml.
CURATEcamp, http://curatecamp.org/.
Digital Curator Vocational Education Europe (DigCurV) Project, http://www
.digcur-education.org/eng/International-Conference
Digital Heritage International Congress 2013, http://www.digitalheritage2013.org/.
Digital Library Federation (DLF) Forum, http://www.diglib.org/.
Digital Preservation 2013, http://www.digitalpreservation.gov/meetings/ndiipp13
.html.
Future Perfect 2012, http://futureperfect.org.nz.
Image and Research Seminar, http://www.girona.cat/sgdap/cat/jornades_presenta
cio_ENG.php.
International CIPA Symposium, http://www.cipa2013.org/ (2013 website).
International Conference on Dublin Core and Metadata Applications, http://dcev
ents.dublincore.org/IntConf/.
Joint Conference on Digital Libraries (JCDL), http://www.jcdl.org/.
Museum and Computer Network (MCN), http://www.mcn.edu/.
Open Repositories Conference, http://sites.tdl.org/openrepositories/.
Personal Digital Archiving Conference http://mith.umd.edu/pda2013/ (2013 web-
site).
Research Data Access and Preservation Summit, http://www.asis.org/rdap (2013
website).
Texas Conference on Digital Libraries, https://conferences.tdl.org/TCDL/.
The Memory of the World in the Digital Age: Digitization and Preservation, http://
www.unesco.org/new/en/communication-and-information/events/calendar-of
-events/events-websites/the-memory-of-the-world-in-the-digital-age-digitization
-and-preservation/ (2012 website).
Theory and Practice of Digital Libraries (TPDL), http://www.tpdl2013.info/ (2013
website).

NOTE

1. About," Digital Preservation Network, s.v. "The DPN Vision," accessed January 1,
2014, http://www.dpn.org/about/.

Glossary

access. The right, opportunity, or means of finding, using, or approaching documents and/or information. [InterPARES2 Project glossary]

Access Functional Entity. The OAIS functional entity that contains the services and functions that make the archival information holdings and related services visible to consumers. [OAIS Reference Model]

Administrative. The OAIS functional entity that contains the services and functions needed to control the operation of the other OAIS functional entities on a day-to-day basis. [OAIS Reference Model]

administrative metadata. The additional information necessary to facilitating the use of the item being described.

analog. A colloquial term used to represent physical containers of information that are not in digital format. Examples include books, paintings, paper, and microforms.

application profile. A fully conforming instantiation of an element set for a particular community, created to adapt an element set into a package tailored to the functional requirements of a particular application while retaining interoperability with the base standard. Can involve mixing and matching terms from multiple standards to meet the descriptive needs of a particular project or service. [InterPARES2 Project glossary]

archival document. *See* **record**.

Archival Information Packages (AIPs). Information packages used within the OAIS system containing Content Information including descriptive metadata. [OAIS Reference Model] *See also* **Information Packages**.

Archival Storage Functional Entity. The OAIS functional entity that contains the services and functions used for the storage and retrieval of Archival Information Packages. [OAIS Reference Model]

Archive. An organization that intends to preserve information for access and use by a Designated Community. [OAIS Reference Model]

archive. 1. A collection of data objects, perhaps with associated metadata, in a storage system whose primary purpose is the long-term preservation and retention of that data. 2. Synonym for data ingestion. [SNIA dictionary]

authenticity. The trustworthiness of a record as a record—that is, the quality of a record that is what it purports to be and that is free from tampering or corruption. [InterPARES2 Project glossary]

back-up copy. *See* **backup**.

backup. Short-term procedure ensuring bit stream preservation (preserving the ones and zeros that make up a digital file) but not addressing things like the availability of software to access the file, obsolete file formats, questions of rights, and issues of authenticity and provenance.

BagIt. A hierarchical file packaging format developed by the Library of Congress and the California Digital Library to transfers large amounts of data between cultural institutions. Transfers can be done using physical media, such as disk drives, or over a network. BagIt is an Internet Engineering Task Force Internet-draft specification.

best practice. In the application of theory to real-life situations, a procedure that, when properly applied, consistently yields superior results and is therefore used as a reference point in evaluating the effectiveness of alternative methods of accomplishing the same task. [InterPARES2 Project glossary]

big data. A collection of data or data sets that is so large that it is difficult to manage and process using traditional database management techniques and data processing applications. Big data is generally characterized by the 3Vs: volume, variety, and velocity.

binary bit. *See* **bit**.

bit. The smallest unit of data (represented by 0 or 1) that a computer can hold in its memory. [InterPARES2 Project glossary]

bit stream preservation. The process of storing and maintaining digital objects over time, ensuring that there is no loss or corruption of the bits making up those objects. [LIFE]

bit rot. An event that occurs, usually gradually, when bits of a file change over time. Bit rot can be due to physical deterioration of memory in storage media or to environmental factors affecting that media. Over time bit rot may cause the data or files to become unreadable. *See also* **media decay**.

checksum. An error-detection scheme used to ensure the integrity of data (or portions of data) for data transmission or storage. Checksums are calculated using algorithms.

collection. A set of objects that is organized, described, and made available through LAMs and overseen by Archives professionals.

collection development. The selection and deselection of objects for a collection. Museums may use the term *curation*; in archival science, sometimes the word *appraisal* is used.

compression. Method of making files smaller, reducing the amount of storage necessary; when files are compressed, information can be lost. *See also* **lossy compression, lossless compression**.

Consumer. The role played by those persons, or client systems, who interact with OAIS services to find preserved information of interest and to access that information in detail. This can include other OAISes, as well as internal OAIS persons or systems.

Content Information. A set of information that is the original target of preservation or that includes part or all of that information. It is an Information Object composed of its Content Data Object and its Representation Information. [OAIS Reference Model]

content item. *See* **digital object**.

crosswalk. A chart or table that represents the semantic mapping of fields or data elements in one metadata standard to fields or data elements in another standard that has a similar function or meaning. [InterPARES2 Project glossary]

dark archives. Information repositories only accessible by authorized users. Dark archives, for example, may not be freely available on the Web but instead may be password protected or housed behind closed doors.

data. The smallest meaningful units of information. [InterPARES2 Project glossary]

Data Management Functional Entity. The OAIS functional entity that contains the services and functions for populating, maintaining, and accessing a wide variety of information. Some examples of this information are catalogs and inventories on what may be retrieved from Archival Storage, processing algorithms that may be run on retrieved data, Consumer access statistics, Consumer billing, Event Based Orders, security controls, and OAIS schedules, policies, and procedures. [OAIS Reference Model]

descriptive metadata. Metadata that describe a resource for purposes such as discovery and identification. They can include elements such as title, abstract, author, and keywords. [NISO]

Designated Community. An identified group of potential Consumers who should be able to understand a particular set of information. The Designated Community may be composed of multiple user communities. A Designated Community is defined by the Archive, and this definition may change over time. [OAIS Reference Model]

digital archive. A repository for the long-term maintenance of digital resources and making them available. [Archives New Zealand] *See also* **archive**.

digital asset. Digital versions of (museum) artifacts; digital assets may be housed in a digital asset management system.

digital asset management systems. Digital library systems that are not normally expected to provide support for digital preservation. In some cases these systems are being retrofitted for digital preservation and preservation components can be purchased for an additional fee, or, in the case of some open source systems, add-ons can be installed to assist with digital preservation.

digital collection. A collection of digital objects made accessible through a digital library interface.

digital curation. The selection, archiving, preservation, and management of digital objects throughout the life cycle of the object. *See also* **digital preservation**.

digital humanities. The application of computing power to humanities research in a way that promotes new discoveries that traditionally would have been impossible. Not a single, standardized approach, digital humanities represents instead a new and somewhat customizable paradigm in humanities research.

digital library. A collection of digital objects that has been created, stored, and organized in some way that promotes access. A digital library may include preservation components.

digital object. A unit of content managed by a digital archive. Digital objects have as one of their attributes an Identifier. They can be seen to be the atomic level of content. Smaller units can be contained within them, but the repository manages the digital object in a singular fashion. [Archives New Zealand] *See also* **item**.

digital preservation. The activities necessary to ensure continued access to digital materials for as long as necessary.

digital preservationist. Information professional typically working in a library, archive, or museum, responsible for the digital preservation of electronic content.

digital preservation system. Digital library software that includes a preservation component. *See also* **Open Archival Information System (OAIS)**.

Dissemination Information Packages (DIPs). An Information Package derived from one or more AIPs and sent by Archives to the Consumer in response to a request to the OAIS. [OAIS Reference Model]

document. *See* **File**.

documentation. The information provided by a creator and the repository that provides enough information to establish provenance, history, and context and to enable its use by others. [DPC Handbook]

economic sustainability. The set of business, social, technological, and policy mechanisms that encourage the gathering of important information assets into digital preservation systems and that support the indefinite persistence of digital preservation systems, enabling access to and use of the information assets into the long-term future. [BRTF-SDPA]

electronic. Not analog; digital.

element set. A grouping of metadata elements along with their attributes—such as name, identifier, definition, or relationship to other concepts—collated for a specific purpose, community, or domain surrogate. [InterPARES2 Project glossary]

emulation. One of two primary approaches to overcoming format obsolescence in digital preservation. Emulation is the recreation of the original operating environment using modern technology.

File. Named and ordered sequence of Bytes that is known by an operating system. A File can be zero or more Bytes, has access permissions, and has file system statistics such as size and last modification date. A File also has a Format. [PREMIS]

file format. The organization of data within digital objects, usually designed to facilitate the storage, retrieval, processing, presentation, and/or transmission of the data by software. [InterPARES2 Project glossary]

fixity. The quality of a record that makes it immutable and requires changes to be made by appending an update or creating a new version. [InterPARES2 Project glossary]

fonds. The whole of the records that a physical or juridical person accumulates by reason of its function or activity; the highest-level archival aggregation. [InterPARES2 Project glossary]

guidelines. *See* **plans.**

hardware obsolescence. Hardware that is no longer in use or available because of the development of an improved or superior way of achieving the same goal. The obsolete hardware is no longer supported. [National Archives of Australia] *See also* **obsolescence** or **software obsolescence.**

humanities. The branches of knowledge concerned with human constructs, thoughts, and culture, such as philosophy, languages, and art.

Information Packages. Information or data exchanged within an OAIS or provided to, or submitted by, external users and systems. [OAIS Reference Model]

information professional. LAM professionals, especially those working in libraries and archives, and employees specialized in providing access to content for users.

ingest. The process by which a digital object or metadata package is absorbed by a different system than the one that produced it. [LIFE]

Ingest Functional Entity. The OAIS functional entity that contains the services and functions that accept Submission Information Packages from Producers, prepares Archival Information Packages for storage, and ensures that Archival Information Packages and their supporting Descriptive Information become established within the OAIS. [OAIS Reference Model]

institutional repository. A digital library dedicated to a certain institution's (i.e., a university's) digital content.

intellectual property rights (IPR). The rights of individuals or organizations to control the use or dissemination of ideas or information. They include copyright, trademarks, and patents. [InterPARES2 Project glossary]

item. The smallest discrete unit of record material that accumulates to form a series (i.e., a file or part file in a series of files; a volume in a series of volumes, etc.). Sometimes the term is also used as equivalent to *Document.* [DPGlossary] *See also* **digital object.**

LAM. Acronym for *libraries, archives, and museums.*

life cycle collection management. Life cycle collection management is a way of taking a long-term approach to the stewardship of collections. It defines the different stages in a collection item's existence over time. Life cycle collection management seeks to identify the costs of each stage to define the economic interdependencies between the stages. [LIFE]

life cycle (conceptual). The life cycle approach is a philosophy that aims to observe all the stages of a process or object, to understand that process or object better. Life cycle costing enables quantification of all the expenditures associated with the stewardship of an object. [LIFE]

LOCKSS (Lots Of Copies Keeps Stuff Safe). An open source software program that replicates digital content across a network of computers that are running the software. LOCKSS is built on the principle that "lots of copies keeps stuff safe." LOCKSS can be used for bit stream preservation.

long term. A period of time long enough for there to be concern about the impacts of changing technologies, including support for new media and data formats, and of a changing Designated Community, on the information being held in an OAIS. This period extends into the indefinite future. [DPGlossary]

long-term preservation. The act of maintaining information, Independently Understandable by a Designated Community, and with evidence supporting its Authenticity, over the Long Term. [DPGlossary]

lossless compression. A data compression method that allows for the original data to be reconstructed in full.

lossy compression. A data compression method that only allows for an approximation of the original data to be reconstructed. Lossy compression is often used for images, audio, and video files because it can result in smaller file sizes then lossless compression.

Lots Of Copies Keeps Stuff Safe. *See* **LOCKSS.**

Management. The role played by those who set overall OAIS policy as one component in a broader policy domain—for example, as part of a larger organization. [OAIS Reference Model]

mandatory responsibilities. The OAIS Reference Model requires that an OAIS be responsible for (1) negotiating for and accepting information, (2) obtaining sufficient control for preservation, (3) determining the designated community, (4) ensuring information is independently understandable, (5) following established preservation policies and procedures, and (6) making the information available. [OAIS Reference Model]

media decay. The tendency to physical failure and bit rot that makes digital media unreliable. *See also* **bit rot.**

memorandum of understanding. *See* **MOU.**

metadata. 1. Structured, encoded data that describes characteristics of information-bearing entities (including individual objects, collections, or systems) to aid in the identification, discovery, assessment, management, and preservation of the described entities. [Zeng and Qin]. 2. Information that describes significant aspects of a resource. [DPC Handbook]

metadata crosswalk. *See* **crosswalk.**

metadata for preservation. The suite of all metadata that will permit over time the long-term access to electronic files. This includes descriptive metadata, administrative metadata, technical metadata, and preservation metadata.

metadata schema. A framework that specifies and describes a standard set of metadata elements and their interrelationships that need to be recorded to ensure the identification of records and their authenticity. Schemas provide a formal syntax (or structure) and semantics (or definitions) for the metadata elements. [Inter-PARES2 Project glossary]

migration. One of two primary approaches to overcoming format obsolescence in digital preservation, migration is when obsolete files whose formats are no longer viable are recreated in a current file format. *See also* **normalization**.

MOU (memorandum of understanding). An agreement that describes the collection and the responsibilities of both the department in charge of the digital preservation system and the originator of the content.

namespace. A collection of names, identified by a URL reference, used as element types and attribute names. [InterPARES2 Project glossary]

normalization. Migrating digital objects to a limited number of standard formats. *See also* **migration**.

OAIS. *See* **Open Archival Information System (OAIS)**.

OAIS Functional Model. Describes seven main functional entities (Ingest, Archival Storage, Data Management, Administration, Preservation Planning, and Access) and how they interact with each other. [OAIS Reference Model]

obsolescence. When hardware, software, file formats, or other technology are no longer viable even if they are in working order. *See also* **hardware obsolescence** *or* **software obsolescence**.

open access. Immediate, free availability on the public Internet, permitting any users to read, download, copy, distribute, print, search, or link to the full text of these articles, crawl them for indexing, pass them as data to software, or use them for any other lawful purpose. [SPARC]

open access repository. Digital repositories that are either institutional- or subject-based that provide scholarly content to the general public under Open Access terms.

Open Archival Information System (OAIS). An Archive, consisting of an organization, which may be part of a larger organization, of people and systems, that has accepted the responsibility to preserve information and make it available for a Designated Community. It meets a set of responsibilities, as defined in section 4 of the OAIS Reference Model, that allows an OAIS Archive to be distinguished from other uses of the term *archive*. The term *open* in OAIS is used to imply that this Recommendation and future related Recommendations and standards are developed in open forums, and it does not imply that access to the Archive is unrestricted. [OAIS Reference Model] *See also* **digital preservation system**.

original order. The order in which records and archives were kept when in active use—that is, the order of accumulation as they were created, maintained, and used. The principle of original order requires that the original order be preserved or reconstructed. [DPGlossary]

outreach. A set of organized activities of a digital preservation program intended to acquaint stakeholders and potential stakeholders with digital preservation and its value.

physical object. An object (such as a moon rock, biospecimen, or microscope slide) with physically observable properties that represent information that is considered suitable for being adequately documented for preservation, distribution, and independent usage. [DPGlossary]

plans. Documentation that is directly actionable and can be case- (or collection-) specific; plans are not voted on or approved at a high level and are often very specific in nature. Alternatively, plans can also be directly based on missions, goals, or objectives of an institution, bypassing a formal written policy. *See also* **policies**.

policies. High-level documents reflecting the mission of the institution that guide in the creation of action plans or guidelines and best practices; policies provide an overarching approach that is technology-independent. *See also* **plans**.

preservation. The whole of the principles, policies, rules, and strategies aimed at prolonging the existence of an object by maintaining it in a condition suitable for use, either in its original format or in a more persistent format, while leaving intact the object's intellectual form. [InterPARES2 Project glossary]

Preservation Description Information (PDI). The information that is necessary for adequate preservation of the Content Information and that can be categorized as Provenance, Reference, Fixity, Context, and Access Rights Information. [OAIS Reference Model]

preservation metadata. Information a Preservation Repository uses to support the digital preservation process. [PREMIS] *See also* **metadata for preservation**.

Preservation Planning Functional Entity. The OAIS functional entity that provides the services and functions for monitoring the environment of the OAIS and that provides recommendations and preservation plans to ensure that the information stored in the OAIS remains accessible to, and understandable by and sufficiently usable by, the Designated Community over the Long Term, even if the original computing environment becomes obsolete. [OAIS Reference Model]

preservation repository. *See* **digital preservation system**.

provenance. The relationships between records and the organizations or individuals that created, accumulated, and/or maintained and used them in the conduct of personal or corporate activity. [InterPARES2 Project glossary]

record. A document made or received in the course of a practical activity as an instrument or a by-product of such activity, set aside for action or reference. [InterPARES2 Project glossary]

repository. A system to store and allow access to digital objects. [LIFE]

rights. Assertions of one or more rights or permissions pertaining to a Digital Object and/or an Agent. [PREMIS]

risk. According to the IEEE 13335-1:1996, the potential that a given threat will exploit vulnerabilities of an asset or group of assets to cause loss or damage to the assets. [SNIA dictionary]

risk management. According to the IEEE 13335-1:1996, the process of assessing and quantifying risk and establishing an acceptable level of risk for the organization. [SNIA dictionary]

science. The body of knowledge comprising measurable or verifiable facts acquired through application of the scientific method and generalized into scientific laws or principles. [InterPARES2 Project glossary]

short-term preservation. Access to digital materials either for a defined period of time while use is predicted but that does not extend beyond the foreseeable future and/or until it becomes inaccessible because of changes in technology. [DPGlossary]

software obsolescence. The phenomenon of software being rendered obsolete because newer versions are not "backwardly compatible" (able to read older versions of that software), the software is no longer used and has been superseded by other software, or it cannot function with newer equipment or software. [National Archives of Australia] *See also* **obsolescence** or **hardware obsolescence.**

stakeholder. Interested parties including producers of content, a collection's Designated Community, and an Archive's funders. Can also include those with a vested professional interest in the digital preservation of content, such as the digital preservationist and other employees of the Archive.

standard. The complex of established norms aiming to make the characteristic of a product, process, or service uniform within or across a sector, a country, or a system. [InterPARES2 Project glossary]

standards. Sets of rules or guidelines cooperatively adhered to by peer entities. [InterPARES2 Project glossary]

structural metadata. Describes the internal structure of digital resources and the relationships between their parts. It is used to enable navigation and presentation. (From NINCH Guide to Good Practice: www.nyu.edu/its/humanities/ninch-guide/appendices/metadata.html.) [PREMIS]

Submission Information Packages (SIPs). An Information Package that is delivered by the Producer to the OAIS for use in the construction or update of one or more AIPs and/or the associated Descriptive Information. [OAIS Reference Model]

technical metadata. Information necessary for accessing the item being described if that item is electronic.

trust. The belief in the reliability, truth, ability, or strength of someone or something. A trusted system is believed to have the ability to function as expected and to not misbehave. [SNIA dictionary]

trusted digital repository. A repository "whose mission is to provide reliable, long-term access to managed digital resources to its designated community, now and in the future." In order to be considered a trusted digital repository, the repository must have the following seven attributes: compliance with the reference model for an Open Archival Information System (OAIS), administrative responsibility, organizational viability, financial sustainability, technological and procedural suitability, system security, and procedural accountability. (Research Libraries Group (RLG). *Trusted Digital Repositories: Attributes and Responsibilities; An RLG-OCLC Report.* Mountain View, Calf.: Research Libraries Group, 2002. http://www.oclc.org/resources/research/activities/trustedrep/repositories.pdf.)

trusted preservation system. The whole of the rules that control the preservation and use of the records of the creator and provide a circumstantial probability of the authenticity of the records, and the tools and mechanisms used to implement those rules. [InterPARES2 Project glossary]

value vocabulary. Definition of resources (such as instances of topics, art styles, or authors) that are used as values for elements in metadata records. Typically a value vocabulary does not define bibliographic resources, such as books, but rather concepts related to bibliographic resources (persons, languages, countries, etc.). [Library Linked Data Incubator Group]

version control. *See* **versioning**.

versioning. A formal representation of the sequence of changes within a digital file; a system for tracking and managing such changes explicitly so as to avoid accidentally replacing a current file with an obsolete previous version and so as to permit comparison of different versions, reversion to an earlier state of the file, and similar actions.

[Archives New Zealand] Archives New Zealand, "Glossary Definitions Full List," accessed February 2, 2014, http://archives.govt.nz/advice/continuum-resource-kit/glossary/definitions-full-list.

[BRTF-SDPA] Blue Ribbon Task Force on Sustainable Digital Preservation and Access (BRTF-SDPA), "Economic Sustainability in a Digital Preservation Context," accessed February 2, 2014, http://brtf.sdsc.edu/econ_sustainability.html.

[DPC Handbook] Digital Preservation Coalition. "Introduction: Definitions and Concepts." Accessed August 2, 2013. http://www.dpconline.org/advice/preservationhandbook/introduction/definitions-and-concepts.

[DPGlossary] Alliance for Permanent Access, "DPGlossary," accessed February 2, 2014, http://www.alliancepermanentaccess.org/index.php/knowledge-base/dpglossary/.

[InterPARES2 Project glossary] International Research on Permanent Authentic Records in Electronic Systems, "The InterPARES 2 Project Glossary," accessed February 2, 2014, http://www.interpares.org/ip2/ip2_terminology_db.cfm.

[Library Linked Data Incubator Group] Library Linked Data Incubator Group, "Datasets, Value Vocabularies, and Metadata Element Sets," modified October 25, 2011, http://www.w3.org/2005/Incubator/lld/XGR-lld-vocabdataset-20111025/.

[LIFE] LIFE (Life Cycle Information for E-Literature), "LIFE: Glossary and Reference," accessed, February 2, 2014, http://www.life.ac.uk/glossary/.

[National Archives of Australia] National Archives of Australia, "Glossary," accessed February 2, 2014, http://www.naa.gov.au/records-management/publications/glossary.aspx.

[NISO] National Information Standards Organization (NISO), *Understanding Metadata* (Bethesda, Md.: NISO Press, 2004), 1, http://www.niso.org/publications/press/UnderstandingMetadata.pdf.

[PREMIS] PREMIS Editorial Committee. "Glossary" in *PREMIS Data Dictionary for Preservation Metadata, Version 2.2. Washington, D.C.: Library of Congress, 2012, 257-263, http://www.loc.gov/standards/premis/v2/premis-2-2.pdf.*

[OAIS Reference Model] Consultative Committee for Space Data Systems (CCSDS), *Reference Model for an Open Archival Information System (OAIS): Recommended Practice CCSDS 650.0-M-2; Recommendation for Space Data System Practices*, Magenta Book, Recommended Practice, issue 2 (Washington, D.C.: CCSDS Secretariat, June 2012), pp. 1–8, 1–16, http://public.ccsds.org/publications/archive/650x0m2.pdf.

[SNIA] Storage Networking Industry Association, *2013 SNIA Dictionary*. San Francisco, Ca.: SNIA, 2013), http://snia.org/sites/default/files/SNIADictionary2013.pdf.

[SPARC] SPARC, "Why Open Access?" accessed February 2, 2014, http://www.sparc.arl.org/resources/open-access/why-oa

[Zeng and Qin] Zeng, Marcia Lei, and Jian Qin. *Metadata*. New York: Neal-Schuman, 2008.

Bibliography

CHAPTER 1

AHDS History/UK Data Archive. "Planning Historical Digitisation Projects." Last modified June 21, 2005. http://chnm.gmu.edu/digitalhistory/links/pdf/preserving/8_32.pdf.

American Library Association (ALA). "ALA Preservation Policy." 2001. http://www.ala.org/alcts/resources/preserv/01alaprespolicy.

———. "Core Values of Librarianship: Preservation." Accessed June 8, 2013. http://www.ala.org/advocacy/intfreedom/statementspols/corevalues#preservation.

Baudoin, Patsy. "The Principle of Digital Preservation." *The Serials Librarian* 55, no. 4 (2008): 556–59. doi:10.1080/03615260802291212.

Blue Ribbon Task Force on Sustainable Digital Preservation and Access (BRTF-SDPA). *Sustainable Economics for a Digital Planet: Ensuring Long Term Access to Digital Information.* San Diego: San Diego Supercomputer Center, 2010. http://brtf.sdsc.edu/biblio/BRTF_Final_Report.pdf.

Breeding, Marshall. "From Disaster Recovery to Digital Preservation." *Computers in Libraries* 32, no. 4 (May 2012): 22–25.

British Broadcasting Corporation (BBC). "Story of Domesday." Accessed August 1, 2013. http://www.bbc.co.uk/history/domesday/story.

Brown, Douglas. "Lost in Cyberspace: The BBC Domesday Project and the Challenge of Digital Preservation." *CSA Discovery Guides.* June 2003. http://www.csa.com/discoveryguides/cyber/overview.php.

"Digital Archiving: History Flushed." *Economist*, April 28, 2012. http://www.economist.com/node/21553410.

Digital Preservation Coalition (DPC). *Digital Preservation Handbook.* York, Eng.: DPC, 2008. Accessed September 1, 2012. http://www.dpconline.org/advice/preservationhandbook.

Eve, Martin Paul. "The Problems for Small Open Access Journals in Terms of Digital Preservation." *Martin Paul Eve*, March 30, 2012. Accessed August 21, 2012. https://www
.martineve.com/2012/03/30/the-problems-for-small-open-access-journals-in-terms-of-di
gital preservation/.

Evens, Tom, and Laurence Hauttekeete. "Challenges of Digital Preservation for Cultural
Heritage Institutions." *Journal of Librarianship and Information Science* 43, no. 3 (2011):
157–65.

Factor, Michael. "Long Term Digital Preservation." Paper presented at IBM Haifa Research
Lab, Haifa, Israel, November 2008. Accessed August 30, 2012. http://www.ndpp.in/pre
sentation/National_Workshop2008/Mr._Vijay_K_Garg.pdf.

Gilliland-Swetland, Anne J. *Enduring Paradigm, New Opportunities: The Value of the Archival
Perspective in the Digital Environment*. Washington, D.C.: Council on Library and Information Resources, 2000. http://www.clir.org/pubs/abstract/pub89abst.html.

Jisc. *JISC Beginner's Guide to Digital Preservation*. Accessed September 1, 2012. http://blogs.
ukoln.ac.uk/jisc-beg-dig-pres/.

Knight, Steve. "Securing the Future: Digital Preservation at the National Library of New
Zealand." Paper presented at the annual conference of the International Group of ex Libris
(IGeLU), Madrid, September 8–10, 2008. Accessed September 1, 2012. http://igelu.org/
wp-content/uploads/2010/10/12a_knight.pdf.

Krtalic, Maja, and Damir Hasenay. "Exploring a Framework for Comprehensive and Successful Preservation Management in Libraries." *Journal of Documentation* 68, no. 3 (2012):
353–77.

Li, Yuan, and Meghan Banach. "Institutional Repositories and Digital Preservation: Assessing
Current Practices at Research Libraries." *D-Lib Magazine* 17, no. 5–6 (2011). http://www
.dlib.org/dlib/may11/yuanli/05yuanli.html.

Library of Congress (LOC). "About Digital Preservation." Accessed September 29, 2013.
http://www.digitalpreservation.gov/about/.

———. *On the Record: Report of the Library of Congress Working Group on the Future of Bibliographic Control*. Washington, D.C.: Library of Congress, 2008. http://www.loc.gov/
bibliographic-future/news/lcwg-ontherecord-jan08-final.pdf.

———. "Why Digital Preservation Is Important for Everyone." Accessed September 1, 2012.
http://www.digitalpreservation.gov/multimedia/videos/digipres.html.

Life Cycle Information for E-literature (LIFE). "LIFE: Glossary and Reference." Accessed July
15, 2013. http://www.life.ac.uk/glossary/.

McKie, Robin, and Vanessa Thorpe. "Digital Domesday Book Lasts 15 Years Not 1000." *Observer*, March 3, 2003. Accessed August 20, 2012. http://observer.guardian.co.uk/uk_news/
story/0,6903,661093,00.html.

Meador, John M. Jr., and Edward M. Corrado. "Rosetta and the 21st Century Academic
Digital Library." Paper presented at the annual conference of the International Group of ex
Libris Users (IGeLU), Zurich, September 11–13, 2012.

Meador, John M. Jr., Edward M. Corrado, and Sandy Card. "Building Our Digital Library
Using Rosetta and Primo: The First Year." Paper presented at the annual meeting of the
Rosetta Advisory Group, Hannover, Ger., July 17, 2012.

National Archives. "Domesday Preserved in New BBC Project." May 12, 2011; accessed September 29, 2013. http://www.nationalarchives.gov.uk/news/573.htm.

Online Computer Library Center, Inc., (OCLC) and the Center for Research Libraries.
Trustworthy Repositories Audit and Certification: Criteria and Checklist. Chicago and Dublin,

Ohio: OCLC and the Center for Research Libraries, 2007. http://www.crl.edu/PDF/trac .pdf.

PDF Standards. "PDF/A." Accessed July 15, 2013. http://pdf.editme.com/pdfa.

Research Libraries Group (RLG). *Trusted Digital Repositories: Attributes and Responsibilities; An RLG-OCLC Report.* Mountain View, Calf.: Research Libraries Group, 2002. http://www .oclc.org/resources/research/activities/trustedrep/repositories.pdf.

Scholarly Publishing and Academic Resources Coalition (SPARC). "Abstracts." *Digital Repositories Meeting 2010.* Accessed September 1, 2012. http://www.arl.org/sparc/meet ings/dr10/drabstracts/index.shtml. This Website is no longer available but the contents can be viewed using the Internet Archive's Wayback Machine at http://web.archive.org/ web/20110928061108/http://www.arl.org/sparc/meetings/dr10/drabstracts/index.shtml (last accessed September 29, 2013).

———. "Open Access." Accessed September 1, 2012. http://www.sparc.arl.org/issues/open access.

Sierman, Barbara. "Organizing Digital Preservation." In *Business Planning for Digital Libraries: International Approaches*, edited by Mel Collier, 113–22. Leuven, Belg.: Leuven University Press, 2010.

Wheatley, Paul. "Digital Preservation and BBC Domesday." Paper presented at the annual meeting of the Electronic Media Group's American Institute for Conservation of Historic and Artistic Works, Portland, June 14, 2004. Accessed September 1, 2012. http://cool .conservation-us.org/coolaic/sg/emg/library/pdf/wheatley/Wheatley-EMG2004.pdf.

Wikipedia, s.v. "Digital Asset Management." Accessed August 13, 2012. http://en.wikipedia .org/w/index.php?title=Digital_asset_management&oldid=507130560.

CHAPTER 2

Anderson, Martha. "B Is for Bit Preservation." *The Signal*, September 7, 2011. http://blogs .loc.gov/digitalpreservation/2011/09/b-is-for-bit-preservation/.

Beagrie, Neil. "Keeping Research Data Safe: Costs of Research Data Preservation." Paper presented at the Preservation and Archiving Special Interest Group (PASIG) Conference, Dublin, October 2012. http://lib.stanford.edu/files/pasig-oct2012/12-Beagrie-PA SIG-1012_CB_costs2.pdf.

Beagrie, Neil, Brian Lavoie, and Matthew Woolard. *Keeping Research Data Safe 2: Final Report.* Salisbury, Eng.: Charles Beagrie Limited, 2010. http://www.jisc.ac.uk/media/documents/ publications/reports/2010/keepingresearchdatasafe2.pdf.

Becker, Christoph, Hannes Kulovits, Mark Guttenbrunner, Stephan Strodl, Andreas Rauber, and Hans Hofman. "Systematic Planning for Digital Preservation: Evaluating Potential Strategies and Building Preservation Plans." *International Journal of Digital Librarianship* 10 (2009): 133–57.

Bellardo, Lewis J., and Lynn Lady Bellardo. *A Glossary for Archivists, Manuscript Curators, and Records Managers.* Chicago: Society of American Archivists, 1992.

Boardman, Michael. "Digital Copyright Protection and Graduated Response: A Global Perspective." *Loyola of Los Angeles International & Comparative Law Review* 33, no. 2 (2011): 223–54.

BusinessDictionary.com, s.v. "Stakeholder." Accessed September 29, 2013, http://www.busi nessdictionary.com/definition/stakeholder.html.

Canadian Heritage Information Network. "Checklist for Creating a Preservation Policy." Last modified February 15, 2013. http://www.pro.rcip-chin.gc.ca/contenu_numerique digital_content/preservation_numerique-digital_preservation/annexeA-appendixA-eng .jsp.

Capalan, Priscilla. "DAITSS, an OAIS-Based Preservation Repository." In *Proceedings of the 2010 Roadmap for Digital Preservation Interoperability Framework Workshop*, Gaithersburg, Md., March 29-31, 2010, http://daitss.fcla.edu/sites/daitss.fcla.edu/files/DAITSS%20 in%20ACM%20rev_0.pdf.

Corrado, Edward M. "Implementing Rosetta at Binghamton University Libraries." *SUNYergy* 14, no. 1 (2012). http://www.sunyconnect.suny.edu/sunyergy/default52.htm.

DH Curation Guide. *Glossary*, s.v. "Versioning, version control." Accessed September 29, 2013. http://guide.dhcuration.org/glossary.html.

Digital Preservation Management Workshop. "Where to Begin?" Accessed September 29, 2013. http://www.dpworkshop.org/dpm-eng/conclusion.html.

Ex Libris/Rosetta. *The Ability to Preserve a Large Volume of Digital Assets: A Scaling Proof of Concept*. Jerusalem: Ex Libris, Ltd., 2010. http://www.exlibrisgroup.com/files/Products/ Preservation/RosettaScalingProofofConcept.pdf.

Frankel, Susy. "Digital Copyright and Culture." *The Journal of Arts Management, Law, and Society* 40 (2010): 140–56.

Gasaway, Laura N. "Libraries, Digital Content, and Copyright." *Vanderbilt Journal of Entertainment & Technology Law* 12, no. 4 (2010): 755–78.

Goethals, Andrea, Jimi Jones, Carol Kussman, Kate Murry, and Meg Phillips. "Who's Minding the (Data) Store? Results of the NDSA Digital Preservation Staffing Survey." Poster presented at the iPRES 2012 Conference, Toronto, October 1–5, 2012. http://www.digi talpreservation.gov/ndsa/documents/NDSA-staff-survey-poster-ipres2012.pdf.

Hoffmann, Gretchen McCord. "Browsing and Caching." In *Copyright in Cyberspace 2*, edited by Gretchen McCord Hoffmann, 69-80. New York: Neal-Schuman, 2005.

Hole, Brian. "Understanding the True Costs of Digital Preservation: LIFE[3]." Presentation at Decoding the Digital, London, July 27, 2010. http://www.bl.uk/blpac/pdf/decodinghole .pdf.

Hole, Brian, Li Lin, Patrick McCann, and Paul Wheatley. "LIFE[3]: A Predictive Costing Tool for Digital Collections." Paper presented at the iPRES 2010 Conference, Vienna, September 19–24, 2010. http://www.life.ac.uk/3/docs/Ipres2010_life3_submitted.pdf.

International Organization for Standardization (ISO). "ISO 19005-1:2005: Document Management; Electronic Document File Format for Long-Term Preservation, Part 1: Use of PDF 1.4 (PDF/A-1)." Accessed September 29, 2013, http://www.iso.org/iso/iso_catalogue/ catalogue_tc/catalogue_detail.htm?csnumber=38920. Cited in Oettler, Alexandra, *PDF/A in a Nutshell*.

Jones, Sarah. "Small Steps and Lasting Impact: Making a Start with Preservation." Paper presented at Getting Started with Digital Preservation, Glasgow, February 28, 2011. http:// www.bl.uk/blpac/pdf/digitalstartglasjones.pdf.

Kilbride, William. "Introducing Digital Preservation." Paper presented at Getting Started with Digital Preservation, Glasgow, February 28, 2011. http://www.bl.uk/blpac/pdf/digitalstart glaskilbride.pdf.

Library of Congress (LOC). "Library Develops Bagit Specification for Transferring Digital Content." Accessed July 31, 2013. http://www.digitalpreservation.gov/ news/2008/20080602news_article_bagit.html.

———. "Planets." Accessed September 29, 2013, http://www.digitalpreservation.gov/series/edge/planets.html.

Life Cycle Information for E-literature (LIFE). *LIFE: Glossary and Reference*, s.v. "Ingest." Accessed July 15, 2013. http://www.life.ac.uk/glossary/.

———. "LIFE: Life Cycle Information for E-literature." Accessed December 23, 2012. http://www.life.ac.uk/about/.

Madalli, Devika P., Sunita Barve, and Saiful Amin. "Digital Preservation in Open source Digital Library Software." *The Journal of Academic Librarianship* 38, no. 3 (2012): 161–64.

Moulaison, Heather Lea, and Sarah Wenzel. "Who Owns the Eiffel Tower? Issues Surrounding the Digitization of Cultural Heritage in Modern France." *Documents to the People* 39, no. 1 (2011): 21–25.

National Archives. "Welcome to PRONOM." Accessed November 25, 2012. http://www.nationalarchives.gov.uk/PRONOM/Default.aspx.

Oettler, Alexandra. *PDF/A in a Nutshell 2.0: PDF for Long-Term Archiving; The ISO Standard, from PDF/A-1 to PDF/A-3*. Berlin: Association for Digital Document Standards, 2013. http://www.pdfa.org/wp-content/uploads/2013/05/PDFA_in_a_Nutshell_211.pdf.

Patry, William. *How to Fix Copyright*. Oxford: Oxford University Press, 2011.

Reindl, Andreas P. "Choosing Law in Cyberspace: Copyright Conflicts on Global Networks." *Michigan Journal of International Law* 19 (1998): 799–871.

Riestra, Ruben, Xenia Beltran, Panos Georgiou, Giannis Tsakonas, Kirnn Kaur, Susan Reilly, and Karlheinz Schmitt. *Business Preparedness Report*. Dorset, Eng., and The Hague: APARSEN, 2013. APARSEN-REP-D36_1-01-1_0. http://www.alliancepermanentaccess.org/wp-content/uploads/downloads/2013/03/APARSEN-REP-D36_1-01-1_0.pdf.

Rosenstein, Carole. "When Is a Museum a Public Museum? Considerations from the Point of View of Public Finance." *International Journal of Cultural Policy* 16, no. 4 (Nov. 2010): 449–65.

Tessella Digital Preservation. "Basic Repository." Accessed June 15, 2014. http://www.digitalpreservation.com/solution/basic-repository/.

———. "Preservica." Accessed June 15, 2014. http://www.digital preservation.com/solution/preservica/.

U.C. Curation Center and California Digital Library. "Total Cost of Preservation (TCP): Cost Modeling for Sustainable Services, Revision 2.0 (draft) 2012-11-09." U.C. Curation Center and California Digital Library, November 9, 2012. https://wiki.ucop.edu/download/attachments/163610649/TCP-cost-modeling-for-sustainable-services-v2.pdf.

Wheatley, Paul. "Costing the DP Lifecycle More Effectively." Paper presented at iPRES 2008, London, September 29–30, 2008. http://www.bl.uk/ipres2008/presentations_day1/19_Wheatley.pdf.

Wright, Richard, Matthew Addis, and Ant Miller. "The Significance of Storage in the 'Cost of Risk' of Digital Preservation." Presentation at iPRES 2008, London, September 29–30, 2008. http://www.bl.uk/ipres2008/presentations_day1/21_Wright.pdf.

CHAPTER 3

Consultative Committee for Space Data Systems (CCSDS). *Reference Model for an Open Archival Information System (OAIS): Recommended Practice CCSDS 650.0-M-2; Recommendation for Space Data System Practices*, Magenta Book, Recommended Practice, issue 2.

Washington, D.C.: CCSDS Secretariat, June 2012. http://public.ccsds.org/publications/archive/650x0m2.pdf.

Doyle, Julie, Herna Viktor, and Eric Paquet. "Long-Term Digital Preservation: Preserving Authenticity and Usability of 3-D Data." *International Journal on Digital Libraries* 10 (2009): 33–47.

Everybody's Libraries Blog. "What Repositories Do: The OAIS Model." October 13, 2008; accessed September 29, 2013, http://everybodyslibraries.com/2008/10/13/what-repositories-do-the-oais-model/.

Laughton, Paul. "OAIS Functional Model Conformance Test: A Proposed Measurement." *Program: Electronic Library and Information Systems* 46 (2012): 308–20.

Lee, Christopher A. "Open Archival Information System (OAIS) Reference Model." In *Encyclopedia of Library and Information Sciences*, 3rd ed. Boca Raton, Fla.: CRC Press, 2009. doi:10.1081/E-ELIS3-120044377.

Lesk, Michael. *Understanding Digital Libraries*. Boston: Elsevier, 2004.

Ockerbloom, John Mark. "What Repositories Do: The OAIS Model." *Everybody's Libraries Blog*, October 13, 2008. Accessed September 29, 2013, http://everybodyslibraries.com/2008/10/13/what-repositories-do-the-oais-model/.

Paradigm. "Workbook on Digital Private Papers." Accessed June 1, 2013. http://www.paradigm.ac.uk/workbook/index.html.

CHAPTER 4

Caplan, Priscilla. "Digital Preservation." *Library Technology Reports* 44, no. 2 (Feb./Mar. 2008).

Digital Curation Centre. "Curation Journals." Accessed September 29, 2013. http://www.dcc.ac.uk/resources/curation-journals.

———. "Events." Accessed September 29, 2013 http://www.dcc.ac.uk/events.

Distributed Data Curation Center. "About Us." Accessed September 29, 2013. http://d2c2.lib.purdue.edu/about.

EZID. "EZID Homepage." Accessed September 29, 2013. http://n2t.net/ezid.

Higgins, Sarah. "Digital Curation: The Emergence of a New Discipline." *International Journal of Digital Curation* 6, no. 2 (2011): 78–88. http://www.ijdc.net/index.php/ijdc/article/download/184/251.

Imaging.org. "Archiving." Accessed September 29, 2013. http://www.imaging.org/ist/conferences/archiving/index.cfm.

New York University. "Moving Image Archive Program." Accessed September 29, 2013. http://www.nyu.edu/tisch/preservation/.

Poole, Alex H., Christopher A. Lee, Heather L. Barnes, and Angela P. Murillo. "Digital Curation Preparation: A Survey of Contributors to International Professional, Educational, and Research Venues: UNC SILS Technical Report 2013-01." April 15, 2013; accessed September 29, 2013, http://sils.unc.edu/sites/default/files/news/SILS%20Report%20TR-2013-01-final.pdf.

Tammaro, Anna Maria, and Melody Madrid. "Digital Curator Education: Professional Identity vs. Convergence of LAM (Libraries, Archives, Museums)." Unpublished manuscript, 2012.

University of California: California Digital Library, "About CDL," accessed September 29, 2013, http://www.cdlib.org/about/.

Weech, Terry. "Convergence of Education for Information Professionals in Libraries, Archives, Museums, and Other Institutions in LIS Schools in Research and Curriculum Offerings: The U.S. and Canadian Experience." PowerPoint presented at the Convergence of Education for Information Professionals workshop, iConference 2013, Fort Worth, Texas, February 2013. https://ideals.illinois.edu/handle/2142/42574.

CHAPTER 5

Billenness, Clive. "Building a Sustainable Model for Digital Preservation Services." Paper presented at the third annual WePreserve Conference, Nice, October 28–30, 2008. http://www.digitalpreservationeurope.eu/preservation-training-materials/files/WEPRE SERVEsustainability.pdf.
Blue Ribbon Task Force on Sustainable Digital Preservation and Access (BRTF-SDPA). "Blue Ribbon Task Force on Sustainable Digital Preservation and Access Homepage." Accessed May 26, 2013. http://brtf.sdsc.edu/index.html.
———. *Sustainable Economics for a Digital Planet: Ensuring Long Term Access to Digital Information.* San Diego: San Diego Supercomputer Center, 2010. http://brtf.sdsc.edu/biblio/ BRTF_Final_Report.pdf.
Burns, C. Sean, Amy Lana, and John M. Budd. "Institutional Repositories: Exploration of Costs and Value." *D-Lib Magazine* 19, no. 1–2 (2013). http://dlib.org/dlib/january13/ burns/01burns.html.
Cardiff University. "Cardiff University Electronic Theses and Dissertations Publication Form." Accessed September 29, 2013. http://www.cf.ac.uk/regis/resources/Electronic%20 Theses%20and%20Dissertations%20Publication%20Form.pdf.
Chen, Su-Shung. "Digital Preservation: Organizational Commitment, Archival Stability, and Technological Continuity." *Journal of Organizational Computing and Electronic Commerce* 17 (2007): 207–15.
Corrado, Edward M. "The Importance of Open Access, Open Source, and Open Standards for Libraries." *Issues in Science and Technology Librarianship* (Spring 2005). http://www.istl .org/05-spring/article2.html.
Cost Model for Digital Preservation. "Cost Model for Digital Preservation (CMDP)." Accessed September 29, 2013. http://costmodelfordigitalpreservation.dk/.
Darby, Nell. "The Cost of Historical Research: Why Archives Need to Move with the Times." *Higher Education Network Blog,* May 23, 2013. Accessed September 29, 2013. http:// www.guardian.co.uk/higher-education-network/blog/2013/may/23/history-research-costs -archive-fees.
Data Archiving and Networked Services (DANS). "Costs of Digital Archiving, vol. 2." Accessed September 29, 2013. http://www.dans.knaw.nl/en/content/categorieen/projecten/ costs-digital-archiving-vol-2.
Evens, Tom, and Laurence Hauttekeete. "Challenges of Digital Preservation for Cultural Heritage Institutions." *Journal of Librarianship and Information Science* 43 (2011): 157–65.
Gibbs, Martin, and Sarah Colley. "Digital Preservation, Online Access and Historical Archaeology 'Grey Literature' from New South Wales, Australia." *Australian Archaeology* 75 (2012): 95–103.
Holdren, John P. "Memorandum for the Heads of Executive Departments and Agencies: Increasing Access to the Results of Federally Funded Scientific Research." February 22,

2013. http://www.whitehouse.gov/sites/default/files/microsites/ostp/ostp_public_access_memo_2013.pdf.

Hubbard, Douglas W. *The Failure of Risk Management: Why It's Broken and How to Fix It.* Hoboken: John Wiley and Sons, 2009.

Katre, Dinesh. "Ecosystems for Digital Preservation in Indian Context: A Proposal for Sustainable and Iterative Lifecycle Model." Paper presented at the Indo–U.S. Workshop on International Trends in Digital Preservation, Prune, India, March 24–25, 2009. http://www.scribd.com/doc/36284662/Indo-US-DP-Proceedings-C-DAC-2009.

Kenney, Anne R., and Nancy Y. McGovern. "The Five Organizational Stages of Digital Preservation." In *Digital Libraries: A Vision for the 21st Century; A Festschrift in Honor of Wendy Lougee on the Occasion of her Departure from the University of Michigan,* edited by Patricia Hodges, Mark Sandler, Maria Bonn, and John Price Wilkin, Ann Arbor: Scholarly Publishing Office, University of Michigan, University Library, 2003. http://quod.lib.umich.edu/s/spobooks/bbv9812.0001.001/1:11?rgn=div1;view=fulltext.

Lavoie, Brian F. "The Fifth Blackbird: Some Thoughts on Economically Sustainable Digital Preservation." *D-Lib Magazine* (March/April 2008). http://www.dlib.org/dlib/march08/lavoie/03lavoie.html.

Lavoie, Brian, Lorraine Eakin, Amy Friedlander, Francine Berman, Paul Courant, Clifford Lynch, and Daniel Rubinfeld. "Sustaining the Digital Investment: Issues and Challenges of Economically Sustainable Digital Preservation." Blue Ribbon Task Force on Sustainable Digital Preservation and Access (BRTF-SDPA). December 2008. http://brtf.sdsc.edu/biblio/BRTF_Interim_Report.pdf.

Lazorchak, Butch. "A Digital Asset Sustainability and Preservation Cost Bibliography." *The Signal: Digital Preservation Blog,* June 26, 2012. Accessed September 29, 2013. http://blogs.loc.gov/digitalpreservation/2012/06/a-digital-asset-sustainability-and-preservation-cost-bibliography/.

Lesk, Michael. *Practical Digital Libraries: Books, Bytes, and Bucks.* San Francisco: Morgan Kaufmann, 1997.

Lyall, Frank, and Paul B. Larsen, *Space Law: A Treatise.* Surrey, Eng.: Ashgate Publishing, 2009.

Maron, Nancy L., K. Kirby Smith, and Matthew Loy. *Sustaining Digital Resources: An On-the-Ground View of Projects Today.* Report prepared by Ithaka with support from U.K. Joint Information Systems Committee (JISC), the U.S. National Endowment for the Humanities, and the U.S. National Science Foundation. April 2009. http://www.jisc.ac.uk/media/documents/publications/general/2009/scaithakaprojectstodayfundersedition.pdf.

Morrissey, Sheila. "The Economy of Free and Open Source Software in the Preservation of Digital Artefacts." *Library Hi Tech* 28 (2010): 211–23.

National Aeronautics and Space Administration (NASA). *NASA Risk Management Handbook.* Version 1.0, NASA/SP-2011-3422. Washington, D.C.: NASA Headquarters, 2011. http://permanent.access.gpo.gov/gpo24492/20120000033-2011025561.pdf.

National Digital Stewardship Alliance. *National Agenda for Digital Stewardship 2014.* Washington, D.C.: Library of Congress, 2014. http://www.digitalpreservation.gov/ndsa/documents/2014NationalAgenda.pdf.

Open Source Initiative. "Open Standards Requirement for Software." Accessed September 29, 2013. http://opensource.org/osr.

OPF Knowledge Base Wiki. "Digital Preservation and Data Curation Costing and Cost Modelling." Last modified April 22, 2013. http://wiki.opf-labs.org/display/CDP/Home.

Palaiologk, Anna, Anastasios A. Economides, Heiko D. Tjalsma, and Laurents B. Sesink. "An Activity-Based Costing Model for Long-Term Preservation and Dissemination of Digital Research Data: The Case of DANS." *International Journal on Digital Libraries* 12 (2012): 195–214. doi:10.1007/s00799-012-0092-1.

Pearson, David. "Sustainable Models for Digital Preservation." Paper presented at the Sustainable Data from Digital Fieldwork International Conference, Sydney, December 4–6, 2006. http://www.nla.gov.au/openpublish/index.php/nlasp/article/viewArticle/920.

Riestra, Ruben, Xenia Beltran, Panos Georgiou, Giannis Tsakonas, Kirnn Kaur, Susan Reilly, and Karlheinz Schmitt. *Business Preparedness Report.* Dorset, Eng., and The Hague: APARSEN, 2013. APARSEN-REP-D36_1-01-1_0. http://www.alliancepermanentaccess .org/wp-content/uploads/downloads/2013/03/APARSEN-REP-D36_1-01-1_0.pdf.

U.S. Environmental Protection Agency. "Sustainability: Basic Information." Accessed May 15, 2013. http://www.epa.gov/sustainability/basicinfo.htm.

Walters, Tyler O., and Katherine Skinner. "Economics, Sustainability, and the Cooperation Model in Digital Preservation." *Library Hi Tech* 28 (2010): 259–72.

Wikipedia, s.v. "Succession Planning." Accessed March 21, 2013. http://em.wikipedia.org/ wiki/Succession_planning.

CHAPTER 6

Alliance Permanent Access to the Records of Science in Europe Network (APARSEN). *Trust Is Fundamental to the Working of Society.* Dorset, Eng., and The Hague: APARSEN, 2012. http://www.alliancepermanentaccess.org/wp-content/uploads/downloads/2012/09/ APARSEN-Trust-Brochure-Low-Res-Web-Version.pdf.

Center for Research Libraries (CRL). "Certification and Assessment." Accessed September 29, 2013. http://www.crl.edu/archiving-preservation/digital-archives/certification-and -assessment-digital-repositories.

———. *Trustworthy Repositories Audit and Certification: Criteria and Checklist (TRAC), Version 1.0.* Chicago and Dublin, Ohio: CRL and OCLC, 2007. http://www.crl.edu/sites/default/ files/attachments/pages/trac_0.pdf.

Chronopolis. "TRAC." Accessed September 29, 2013. http://chronopolis.sdsc.edu/trac/index .html.

Consultative Committee for Space Data Systems (CCSDS). *Audit and Certification of Trust-worthy Digital Repositories: Recommended Practice CCSDS 652.0-M-1; Recommendation for Space Data System Practices,* Magenta Book, Recommended Practice, issue 1. Washington, D.C.: CCSDS Secretariat, 2011. http://public.ccsds.org/publications/archive/652x0m1 .pdf.

Dale, Robin L. "Making Certification Real: Developing Methodology for Evaluating Trustworthiness." *RLG DigiNews* 9, no. 5 (2005). http://www.worldcat.org/arcviewer/1/ OCC/2007/08/08/0000070511/viewer/file3025.html#article2.

Data Seal of Approval. "DSA Guidelines for 2014–2015 Now Available." July 31, 2013. http://datasealofapproval.org/?q=node/95.

———. "Guidelines, Version 1." June 1, 2010. https://assessment.datasealofapproval.org/ guidelines_1/pdf/.

Dobratz, Susanne, and Heike Neuroth. "Nestor: Network of Expertise in Long-Term STOr-age of Digital Resources; A Digital Preservation Initiative for Germany." *D-Lib Magazine* 10, no. 4 (April 2004). http://www.dlib.org/dlib/april04/dobratz/04dobratz.html.

Dictionary.com, s.v. "Trust." Accessed September 29, 2013. http://dictionary.reference.com/browse/trust.

Digital Repository Audio Method Based on Risk Assessment (DRAMBORA). "A Risk-Aware Path to Self-Assurance and Partner Confidence for Digital Repositories." Flyer. Accessed June 8, 2013. http://www.repositoryaudit.eu/img/drambora_flyer.pdf.

Hardman, Catherine. "Case Study ADS: Presentation 4." Presentation at the Data Seal of Approval Conference 2012, Florence, December 10, 2013. http://www.datasealofapproval.org/sites/default/files/4_ADS_DSA_Florence2012-Cathrine_Hardman.ppt.

Ketal, Christian. "DIN Standard 31644 and Nestor Certification." Paper presented at the Fondazione Rinascimento Digitale 2012, Florence, December 11–12, 2013. http://www.rinascimento-digitale.it/conference2012/paper_ic_2012/keitel_paper.pdf.

Nestor. "About Us." Last modified March 30, 2012. http://www.langzeitarchivierung.de/Subsites/nestor/EN/Header/AboutUs/ueberuns_node.html.

———. "Standardisation." Last modified March 30, 2012. http://www.langzeitarchivierung.de/Subsites/nestor/EN/Standardisation/standardisation.html

———. "Nestor Homepage." Accessed September 29, 2013. http://www.langzeitarchivierung.de/Subsites/nestor/EN/Home/home_node.html.

Research Libraries Group–Online Computer Library Center (RLG-OCLC). *Trusted Digital Repositories: Attributes and Responsibilities; An RLG-OCLC Report.* Mountain View, Calif.: RLG, 2002. http://www.oclc.org/content/dam/research/activities/trustedrep/repositories.pdf.

Speck, Jason G. "Protecting Public Trust: An Archival Wake-Up Call." *Journal of Archival Organization* 8 (2010): 31–53.

Task Force on Archiving of Digital Information. "Preserving Digital Information: Report of the Task Force on Archiving of Digital Information." Commissioned by the Commission on Preservation and Access and the Research Libraries Group. May 1, 1996. http://www.oclc.org/content/dam/research/activities/digpresstudy/final-report.pdf.

TrustedDigitalRepository.eu. "Trusted Digital Repository Homepage." Accessed September 29, 2013. http://www.trusteddigitalrepository.eu/Site/Trusted%20Digital%20Repository.html.

CHAPTER 7

Baudoin, Patsy. "The Principle of Digital Preservation." *The Serials Librarian* 55, no. 4. (2008): 556–59. doi:10.1080/03615260802291212.

Campbell, D. Grant. "Metadata, Metaphor, and Metonymy." In *Metadata: A Cataloger's Primer*, edited by Richard P. Smiraglia, 57-73. New York: Routledge, 2005.

Caplan, Priscilla. *Understanding PREMIS*. Washington, D.C.: Library of Congress, 2009. http://www.loc.gov/standards/premis/understanding-premis.pdf.

Caplan, Priscilla, and Rebecca Gunther. "Practical Preservation: The PREMIS Experience." *Library Trends* 54, no. 1 (2005): 111–24.

Chen, Mingyu, and Michele Reilly. "Implementing METS, MIX, and DC for Sustaining Digital Preservation at the University of Houston Libraries." *Journal of Library Metadata* 11 (2011): 83–99.

Consultative Committee for Space Data Systems (CCSDS). *Reference Model for an Open Archival Information System (OAIS): Recommended Practice CCSDS 650.0-M-2; Recommendation for Space Data System Practices*, Magenta Book, Recommended Practice, issue 2. Washington, D.C.: CCSDS Secretariat, June 2012. http://public.ccsds.org/publications/archive/650x0m2.pdf.

California Digital Library (CDL). *CopyrightMD User Guidelines, Version 0.91*. Oakland, Calif.: CDL, 2009. http://www.cdlib.org/groups/rmg/docs/copyrightMD_user_guidelines.pdf.

Caplan, Priscilla. *Understanding PREMIS*. Washington, D.C.: Library of Congress, 2009. http://www.loc.gov/standards/premis/understanding-premis.pdf.

Chen, Mingyu, and Michele Reilly. "Implementing METS, MIX, and DC for Sustaining Digital Preservation at the University of Houston Libraries." *Journal of Library Metadata* 11 (2011): 83–99.

Coyle, Karen. "Understanding the Semantic Web: Bibliographic Data and Metadata." *Library Technology Reports* 46, no. 1 (2010): 5–31.

Cundiff, Morgan. "METS Application Profiles." (PowerPoint presented at the METS Opening Day Program, Washington, D.C.: Library of Congress, October 27-28, 2003),. www.loc.gov/standards/mets/presentations/cundiff.ppt.

Cutter, Charles A. *Rules for a Dictionary Catalog*. 4th ed., rewritten. Washington, D.C.: Government Printing Office, 1904. http://digital.library.unt.edu/ark:/67531/metadc1048/.

Dietrich, Chris. "Forbearing the Digital Dark Ages: Capturing Metadata for Digital Objects." Webinar PowerPoint presentation for the Association of Southeastern Research Libraries, April 9, 2013. http://www.aserl.org/wp-content/uploads/2013/04/Intro_DP_2013-2_DigitalObjectMetadata.pdf.

Digital Preservation Coalition. "Introduction: Definitions and Concepts." Accessed August 2, 2013. http://www.dpconline.org/advice/preservationhandbook/introduction/definitions-and-concepts.

———. *Preservation Management of Digital Materials: The Handbook*. In collaboration with the National Library of Australia and the PADI (Preserving Access to Digital Information) Gateway. York, Eng.: Digital Preservation Coalition, 2008. http://www.dpconline.org/component/docman/doc_download/299-digital preservation-handbook.

Dublin Core Metadata Initiative. "Dublin Core Metadata Element Set, Version 1.1." Accessed September 29, 2013. http://dublincore.org/documents/dces/.

———. "Dublin Core Qualifiers (SUPERSEDED, SEE DCMI Metadata Terms)." July 11, 2000. http://dublincore.org/documents/2000/07/11/dcmes-qualifiers/.

Gilliland-Swetland, Anne J. *Enduring Paradigm, New Opportunities: The Value of the Archival Perspective in the Digital Environment*. Washington, D.C.: Council on Library and Information Resources, 2000. http://www.clir.org/pubs/reports/pub89/pub89.pdf.

Guenther, Rebecca, and Jackie Radebaugh. "What Is METS? (Schema)." PowerPoint presented at the Standards Showcase: MODS, METS, MARCXML, the annual conference of the American Library Association, New Orleans, June 23–27, 2006. http://www.loc.gov/standards/mods/mods-mets-ala/pages/Slide21-th_gif.html.

Habing, Thomas. "METS, MODS and PREMIS, Oh My!" PowerPoint presented at the annual conference of the American Library Association, Washington, D.C., June 21–27, 2007. http://www.loc.gov/standards/mods/presentations/habing-ala07/.

Hackney, Douglas. "Digital Photography Meta Data Overview: Document Version 1.2." N.p.: Douglas Hackney, 2008. http://www.hackneys.com/travel/docs/metadataoverview .pdf.

Hillmann, Diane. "Using Dublin Core: The Elements." *Dublin Core Metadata Initiative*, August 26, 2003. http://dublincore.org/documents/2003/08/26/usageguide/elements.shtml.

Howe, Denis, ed. *The Free On-line Dictionary of Computing*, s.v. "Data." Last modified September 10, 2007. http://foldoc.org/data.

International Federation of Library Associations and Institutions' (IFLA) Study Group on the Functional Requirements for Bibliographic Records. "Functional Requirements for Bibliographic Records: Final Report." September 1997; last modified February 2009. http:// www.ifla.org/files/cataloguing/frbr/frbr_2008.pdf.

Lavoie, Brian, and Richard Gartner. *Preservation Metadata: Digital Preservation Coalition Technology Watch Report 13-03*, 2nd ed. Great Britain: Digital Preservation Coalition in association with Charles Beagrie, Ltd., 2013. http://dx.doi.org/10.7207/twr13-03.

Lazinger, Susan. *Digital Preservation and Metadata: History, Theory, Practice.* Englewood, Colo.: Libraries Unlimited, 2001.

Library of Congress (LOC). "DigiProv Data Dictionary: Audio-Visual Prototyping Project." Last modified August 31, 2010. http://www.loc.gov/rr/mopic/avprot/DD_PMD.html.

———. "DIGIPROVMD: Digital Production and Provenance Metadata Extension Schema." Last modified August 23, 2002. http://lcweb2.loc.gov/mets/Schemas/PMD.xsd.

———. "Explanation: DigiProv (Digital Provenance) Extension Schema." AV Prototype Project Working Documents. February 2003; last modified August 31, 2010. http://www.loc .gov/rr/mopic/avprot/digiprov_expl.html.

———. "Rights Data Dictionary." Last modified August 31, 2010. http://www.loc.gov/rr/ mopic/avprot/DD_RMD.html.

———. "TextMD: Technical Metadata for Text." Accessed May 13, 2013. http://www.loc.gov/ standards/textMD/.

"METS Editorial Board Endorses VRA Core 4.0 Schema: November 7, 2007." *VRA Core News*, November 8, 2012. Accessed September 29, 2013. http://vracorenews.blogspot .com/2012/11/mets-editorial-board-endorses-vra-core.html.

Millar, Laura. "The Death of the Fonds and the Resurrection of Provenance: Archival Context in Space and Time." *Archivaria* 53, no. 6 (2002): 1–15.

National Information Standards Organization (NISO). *Understanding Metadata.* Bethesda, Md.: NISO Press, 2004. http://www.niso.org/publications/press/UnderstandingMetadata .pdf.

Novak, Audrey. "Fixity Checks: Checksums, Message Digests, and Digital Signatures." Committee report, Yale University Digital Preservation Committee, November 2006.

Open Provenance Model. "The OPM Provenance Model (OPM)." Accessed June 7, 2013. http://openprovenance.org/.

Open-biomed. "Open Provenance Model Vocabulary Specification." October 6, 2010; last modified June 4, 2012. http://open-biomed.sourceforge.net/opmv/ns.html.

PBCore.org. "What Is a Metadata Dictionary?" Accessed September 29, 2013. http://pbcore .org/PBCore/PBCorePrimer.html#02.

Pearce, Judith, David Pearson, Megan Williams, and Scott Yeadon. "The Australian METS Profile: A Journey about Metadata." *D-Lib Magazine* 14, no. 3–4 (March/April 2008). http://www.dlib.org/dlib/march08/pearce/03pearce.html.

PREMIS Editorial Committee. *PREMIS Data Dictionary for Preservation Metadata, Version 2.2.* Washington, D.C.: Library of Congress, 2012. http://www.loc.gov/standards/premis/v2/premis-2-2.pdf.

Romary, Laurent. "Data Management in the Humanities." *ERCIM News* 89 (April 2012). http://ercim-news.ercim.eu/images/stories/EN89/EN89-web.pdf.

Seaman, David, "XML in Action: TEI." Course presented at Rare Book School, Charlottesville, Va., June 2012.

Smith, Abby. "Preface." In *Enduring Paradigm, New Opportunities: The Value of the Archival Perspective in the Digital Environment*, Anne J. Gilliland-Swetland, iv. Washington, D.C.: Council on Library and Information Resources, 2000. http://www.clir.org/pubs/reports/pub89/pub89.pdf.

Society of American Archivists. *A Glossary of Archival and Records Terminology*, s.v. "Data." accessed September 29, 2013, http://www2.archivists.org/glossary/terms/d/data.

Sweeney, Shelley. "The Ambiguous Origins of the Archival Principle of 'Provenance.'" *Libraries & the Cultural Record* 43, no. 2 (2008): 193–213. doi:10.1353/lac.0.0017.

Taylor, Arlene G., and Daniel N. Joudrey. *The Organization of Information*. Westport, Conn.: Libraries Unlimited, 2009.

W3C. "Extensible Markup Language (XML)." Last modified June 4, 2013. http://www.w3.org/XML/.

———. "PROV Model Primer." Last modified April 30, 2013. http://www.w3.org/TR/2013/NOTE-prov-primer-20130430/.

———. "PROV-Overview." April 30, 2013; accessed June 7, 2013. http://www.w3.org/TR/2013/NOTE-prov-overview-20130430/.

W3Schools.com. "PROV-XML: The PROV XML Schema." April 30, 2013; accessed June 7, 2013. http://www.w3.org/TR/prov-xml/.

———. "XML Validation." Accessed September 29, 2013. http://www.w3schools.com/xml/xml_dtd.asp.

———. "XSLT Introduction." Accessed September 29, 2013. http://www.w3schools.com/xsl/xsl_intro.asp.

Whalen, Maureen. "Rights Metadata Made Simple." In *Introduction to Metadata*, version 3.0, edited by Murtha Baca, 1-8. Los Angeles: J. Paul Getty Trust/Gregory M. Britton, 2008. http://www.getty.edu/research/publications/electronic_publications/intrometadata/rights.pdf.

Yale University Library. "Digital Preservation Policy." November 2005; last modified February 2007. http://www.library.yale.edu/iac/DPC/final1.html.

Zeng, Marcia Lei, and Jian Qin. *Metadata*. New York: Neal-Schuman, 2008.

CHAPTER 8

Abrams, Stephen. "DCC | Digital Curation Manual: Instalment on 'File Formats.'" Edinburgh Research Archive. Last modified October 2007. http://lac-repo-https://www.era.lib.ed.ac.uk/bitstream/1842/3351/1/Abrams%20file formats.pdf.

Adobe. "About Adobe PDF." Accessed September 29, 2013. http://www.adobe.com/products/acrobat/adobepdf.html.

Apache Software Foundation. "Apache Tika." Accessed April 23, 2013. http://tika.apache.org/.

Arms, Caroline, and Carl Fleischhauer. "Digital Formats: Factors for Sustainability, Functionality, and Quality." Paper presented at the Imaging Science and Technology (IS&T) Archiving 2005 Conference, Washington, D.C., April 26–29, 2005. http://memory.loc.gov/ammem/techdocs/digform/Formats_IST05_paper.pdf.

Ball, Alex. "Briefing Paper: File Format and XML Scheme Registries." May 31, 2006. http://www.ukoln.ac.uk/projects/grand-challenge/papers/registryBriefing.pdf.

Barth, Adam, Juan Caballero, and Dawn Song. "Secure Content Sniffing for Web Browsers, or How to Stop Papers from Reviewing Themselves." Paper presented at the thirtieth IEEE Symposium on Security and Privacy, Oakland, Calif., May 2009. Washington, D.C.: IEEE Computer Society, 2009, 360–71. doi:10.1109/SP.2009.3.

Binghamton University Library. "Digital Preservation Levels Based on Format." Accessed September 30, 2013. http://www.binghamton.edu/libraries/technology/digital preservation/levels-based-on-format.html.

Bitbucket. "JHOVE2 Frequently Asked Questions (FAQ)." Last modified March 18, 2013. https://bitbucket.org/jhove2/main/wiki/JHOVE2_Frequently_Asked_Questions_%28FAQ%29.

Clausen, Lars R. *Handling File Formats.* Copenhagen: n.p., 2004. http://citeseerx.ist.psu.edu/viewdoc/download?doi=10.1.1.2.1801&rep=rep1&type=pdf.

Clipsham, David. "Bring Out Your Dead (Files)." *National Archives Blog*, February 8, 2013. http://blog.nationalarchives.gov.uk/blog/bring-out-your-dead-files/.

———. "Recent Developments in DROID and PRONOM: What Happened in 2012?" Presentation for the National Archives, January 28, 2013. http://www.dpconline.org/component/docman/doc_download/813-2013fileformatsclipsham.

Dappert, Angela. "The PREMIS Data Dictionary: Information You Need to Know for Preserving Digital Documents." Paper presented in Prague, October 14, 2008.

Darwin, Ian F. "Fine Free File Command." *Darwynsys.com.* Accessed August 1, 2013. http://darwinsys.com/file/.

DBpedia. "About." Accessed April 23, 2013. http://dbpedia.org/About.

ECMA International. "Standard ECMA-376: Office Open XML File Formats." Accessed September 29, 2013. www.ecma-international.org/publications/standards/Ecma-376.htm.

ExifTool by Phil Harvey. "ExifTool by Phil Harvey: Read, Write, and Edit Meta Information!" Accessed April 23, 2013. http://www.sno.phy.queensu.ca/~phil/exiftool/.

Farquhar, Adam. "Fido: A High Performance Format Identifier for Digital Objects." *Adam Farquhar's Blog*, November 3, 2010. http://www.openplanetsfoundation.org/blogs/2010-11-03-fido-%E2%80%93-high-performance-format-identifier-digital objects.

FFmpeg. "About FFmpeg." Accessed April 23, 2013. http://www.ffmpeg.org/about.html.

Fileformats.archiveteam.org. "Statement of Project." Last modified October 28, 2012. http://fileformats.archiveteam.org/wiki/Statement_of_Project.

FileInfo.com. ".DOC File Extension." Accessed April 23, 2013. http://www.fileinfo.com/extension/doc.

Global Digital Format Registry. "Format Registry Ontology." Last modified March 10, 2003. http://www.gdfr.info/docs/Ontology-v1-2003-03-10.pdf.

Internet Assigned Numbers Authority. "MIME Media Types." Last modified January 30, 2013. http://www.iana.org/assignments/media-types.

Library and Archives Canada. "Library and Archives Canada, Local Digital Format Registry (LDFR) File Format Guidelines for Preservation and Long-term Access Version 1.0." Accessed April 23, 2013. http://www.collectionscanada.gc.ca/obj/012018/f2/012018-2200-e.pdf.

Library of Congress (LOC). "Formats, Evaluation Factors, and Relationships." Last modified March 20, 2013. http://www.digitalpreservation.gov/formats/intro/format_eval_rel.shtml.

LinkedIn. "Stephen Abrams." Accessed April 13, 2013. http://www.linkedin.com/pub/stephen-abrams/11/370/591.

Marc Rochkind's Apps and Books. "ImageVerifier." Accessed April 23, 2013. http://basepath.com/site/detail-ImageVerifier.php.

McGath, Gary. "Defining the File Format Registry Problem." *File Formats Blog*, September 3, 2013. http://fileformats.wordpress.com/2012/09/03/registry-problem/.

———. "Format Registries Don't SPARQL." *File Formats Blog*. September 6, 2012. http://fileformats.wordpress.com/2012/09/06/sparql/.

———. "The Format Registry Problem." *Code4Lib Journal* 19. Accessed April 23, 2013. http://journal.code4lib.org/articles/8029.

MediaArea.net. "MediaInfo." Accessed April 23, 2013. http://mediainfo.sourceforge.net/en.

Murray, James D., and William Van Ryper, *Encyclopedia of Graphics File Formats*. Sebastopol, Calif.: O'Reilly & Associates, 1994. Second ed. at http://www.fileformat.info/resource/book/1565921615/index.htm.

National Archives (U.K.). "Download DROID: File Format Identification Tool." Accessed April 23, 2013. http://www.nationalarchives.gov.uk/information-management/projects-and-work/droid.htm.

———. "PRONOM." Accessed April 23, 2013. http://www.nationalarchives.gov.uk/aboutapps/PRONOM/default.htm.

National Archives (U.S.). "Frequently Asked Questions (FAQ) about Digital Audio and Video Records." Accessed April 23, 2012. http://www.archives.gov/records-mgmt/initiatives/davfaq.html.

National Archives of Australia. "Xena Digital Preservation Software." Accessed September 29, 2013. http://xena.sourceforge.net/.

Open Planets Knowledge Base, s.v. "ExifTool." Last modified December 18, 2012. http://wiki.opf-labs.org/display/TR/ExifTool.

———, s.v. "Xpdf." Last modified August 20, 2013. http://wiki.opf-labs.org/display/TR/Xpdf.

Park, Eun G., and Sam Oh. "Examining Attributes of Open Standard File Formats for Long-Term Preservation and Open Access." *Information Technology and Libraries* 31, no. 4 (Dec. 2012): 44–65. doi:10.6017/ital.v31i4.1946.

PDFTron. "PDFTron: PDF/A Manager." Accessed April 23, 2013. http://www.pdftron.com/pdfamanager/.

Rog, Judith, and Caroline van Wijk. *Evaluating File Formats for Long-Term Preservation*. The Hague: National Library of the Netherlands, 2008. http://www.kb.nl/hrd/dd/dd_links_en_publicaties/publicaties/KB_file_format_evaluation_method_27022008.pdf.

Rusbridge, Chris. "Excuse Me . . . Some Digital Preservation Fallacies?" *Adriane* 46 (Feb. 2006). Accessed April 23, 2013. http://www.ariadne.ac.uk/issue46/rusbridge.

———. "Response to the Open Letter on Obsolete Microsoft File Formats." *Unsustainable Ideas Blog*, November 26, 2012. http://unsustainableideas.wordpress.com/2012/11/26/response-open-letter-obsolete-ms-formats/.

SourceForge. "Dependency Discovery Tool." Accessed April 23, 2013. http://sourceforge.net/projects/officeddt/.

———. "JHOVE: JSTOR/Harvard Object Validation Environment." Last modified February 25, 2009. http://jhove.sourceforge.net/.

TechNet. "File Format Reference for Office 2013." Accessed April 23, 2013. http://technet.microsoft.com/en-us/library/dd797428.aspx.

U.C. Curation Center. *Unified Digital Format Registry (UDFR) Final Report.* Oakland, Calif.: California Digital Library, 2012. http://udfr.org/project/UDFR-final-report.pdf.

"University Library Receives Grant." *Harvard Gazette*, February 2, 2006. Accessed September 29, 2013. http://news.harvard.edu/gazette/story/2006/02/university-library-receives-grant/.

University of Minnesota Digital Conservancy. "University Digital Conservancy Preservation Policy." Accessed April 23, 2013. http://conservancy.umn.edu/pol-preservation.jsp.

Van der Knijff, Johan. "JPEG 2000 for Long-Term Preservation: JP2 as a Preservation Format." *D-Lib Magazine* 17, no. 5–6 (2011). http://www.dlib.org/dlib/may11/vanderknijff/05vanderknijff.html.

Von Suchodoletz, Dirk. "Practical Issues with Currently Available File Format Software." Comment on *Bill Robert's Blog*, "File Format Registry Report Released," February 16, 2011. http://www.openplanetsfoundation.org/comment/92#comment-92.

Wikipedia, s.v. "File Format." Last modified April 4, 2013. http://en.wikipedia.org/w/index.php?title=File_format&oldid=548699192.

———, s.v. "JPEG 2000: Legal Issues." Accessed September 29, 2013. http://en.wikipedia.org/wiki/JPEG_2000#Legal_issues.

———, s.v. "List of File Formats (Alphabetical)." Last modified April 15. 2013. http://en.wikipedia.org/wiki/List_of_file_formats_%28alphabetical%29.

———, s.v. "Microsoft Word: File Formats." Accessed April 23, 2013. http://en.wikipedia.org/wiki/Microsoft_Word#File_formats.

———, s.v. "PRONOM." Accessed April 23, 2013. http://en.wikipedia.org/w/index.php?title=PRONOM&oldid=534676523.

CHAPTER 9

Alliance Permanent Access to the Records of Science in Europe Network (APARSEN). *Trust Is Fundamental to the Working of Society.* Dorset, Eng., and The Hague: APARSEN, 2012. http://www.alliancepermanentaccess.org/wp-content/uploads/downloads/2012/09/APARSEN-Trust-Brochure-Low-Res-Web-Version.pdf.

Berman, Francine. "Got Data?" *Communications of the ACM* 51 (Dec. 2008): 50. http://portal.acm.org/citation.cfm?id=1409360.1409376.

Blue Ribbon Task Force on Sustainable Digital Preservation and Access (BRTF-SDPA). *Sustainable Economics for a Digital Planet: Ensuring Long Term Access to Digital Information.* San Diego: San Diego Supercomputer Center, 2010. http://brtf.sdsc.edu/biblio/BRTF_Final_Report.pdf.

Consultative Committee for Space Data Systems (CCSDS). *Reference Model for an Open Archival Information System (OAIS): Recommended Practice CCSDS 650.0-M-2; Recommendation for Space Data System Practices*, Magenta Book, Recommended Practice, issue 2. Washington, D.C.: CCSDS Secretariat, June 2012. http://public.ccsds.org/publications/archive/650x0m2.pdf.

IBM, "Big Data at the Speed of Business," para. 1, accessed August 13, 2013. http://www-01.ibm.com/software/data/bigdata/.

Kastellec, Mike. "Practical Limits to the Scope of Digital Preservation." *Information Technology and Libraries* 31 (June 2012).

University of Oregon Libraries. "Instruction and Outreach." Accessed June 8, 2013. http://library.uoregon.edu/diglib/instruction.html.

CHAPTER 10

Australia National Data Service. "Register My Data." Accessed September 29, 2013. http://www.ands.org.au/services/register-my-data.html.

———. "Research Data Australia." Accessed September 29, 2013. http://www.ands.org.au/guides/research-data-australia.html.

Biodiversity Information Standards: TDWG. "About Us." Last modified January 13, 2011. http://www.tdwg.org/about-tdwg/.

———. "Darwin Core." Last modified October 8, 2009. http://rs.tdwg.org/dwc/.

———. "Darwin Core Terms: A Quick Reference Guide." February 12, 2009; last modified October 26, 2011. http://rs.tdwg.org/dwc/terms/.

Biotechnology and Biological Sciences Research Center (BBSRC). *BBSRC Data Sharing Policy, Version 1.1.* Swindon, Eng.: BBSRC, June 2010. http://www.bbsrc.ac.uk/web/FILES/Policies/data-sharing-policy.pdf.

boyd, danah, and Kate Crawford. "Critical Questions for Big Data." *Information, Communication & Society* 15, no. 5 (2012): 662–79.

Bush, Vannavar. "As We May Think." *Atlantic Monthly* 176, no. 1 (July 1945): 101–8. http://www.theatlantic.com/magazine/archive/1945/07/as-we-may-think/303881/.

CITI Collaborative Institutional Training Initiative. "CITI Human Subjects Research Educational Program Information (CITI)." Accessed September 29, 2013. https://www.citiprogram.org/citiinfo.asp.

Corrado, Edward M. "Preservation and Research Data at Binghamton University Libraries." Presented at the University at Albany Libraries' Open Access Week, Albany, October 23, 2012. http://codabox.org/114/.

DataCite. "DataCite Services." Accessed June 7, 2013. http://datacite.org/services.

Dietrich, Dianne. "Metadata Management in a Data Staging Repository." *Journal of Library Metadata* 10, no. 2–3 (2010): 79–98.

Digital Curation Centre. "Biology." Accessed September 29, 2013. http://www.dcc.ac.uk/resources/subject-areas/biology.

———. "Earth Science." Accessed September 29, 2013. http://www.dcc.ac.uk/resources/subject-areas/earth-science.

Doctorow, Cory. "Welcome to the Petacentre." *Nature* 455, no. 4 (Sept. 2008): 16–21. http://www.nature.com/news/2008/080903/full/455016a.html.

Dryad. Home page. Accessed March 24, 2013. http://datadryad.org/.
———. "Joint Data Archiving Policy (JDAP)." Last modified April 7, 2013. http://datadryad
.org/pages/jdap.
Federal Geographic Data Committee. "Geospatial Metadata Standards: The Content Stan-
dard for Digital Geospatial Metadata (CSDGM)." Last modified September 6, 2012.
http://www.fgdc.gov/metadata/geospatial-metadata-standards#csdgm.
Glinos, Kostas. "Keynote: E-infrastructures for Big Data: Opportunities and Challenges."
ERICM News 89 (2012): 2–3. http://ercim-news.ercim.eu/images/stories/EN89/EN89
-web.pdf.
Global Change Master Directory. "Metadata Protocol and Standards." Last modified June
2013. http://gcmd.nasa.gov/add/standards/index.html.
———. "What Is the Global Change Master Directory (GCMD) and How Can It Help Me?"
Last modified June 2013. http://gcmd.nasa.gov/learn/faqs/about.html.
———. Write a DIF (Version 6)." November 2010. http://gcmd.nasa.gov/add/difguide/
WRITEADIF.pdf.
Health Insurance Portability and Protection Act (HIPPA). "HIPAA 'Protected Health In-
formation': What Does PHI Include?" Accessed September 29, 2013. http://www.hipaa
.com/2009/09/hipaa-protected-health-information-what-does-phi-include/.
Heidorn, P. Bryan. "Shedding Light on the Dark Data in the Long Tail of Science." *Library
Trends* 57, no. 2 (2008): 280–99. doi:10.1353/lib.0.0036.
Howard Hughes Medical Institute (HHMI). "Research Policies: Sharing of Publication-
Related Materials, Data and Software (SC-300)." Accessed September 29, 2013. http://
www.hhmi.org/about/research/sc_300.pdf.
Institute of Education Sciences (IES) Centers. "Policy Statement on Data Sharing in IES
Research Centers." Accessed September 29, 2013. http://ies.ed.gov/funding/datashar
ing_policy.asp.
———. "Resources for Researchers: Data Sharing Implementation Guide." Accessed Septem-
ber 29, 2013. http://ies.ed.gov/funding/datasharing_implementation.asp.
Internet Archive. "About the Internet Archive." Accessed September 29, 2013. http://archive
.org/about/.
———. "Audio Archive." Accessed September 29, 2013. http://archive.org/details/audio/.
———. "Movie Archive." Accessed September 29, 2013. http://archive.org/details/movies/.
———. "Ebook and Texts Archive." Accessed September 29, 2013. http://archive.org/details/
texts/.
Inter-University Consortium for Political and Social Research (ICPSR). "About ICPSR." Ac-
cessed September 29, 2013. http://www.icpsr.umich.edu/icpsrweb/content/membership/
about.html.
King, Ross, Rainer Schmidt, Christoph Becker, and Sven Schlarb. "SCAPE: Big Data Meets
Digital Preservation." *ERCIM News* 89 (April 2012): 30–31. http://ercim-news.ercim.eu/
images/stories/EN89/EN89-web.pdf.
Laney, Doug. "3D Data Management: Controlling Data Volume, Velocity, and Variety."
META Group Application Delivery Services. File 949. February 6, 2001. Stamford, Conn.:
Meta Group, Inc., 2001. http://blogs.gartner.com/doug-laney/files/2012/01/ad949-3D
-Data management-Controlling-Data-Volume-Velocity-and-Variety.pdf.
Lemire, Daniel, and Andre Vellino. "Extracting, Transforming and Archiving Scientific Data."
Paper presented at the fourth Workshop on Very Large Digital Libraries, Berlin, September
29, 2011. http://arxiv.org/abs/1108.4041.

Library of Congress (LOC). "Bill Summary and Status: 113th Congress (2013–2014); H.R.708." Accessed September 29, 2013. http://thomas.loc.gov/cgi-bin/bdquery/z?d113:h.r.708:.

———. "Bill Summary and Status: 113th Congress (2013–2014); S.350." Accessed September 29, 2013. http://thomas.loc.gov/cgi-bin/bdquery/z?d113:s.350:.

———. "Bill Text: 113th Congress (2013–2014); S.350.IS." Accessed September 29, 2013. http://thomas.loc.gov/cgi-bin/query/z?c113:S.350:.

Lohr, Steve. "The Age of Big Data." *New York Times*, February 13, 2012. Accessed September 29, 2013. http://www.nytimes.com/2012/02/12/sunday-review/big-datas-impact-in-the-world.html.

———. "Big Data Is Opening Doors, but Maybe Too Many." *New York Times*, March 23, 2013. Accessed September 29, 2013. http://www.nytimes.com/2013/03/24/technology/big-data-and-a-renewed-debate-over-privacy.html.

Lynch, Clifford. "Big Data: How Do Your Data Grow?" *Nature* 455, no. 4 (2008): 28–29. http://www.nature.com/nature/journal/v455/n7209/pdf/455028a.pdf.

Markoff, John. "Unreported Side Effects of Drugs Are Found Using Internet Search Data, Study Finds." *New York Times Online*, March 6, 2013. Accessed September 29, 2013. http://www.nytimes.com/2013/03/07/science/unreported-side-effects-of-drugs-found-using-internet-data-study-finds.html.

Matthews, Brian, Shoaib Sufi, Damian Flannery, Laurent Lerusse, Tom Griffin, Michael Gleaves, and Kerstin Kleese. "Using a Core Scientific Metadata Model in Large-Scale Facilities." *The International Journal of Digital Curation* 5, no. 1 (2010). http://www.ijdc.net/index.php/ijdc/article/view/149/211.

Medical Research Council (MRC). "Data Sharing." Accessed September 29, 2013. http://www.mrc.ac.uk/Ourresearch/Ethicsresearchguidance/datasharing/index.htm.

———. "MRC Guidance in Data Management Plans." Accessed September 29, 2013. http://www.mrc.ac.uk/Ourresearch/Ethicsresearchguidance/datasharing/DMPs/index.htm.

Mudge, Mark, Michael Ashley, Carla Schroer, and Cultural Heritage Imaging. "A Digital Future for Cultural Heritage." Edited by A. Georgopoulos and N. Agriantonis. Paper presented at Cipa 2007: Anticipating the Future of the Cultural Past, Athens, October 1–7, 2007. http://culturalheritageimaging.org/What_We_Do/Publications/cipa2007/CIPA_2007.pdf.

National Digital Stewardship Alliance. "National Agenda for Digital Stewardship 2014." Accessed September 29, 2013. http://www.digitalpreservation.gov/ndsa/documents/2014NationalAgenda.pdf.

National Institutes of Health. "NIH Data Sharing Policy and Implementation Guidance: Goals of Data Sharing." Last modified March 5, 2003. http://grants.nih.gov/grants/policy/data_sharing/data_sharing_guidance.htm#goals.

National Science Foundation (NSF). *Proposal and Award Policies and Procedures Guide.* NSF 13-1, OMB Control Number: 3145-0058. Washington, D.C.: NSF, 2012. http://www.nsf.gov/pubs/policydocs/pappguide/nsf13001/nsf13_1.pdf.

Oai.datacite.org. "OAI-PMH Data Provider (Beta)." Accessed June 7, 2013. http://oai.datacite.org/.

Olsen, Lola. "What Is a DIF? A Short History of the Directory Interchange Format (DIF)." *Global Change Master Directory: Discover Earth Science Data and* Services. Last modified June 2013. http://gcmd.gsfc.nasa.gov/add/difguide/whatisadif.html.

Organisation for Economic Co-operation and Development (OECD). *OECD Principles and Guidelines for Access to Research Data from Public Funding.* Paris: OECD, 2007. http://www .oecd.org/sti/sci-tech/38500813.pdf.

Research Councils UK "RCUK Policy on Open Access and Supporting Guidance." Accessed September 29, 2013. http://www.rcuk.ac.uk/documents/documents/RCUKOpenAccess Policy.pdf.

SCAlable Preservation Environments (SCAPE). "Preservation." Accessed September 29, 2013. http://www.scape-project.eu/about/preservation.

———. "SCAlable Preservation Environments." Accessed September 29, 2013. http://www .scape-project.eu/.

Toronto International Data Release Workshop Authors. "Prepublication Data Sharing." *Nature* 461 (Sept. 2009): 168–70. doi:10.1038/461168a. http://www.nature.com/nature/ journal/v461/n7261/full/461168a.html.

U.S. Department of Health and Human Services (HHS). "Code of Federal Regulations: §46.102 Definitions." Accessed September 29, 2013. http://www.hhs.gov/ohrp/humansub jects/guidance/45cfr46.html#46.102.

———. "§46.101 To What Does This Policy Apply?" In *Code of Federal Regulations: Title 45, Public Welfare; Part 46, Protection of Human Subjects.* Washington, D.C.: HHS, 2009. http://www.hhs.gov/ohrp/policy/ohrpregulations.pdf.

U.S. Department of Health and Human Services (HHS): Office for Human Research Protections (OHRP). *Institutional Review Board Guidebook*, s.v. "Confidentiality." Last modified 1993. http://www.hhs.gov/ohrp/archive/irb/irb_glossary.htm.

Vines, Timothy H., Rose L. Andrew, Dan G. Bock, Michelle T. Franklin, Kimberly J. Gilbert, Nolan C. Kane, Jean-Sébastien Moore, Brook T. Moyers, Sébastien Renaut, Diana J. Rennison, Thor Veen, and Sam Yeaman. "Mandated Data Archiving Greatly Improves Access to Research Data." *The FASEB Journal* 27, no. 4 (April 2013): 1304–8. doi:10.1096/fj.12 -218164. http://www.fasebj.org/content/early/2013/01/07/fj.12-218164.full.pdf.

Wellcome Trust. "Policy on Data Management and Sharing." August 2010. http://www.well come.ac.uk/About-us/Policy/Policy-and-position-statements/WTX035043.htm.

Wieczorek, John, David Bloom, Robert Guralnick, Stan Blum, Markus Döring, Renato Giovanni, Tim Robertson, and David Vieglais. "Darwin Core: An Evolving Community-Developed Biodiversity Data Standard." *PLoS ONE* 7, no. 1 (2012) doi:10.1371/jour nal.pone.0029715. http://www.plosone.org/article/info%3Adoi%2F10.1371%2Fjournal .pone.0029715.

Working Group on Expanding Access to Published Research Findings. "Accessibility, Sustainability, Excellence: How to Expand Access to Research Publications" ["The Finch Report"]. *Research Information Network*, June 2012. http://www.researchinfonet.org/wp-content/ uploads/2012/06/Finch-Group-report-FINAL-VERSION.pdf.

World Economic Forum, in collaboration with The Boston Consulting Group. "Unlocking The Values of Personal Data: From Collection to Usage." February 2013. http://www3.weforum .org/docs/WEF_IT_UnlockingValuePersonalData_CollectionUsage_Report_2013.pdf.

CHAPTER 11

Adams, Jennifer L., and Kevin B. Gunn. "Keeping Up with . . . Digital Humanities." *Keeping Up With* (April 2013). Association of College and Research Libraries. Accessed May 12, 2013. http://www.ala.org/acrl/publications/keeping_up_with/digital_humanities.

Cataloging Cultural Objects. "Brochure." Accessed September 29, 2013. http://www.vraweb .org/ccoweb/cco/about.html.

CHIN's Professional Exchange. "Recommendations for Museums." Last modified February 15, 2013. http://www.pro.rcip-chin.gc.ca/contenu_numerique-digital_content/preserva tion_numerique-digital_preservation/recommand-recommend-eng.jsp.

———. "Checklist for Creating a Preservation Policy." Last modified February 2, 2013. http:// www.pro.rcip-chin.gc.ca/contenu_numerique-digital_content/preservation_numerique-digital_preservation/annexeA-appendixA-eng.jsp.

Crane, Gregory. "Give Us Editors! Re-inventing the Edition and Rethinking the Humanities." *Connexions*. Last modified by Ben Allen on May 14, 2010. http://cnx.org/content/m34316/1.2/.

Digital Curation Centre (DCC). "Social Science and Humanities." Accessed September 29, 2013. http://www.dcc.ac.uk/resources/subject-areas/social-science-humanities.

Doyle, Julie, Herna Viktor, and Eric Paquet. "Long-Term Digital Preservation: Preserving Authenticity and Usability of 3-D Data." *International Journal on Digital Libraries* 10 (2009): 33–47.

Glinos, Kostas. "Keynote: E-infrastructures for Big Data: Opportunities and Challenges." *ERICM News* 89 (2012): 2–3. http://ercim-news.ercim.eu/images/stories/EN89/EN89 -web.pdf.

Gold, Matthew K. "The Digital Humanities Movement." In *Debates in the Digital Humanities*, edited by Matthew K. Gold, ix-xvi. Minneapolis: University of Minnesota Press, 2012. A digital edition is also available at http://dhdebates.gc.cuny.edu/debates.

Guenther, Rebecca. "The Metadata Object Description Schema (MODS)." PowerPoint presented at the NISO Metadata Workshop, Washington, D.C., May 20, 2004. www.loc.gov/ standards/mods/presentations/niso-mods.ppt.

Guidi, Gabriele, J.-Angelo Beraldin, and Carlo Atzeni. "High-Accuracy 3-D Modeling of Cultural Heritage: The Digitizing of Donatello's 'Maddalena.'" *IEEE Transactions on Image Processing* 13, no. 3 (March 2004): 370–80. doi:10.1109/TIP.2003.822592.

Humanities Blast. "The Digital Humanities Manifesto 2.0." Accessed May 1, 2013. http:// www.humanitiesblast.com/manifesto/Manifesto_V2.pdf.

J. Paul Getty Trust. "Categories for the Description of Works of Art: CDWA Lite." Last modified February 7, 2011. http://www.getty.edu/research/publications/electronic_publications/ cdwa/cdwalite.html.

———. "Categories for the Description of Works of Art: Introduction." Last modified March 11, 2009. http://www.getty.edu/research/publications/electronic_publications/cdwa/intro duction.html.

Kretzschmar, William A. and William Gray Potter. "Library Collaboration with Large Digital Humanities Projects." *Literary and Linguistic Computing* 25 no. 4 (Sept. 2010): 439–45. doi:10.1093/llc/fqq022.

Library of Congress (LOC). "About EAD." Last Modified, July 11, 2012. http://www.loc .gov/ead/eadabout.html.

———. "Design Principles for Enhancements to MODS and MADS." September 2009; last modified October 18, 2010. http://www.loc.gov/standards/mods/design-principles-mods -mads.html.

———. "Development of the Encoded Archival Description DTD." Last revised December 2002. http://www.loc.gov/ead/eaddev.html.

———. "EAD 2002 Schema." Last modified July 17, 2012. http://www.loc.gov/ead/ead schema.html.

———. "EAD Revision Under Way." Last modified November 8, 2013. http://www.loc.gov/ead/eadrevision.html.

———. MIX." Accessed September 29, 2013. http://www.loc.gov/standards/mix/.

———. MODS: Metadata Object Description Schema." Accessed September 29, 2013. http://www.loc.gov/standards/mods/.

———. "Other Web Sites Related to EAD." Accessed September 29, 2013. http://www.loc.gov/ead/eadother.html.

———. "VRA Core 4.0." March 9, 2007. http://www.loc.gov/standards/vracore/VRA_Core4_Intro.pdf.

———. "VRA CORE Schemas and Documentation." Last modified April 16, 2012. http://www.loc.gov/standards/vracore/.

Little, Geoffrey. "We Are All Digital Humanists Now." *The Journal of Academic Librarianship* 37, no. 4 (2011): 352–54. doi:10.1016/j.acalib.2011.04.023.

Merriam-Webster Dictionary, s.v. "Humanity." Accessed May 12, 2013. http://www.merriam-webster.com/dictionary/humanity.

Millon, Emma. "Project Bamboo: Building Shared Infrastructure for Humanities Research." *Blog of the Maryland Institute for Technology in the Humanities*, July 1, 2011. http://mith.umd.edu/project-bamboo-building-shared-infrastructure-for-humanities-research/.

National Information Standards Organization (NISO). *Data Dictionary: Technical Metadata for Digital Still Images*. Bethesda, Md.: NISO Press, 2006. http://www.niso.org/kst/reports/standards/kfile_download?id%3Austring%3Aiso-8859-1=Z39-87-2006.pdf&pt=RkGKiXzW643YeUaYUqZ1BFwDhIG4-24RJbcZBWg8uE4vWdpZsJDs4RjLz0t90_d5_ymGsj_IKVaGZww13HuDlSn6cvwjex0ejiIKSaTYlErPbfamndQa6zkS6rLL3oIr.

———. *Understanding Metadata*. Bethesda, Md.: NISO Press, 2004. http://www.niso.org/publications/press/UnderstandingMetadata.pdf.

NINES. "What Is NINES?" Accessed May 12, 2013. http://www.nines.org/about/what-is-nines/.

PBCore. "Schema." Accessed September 29, 2013. http://www.pbcore.org/schema/.

———. "User Guide to PBCore Public Broadcasting Metadata Dictionary." Accessed September 29, 2013. http://pbcore.org/PBCore/UserGuide.html.

Romary, Laurent. "Data Management in the Humanities." *ERCIM News* 89 (April 2012): 14. http://ercim-news.ercim.eu/images/stories/EN89/EN89-web.pdf.

Rosenbloom, Paul S. "Towards a Conceptual Framework for the Digital Humanities." *Digital Humanities Quarterly* 6, no. 2 (2012). http://www.digitalhumanities.org/dhq/vol/6/2/000127/000127.html.

Ross, Donald Jr. "Computer-Aided Study of Literary Language." *Computer* 11, no. 8 (Aug. 1978): 32–39.

Simon, Herbert A. *The Sciences of the Artificial*. Cambridge: MIT Press, 1969.

Society of American Archivists. "Describing Archives: A Content Standard (DACS)." Accessed September 29, 2013. http://www.archivists.org/governance/standards/dacs.asp.

———. "EAD Beta Scheme Released: Comments Welcome." Accessed September 29, 2013. http://www2.archivists.org/groups/encoded-archival-description-ead-roundtable.

———. "Encoded Archival Description (EAD) Roundtable." Accessed September 29, 2013. http://www2.archivists.org/groups/encoded-archival-description-ead-roundtable.

Suarez, Michael. "Rare Books in a Digital World." Paper presented at Washington University, St. Louis, February 16, 2012.

Text Encoding Initiative (TEI). "TEI: Text Encoding Initiative." Accessed September 29, 2013. http://www.tei-c.org/index.xml.

University of California–Berkeley and University of Chicago. "Bamboo Planning Project: Final Report to the Andrew W. Mellon Foundation." December 21, 2010. https://google drive.com/host/0B3zU098zQ8VMc2xfMUJZaWxXNWs/wp-content/uploads/Project -Bamboo-Planning-Project-Final-Report.pdf.

VRA Core. "Frequently Asked Questions." Accessed September 29, 2013. http://www .vraweb.org/projects/vracore4/vracore_faq.html.

———. "VRA Core Support Pages." Accessed September 29, 2013. http://www.vraweb.org/ projects/vracore4/.

Zeng, Marcia Lei, and Jian Qin. *Metadata*. New York: Neal-Schuman, 2008.

Index

ExifTool, 161
eXtensible Markup Language (XML). *See* XML (eXtensible Markup Language)
EZID, 63, *128*

Fair Access to Science and Technology Research (FASTR) Act, 190
Federal Geographic Data Committee (FGDC), 186
Fedora, 32
Fermilab, xvii
FFmpeg, 163, *164*
FIDO (Format Identification for Digital Objects), 160, 167–8n52
File Extensions Database, 155
file format registries, 34, 143, 156–59
file formats, 34, 82; audio and video, 146–47; definition, 144–45; evaluation of, 149, 153–54; for digital preservation, 145–48; identification of, 159–61; openness of, 145; still images, 146; ubiquity of, 145
FILExt.com, 155
Finch Group, 191
First Monday, 63
fixity, 128, 130, *131,* 148–49
FLAC (Free Lossless Audio Codec), 147, *152*
Florida Center for Library Automation (FCLA), 30, 31
Florida Digital Archive (FDA), 31
FOAF (Friend of a Friend), 121
fonds, 129
Format Identification for Digital Objects (FIDO), 160, 167–68n52
format obsolescence, 7, 34, 69, 127, 145, 149, *150, 174*
FRBR *(Functional Requirements for Bibliographic Records),* 114, 135
free and open source software (FOSS), 82–84
Functional Requirements for Bibliographic Records (FRBR), 114, 135
funding, *174*

Gasaway, Laura, 35, 36
GenBank, 190

GeoTIFF, 156
German Institute for Standardization standard #31644. *See* DIN 31644
German National Library, 103
GIMP (Gnu Image Manipulation Program), 123
Global Change Master Directory (GCMD), 185, 186
Global Digital Format Registry (GDFR), 144, 157
Global LOCKSS Network, 5
GNU/Linux-based operating system, 25, 32
Gold, Matthew, 198
Google (Web search engine), 124, 155, 183
Google Books, 200
Google Documents, 198
Grant Proposal Guide, 188
granularity, 123, 126sb
Grateful Dead, 163, 184
Gray, Jim, xvi
Greenstone, 32
grid resolution, 146
Guardian, 80
Gzip, *131*

Hardman, Catherine, 99
Harvard Graphics file, 159
Harvard University Library's Digital Library program, 156
Harvey, Phil, 161
Hasenay, Damir, 12
HathiTrust, 106
Hauttekeete, Laurence, 9
Health Insurance Portability and Accountability Act (HIPAA) (U.S.), 189
hieroglyphics, xvi
Holdren, John, 81
Howard Hughes Medical Institute (HHMI), 189–90
HTML (Hypertext Markup Language), 112, 123, 146
human resources, xvi, xvii, xx–xxi, 3–5, 11–12, 17, 21, 23, 25–30, 36–37, 43, 48, 51sb, 55–57, 61, 75, 81, 83–84, 87, *88,* 105, 117sb, 125, 147–49, 164, 173, *174*
human subjects, 189, 191–92

Oh, Sam, 153–54, 164
Online Computer Library Center (OCLC), 13, 103, 133, 157
open access, 5, 81, 188, 192
Open Archival Information System (OAIS) Reference Model. *See* OAIS Reference Model
Open Archives Initiative Protocol for Metadata Harvesting (OAI-PMH), 30, 187
open data, 187–91, 192
Open Planets Foundation Digital Preservation Tool Registry, 164
Open Provenance Model (OPM), 121
Open Provenance Model Vocabulary (OPMV), 121
Open Repositories conference, 65
open research, 192
Open Source Initiative, 70
open source software. *See* free and open source software (FOSS)
Open Standards Requirement for Software, 70–71, 83, 84
OpenDocument Spreadsheets (ODS), 146
openness, 44, 83, 145, 149, 154, 188
ORCID (Open Researcher and Contributor ID), 97
Oregon Arts Commission, 175
Organisation for Economic Cooperation and Development's (OECD), 188
original order, 12, 129
outreach, 29, 173–74

Palaiologk, Anna, 78
Park, Eun, 153–54, 164
Patry, William, 35, 36
PBCore schema, 120, 205–6
PDF (Adobe's Portable Document Format), 9, 145–46, 147, *151*, 162
PDF Toolkit (PDFtk), 162
PDF/A, 9, 33, 34, 145–46, *150*, 164
PDF/A Manager, 162
PDF/Archive. *See* PDF/A
PDF/X, 145
PDFTron, 162
performance art, digital versions of, 9
Perseus Digital Library, 198

Persistent URL (PURL), 97
Philips, 8
Philips LVROM player, 9
Pink Book (OAIS Reference Model), 44, 53n6. *See also* OAIS Reference Model
Planets (Preservation and Long-term Access through NETworked Services), 22
plans for digital preservation, 22–23
Poole, Alex H., 64
Portable Document Format (PDF). *See* PDF
Portable Network Graphics (PNG), 146
Portico, 106, 160, *174*
PREMIS, 31, 122, 132, 133, *134–35*, 135–36, *136*, 137, 138, 156
PREMIS Data Dictionary, 133, *134–35*, 135
Preservation and Archiving Special Interest Group (PASIG) International Meeting, 64
Preservation and Long-term Access through NETworked Services (Planets), 22
Preservation Education Directory, 60
preservation metadata, 122, 127, 131–32, 135, 138; descriptive metadata as, 132
preservation repositories, 30–32. *See also* digital preservation systems
Preservica (Tessella preservation repository), 31
Primo (Ex Libris discovery layer), 31
principle of provenance, 12
principle of the sanctity of evidence, 12
Principles and Guidelines for Access to Research Data from Public Funding, 188
privacy, 52, 87, 118, 189, 192
Project Bamboo, 199
PRONOM, 34, 157, 158
protected health information (PHI), 189
protocols: need for common, xvii
PROV Data Model (PROV-DM), 121
provenance, 33, 121, 129, 130, 182
Purdue University Library, 63

Qin, Jian, 114, 115, 204
quality, 97, 188

raw data, 182
RealAudio, 147